Robert Payne Smith

Prophecy, a preparation for Christ : eight lectures preached before the University of Oxford in the year 1869

Second Edition

Robert Payne Smith

Prophecy, a preparation for Christ : eight lectures preached before the University of Oxford in the year 1869
Second Edition

ISBN/EAN: 9783337263492

Printed in Europe, USA, Canada, Australia, Japan

Cover: Foto ©Lupo / pixelio.de

More available books at **www.hansebooks.com**

PROPHECY
A PREPARATION FOR CHRIST

EIGHT LECTURES

PREACHED BEFORE THE UNIVERSITY OF OXFORD

IN THE YEAR

1869

ON THE FOUNDATION OF THE LATE REV. JOHN BAMPTON, M.A.

CANON OF SALISBURY

BY

R. PAYNE SMITH, D.D.

Dean of Canterbury

Late Regius Professor of Divinity and Canon of Christ Church, Oxford

SECOND EDITION CORRECTED AND REVISED

London and New York

MACMILLAN AND CO.

1871

OXFORD:

By T. Combe, M.A., E. B. Gardner, and E. Pickard Hall,

PRINTERS TO THE UNIVERSITY.

EXTRACT

FROM THE LAST WILL AND TESTAMENT

OF THE LATE

REV. JOHN BAMPTON,

CANON OF SALISBURY.

——"I give and bequeath my Lands and Estates to the
" Chancellor, Masters, and Scholars of the University of
" Oxford for ever, to have and to hold all and singular the
" said Lands or Estates upon trust, and to the intents and
" purposes hereinafter mentioned; that is to say, I will and
" appoint that the Vice-Chancellor of the University of Ox-
" ford for the time being shall take and receive all the rents,
" issues, and profits thereof, and (after all taxes, reparations,
" and necessary deductions made) that he pay all the
" remainder to the endowment of eight Divinity Lecture
" Sermons, to be established for ever in the said University,
" and to be performed in the manner following:

"I direct and appoint, that, upon the first Tuesday in
" Easter Term, a Lecturer be yearly chosen by the Heads
" of Colleges only, and by no others, in the room adjoining
" to the Printing-House, between the hours of ten in the
" morning and two in the afternoon, to preach eight Divinity
" Lecture Sermons, the year following, at St. Mary's in
" Oxford, between the commencement of the last month in
" Lent Term, and the end of the third week in Act Term.

"Also I direct and appoint, that the eight Divinity Lecture Sermons shall be preached upon either of the following Subjects—to confirm and establish the Christian Faith, and to confute all heretics and schismatics—upon the divine authority of the holy Scriptures—upon the authority of the writings of the primitive Fathers, as to the faith and practice of the primitive Church—upon the Divinity of our Lord and Saviour Jesus Christ—upon the Divinity of the Holy Ghost—upon the Articles of the Christian Faith, as comprehended in the Apostles' and Nicene Creeds.

"Also I direct, that thirty copies of the eight Divinity Lecture Sermons shall be always printed, within two months after they are preached; and one copy shall be given to the Chancellor of the University, and one copy to the Head of every College, and one copy to the Mayor of the city of Oxford, and one copy to be put into the Bodleian Library; and the expenses of printing them shall be paid out of the revenue of the Land or Estates given for establishing the Divinity Lecture Sermons; and the preacher shall not be paid, nor be entitled to the revenue, before they are printed.

"Also I direct and appoint, that no person shall be qualified to preach the Divinity Lecture Sermons, unless he hath taken the degree of Master of Arts at least, in one of the two Universities of Oxford or Cambridge; and that the same person shall never preach the Divinity Lecture Sermons twice."

PREFACE

TO THE FIRST EDITION.

IT has been my object in the following course of Lectures to show that there exists in the Old Testament an element, which no criticism on naturalistic principles can either account for or explain away. That element is Prophecy: and I have endeavoured to prove that its force does not consist merely in its predictions. These are numerous, special, precise, and have been fulfilled with marvellous exactness, and yet not in such a way as any one, Jew or Gentile, had expected before the fulfilment came. But prophecy means more than this. There is throughout the Old Testament a special presence of God preparing for the fulfilment of a gracious purpose on His part to restore man to a higher state of perfection and happiness than that from which he fell. The Bible begins by describing man as standing in a nearer relation to God than any other created being on this earth. It describes his first estate of innocency, his fall, and the promise given by God of his restoration.

We assert that throughout the Old Testament there is an express and manifest working of the Deity for the accomplishment of this promise. Virtually the promise meant that God would give man a true religion: and a true religion implies such a knowledge of God, and of His purposes towards us, and of our relation to Him, as will suffice for the wants of the soul. It implies, too, the bestowal of sufficient aid to enable us to fulfil our obligations to God, and of some means for the purification of the conscience from the stain of sin, and for the raising of the soul from its present degradation to a fitness for the reception of God's mercies. We assert that Christianity is the sole religion upon earth which fulfils these necessary conditions: and farther, that God has given us the sole satisfactory proof that it is the true religion by pledging His own attributes in its behalf.

This pledge He has given in miracle and prophecy, and without it the proof would fall short of our needs. For no religion could claim authority over the conscience which had no higher evidence to offer than the probabilities of human reasoning. There may be such a thing as a merely natural religion, and for such no supernatural proof would be required. But if we are to be brought into nearer contact with God, and find our peace and happiness in union with Him, we want all that Christianity offers us; all that we seem to find in it. But the whole scheme of Christianity is supernatural, and for such a religion a preparation like that in the Old Testament—a preparation commensurate in its greatness with the Christian faith—was necessary. Men could not have believed in a doctrine so marvellous as that of the Divinity of Christ unless the way had been prepared for it by a dispensation in which God's presence was manifested in a supernatural way.

One portion of this proof was discussed with great ability in the Bampton Lectures of 1865[a]: I have endeavoured to show the reality of the other portion, prophecy. But prophecy must not be narrowed down too closely to words. The prophets were God's representatives on earth, and the mediators between Him and man. And thus in the comparison between our Lord and Moses, it seems to me that our Lord is the prophet like unto Moses, more in being the true Mediator between God and man, than even in being the giver of a new dispensation. All the prophets were mediators, but none held so high a place as Moses among God's representatives under the first covenant: in the second covenant Christ is the one Mediator in Whom God and man are made one (John xvii. 21). Prophets, then, we have none now, because we need no other mediator. In the preparatory dispensation it was the office of the prophet to appear as God's representative whenever any new step was to be taken towards the accomplishment of God's purpose. No doubt the very highest duty and glory of the prophet was to declare

[a] Eight Lectures on Miracles, by J. B. Mozley, B.D., Vicar of Old Shoreham, London, 1865.

some new truth, or explain some old truth. He was then directly 'the speaker for God,' the bearer of God's message: but God might and did use the prophets for other purposes. They laboured for the preservation of Israel's political existence, for morality, for education, for everything that tended to raise the social condition of God's people. Finally, they laboured for all mankind, in giving us a record of Israel's history, and written memorials of the truths revealed to them. In these memorials they ever led the minds of the people onward to the time when the preparation would be complete, and God's promise fulfilled in the Advent of the Christ. It is especially in this portion of their labours that we affirm that God's Spirit was with them in a higher way than in His ordinary and natural workings. Whatever new truth they taught was revealed to them directly by God, and not attained to by the unaided workings of their mental powers: in recording or explaining old truths we feel sure that they had such aid given them as at least preserved them from error; and that even in writing history, where the higher gift of revelation was not needed, that nevertheless they had inspired guidance and control.

Now it is plain from this that such of us as believe in inspiration can never consent to treat the Bible as an ordinary book. In one sense, indeed, it is a matter of painful necessity that it must be so treated. It must be subjected to exactly the same tests as any other document. Its claims are a matter of such incalculable importance to every one of us, that they must be closely and critically examined: every possible argument for and against the authenticity and genuineness of every book of the Bible must be closely studied: and history, chronology, philology, must all be made to contribute their aid to the enquiry. Subjective criticism, too, has a right to be heard. The style of these various writings, their inner accord or disagreement, their relation to their supposed date, the degree of knowledge evinced by the writer, the nature of his ideas, his character as incidentally shown by what he says, and his object in writing: all these and many more such things have their weight in the proof. The examination ought to be made seriously, earnestly, impartially, but even where made with hostile view, we yet may be glad that it has been made. For if the Bible be the Word of God, our duty is to bow our wills humbly and obediently before it. But a being made in God's image has no right to abandon his self-mastery except upon the clearest evidence. We may be glad, then, that the examination has been made, and the claims of the Bible closely scrutinized, even if our own reverence for it might have forbidden our entering upon the task. If, indeed, we were placed in such a position, as that our minds could be a *tabula rasa*, utterly devoid of all prepossessions and ideas one way or another, it would be our duty at once to enter dispassionately upon the enquiry, whether there be a true religion upon earth, and if so, which of the various religions here below is the true one, and what is the extent of its claims upon us. We none of us can possibly be in this position, and those of us who have long since arrived at the conclusion that Christianity is God's one religion, may reasonably decline, as far as our own faith is concerned, to re-open a question upon which we have years ago come, upon sufficient evidence, to a definite conclusion.

But there are those who have arrived at an opposite conclusion, and those who are still undecided as to their own duty, and the side which they ought to take. New arguments have been brought forward against the credibility of Holy Scripture, and men do not know what weight ought to be given them. It is necessary, therefore, to examine these arguments, and to state what seem to be valid reasons for adhering to the conclusion that the Bible is, unlike all other books, a book of miracle and prophecy. There are, indeed, critics who deny the use of argument altogether. With them the conclusion is foregone. They assert that miracle and prophecy are absolutely impossible. It is of no use suggesting that the giving of a true religion may be an adequate cause for such an interference—or apparent interference—with the ordinary laws of nature as would give man the requisite proof that God was speaking to him. No cause, they say, is adequate. The soul cannot be of such value as to justify any interference with the laws of nature. Those laws are found to be, in things material, unchanging. They must therefore be so in things spiritual. The laws that are good enough for the body are good enough for the soul. I do not mean that they use just these words; but that, arguing solely from their experience in things material, they do deny the possibility of God's acting in any higher way in the things which belong to an entirely different sphere. Into this argument it is not necessary for me to enter farther than as it concerns prophecy. Of course prophecy is a miracle; the very thing for which we argue is a supernatural presence of God in the words and actions of certain persons who claimed to speak in God's name. Such a claim must be supported by a supernatural proof, and the proof could take no simpler or more cogent form than prediction. The negative critics do not examine this proof; they start with the denial of the possibility of God speaking to man at all. By their own principles, then, they are bound to affirm that every precise prophecy is either an imposture or an artifice. It may take the form of a prediction, but really must be subsequent to the event which it professes to foretell. Isaiah, in the very place where he predicts the capture of Babylon by Cyrus (xli. 23, 25, xliv. 25, 26), stakes his whole argument for God's unity and the vanity of idols upon the fact that the predictions of Jehovah's messengers were confirmed by the event, and those of the worshippers of idols disproved by it. According to the negative critics, that appeal was a specious hypocrisy, and the pretended prophecy of the conquest of Babylon by Cyrus, and of Jerusalem rebuilt by his decree, is proof enough that the last twenty-seven chapters of Isaiah are a forgery, palmed upon the too credulous Jews by some one who wrote at Babylon at the end of the exile.

If the principle were true, critics, having thus discovered the key to settle the date of each portion of Holy Scripture, would in time arrive at some settled conclusions. There would be a consensus among them, or an approach to one, and absolute results would be obtained. If they could not always tell exactly when a book was forged, scholars would at least be certain that it was a forgery. No reasonable man doubts that the Epistles of Phalaris are a forgery; no one doubts that the history of Susannah, and of Bel and the Dragon, are forgeries tacked on to the Book of Daniel at Alexandria; no one doubts that the Gospel of the Infancy, or the Assumption of the Virgin, are forgeries. Fortunately, forgeries are always very easy of detection, and those of ancient date especially so; for men then had neither the means nor the idea of imitating the style and language of other days. But the negative critics agree in nothing else except in denying the authority and inspiration of the Bible. When you ask for any positive results you find a Babel of Ishmaels. Every man's tongue is against every other. If Ewald ascribes Psalm cx. to the time of Solomon, Hitzig, a critic of almost equal reputation, ascribes it to the time of the Maccabee Jonathan. Hitzig says that the last six chapters of Zechariah were written by one and the same author in the days of King Uzziah; Ewald divides them between two different authors, who lived separated from one another by a period of one hundred and forty years. Ewald ascribes to the age of Jeremiah portions of Isaiah which Hitzig says are some of the most ancient writings of Isaiah himself. The Prophecy of Obadiah, according to Ewald, was written during the Babylonian captivity; Hitzig says it belongs to the time of Antigonus[b].

If the results arrived at by the negative critics are thus unsatisfactory, we are justified in inferring that their method is in fault. In spite of the great ability and patient labour of a host of critics, no such conclusions have been obtained as justify their assumption that prophecy is antecedently impossible. It is still a duty, then, to examine the other hypothesis, that God has spoken to man in the Scriptures, and to sift carefully the evidence offered in its behalf. And here we affirm that the prophecies contained in the Old Testament are so numerous, so entirely inwoven with its innermost substance, so consentient with one another, and yet so contrary to the whole tenour of Jewish thought, so marvellously fulfilled in Christianity, and yet in a way so different from every anticipated fulfilment, that while it is unscientific to refuse to listen to

---

[b] See Hofmann, Weissagung, i. 63. He further shows how the same critics arrive at different conclusions in each edition of their works. De Wette began by ascribing numerous Psalms to the Maccabæan age; subsequently he summarily rejected such a conclusion. Psalm xlv. at first he said was written in the time of the Persians, afterwards he ascribed it to the age of Solomon. The second half of Zechariah he once thought was written some of it in Josiah's days, and the rest under Ahaz; soon he modified his views, and could see no reason for a divided authorship. Nor, as he observes, are the critics more successful on the ground of philosophy than on that of history. Conradi and Bauer see in the Book of Proverbs a genuine work of Solomon's time; while Vatke places it and the Book of Job in the fifth century before our Lord.

the proof of their reality because of any *à priori* supposition, it is even worse folly to speak of them as mere forecasts and anticipations. The argument for prophecy does not rest upon a small number of special predictions, but upon a vast preparation for an equally vast result. That preparation claimed to be divine, and offered miracle and prediction as its proof. Farther, it ever asserted that it was but a preparation for something better, and itself described the nature of the dispensation which was to take its place. Let the critics, then, disprove the real inner unity between the two Testaments; let them show that the Christian Church does not answer to, and complete and perfect, the earlier dispensation. Till they do this, it is in vain to put forward the negative criticism as fairly commensurate with the greatness of the thesis which it undertakes to prove. The Bible, it says, is an ordinary book; its miracles are contrary to science; its prophecies the record of facts that had already happened. But they assume all this; they do not attempt to prove it. Surely a criticism of the Bible upon these assumptions is not real criticism. The Bible claims to be not a common book. That is the very point in dispute. A fair judgment can be arrived at only by an examination of the evidence which it offers in support of its claims, and this enquiry should be carried on in a judicial frame of mind. The negative critics begin by denying every one of the claims of the Bible, and affirm that they are so impossible that all argument is worthless.

Still, if criticism carried on upon this assumption

led to satisfactory results, it would be some indication that the assumption was not absolutely false. Hence the importance of the discussion as to the genuineness of the last twenty-seven chapters of Isaiah. The prophecy about Cyrus is not a matter that very directly concerns us; but the question whether every prediction was subsequent to the event is of vital consequence. The prophecies about the Messiah would be as remarkable at Babylon as at the end of Hezekiah's reign, but what would be the value of them if no prophecy is more than a mere human forecast? The question, besides, is one satisfactory to discuss for another reason. The negative critics boast, or did boast, of the dichotomy of Isaiah as their greatest feat. It used to be constantly put forward as a positive and certain result of nineteenth-century criticism. If, however, you boldly face the question, and look at what the German critics say, you will find that no positive result whatsoever has been arrived at. The sole thing in which they agree is the assertion, that as Cyrus is mentioned by name, therefore he must have been living and threatening Babylon, if he had not already conquered it, at the time the prophecy was penned.

Now let us first of all listen to what Ewald, undoubtedly in many respects the first critic in Germany, says of the real Isaiah. 'We cannot but recognize in Isaiah, as the first condition of his peculiar historical greatness, an originality and a vivacity of spirit rare even among the prophets. What is seldom united in the same genius, the deepest prophetic excitement and purest sensibility, the most unwearied and successful activity exerting itself evenly midst all the turmoil and vicissitudes of life, and the truest poetical versatility and beauty joined with vigour and rushing might of description, this triple band we find realized in Isaiah as in no other prophet, and from the evident traces of the constantly combined action of these three powers we draw our conclusions as to the measure of the original greatness of his genius.' (Proph. d. A. B. i. 272, ed. sec.) You have, then, in Isaiah no common writer. His characteristic is the union in due proportion of three very high and remarkable qualities. Wait a little, and you will find that the Book of Isaiah is a miscellany of fugitive pieces, 'flying leaves,' as Ewald terms one part of it, and that twenty nameless writers all possessed this rare combination of unrivalled native power tempered by the most exquisite judgment.

Let me give the various stages by which this marvellous conclusion was reached. Less, then, than a hundred years ago the suggestion was first made by Koppe, and soon afterwards repeated by Döderlein, that the last twenty-seven chapters of Isaiah are not genuine. The theory was at first very simple, namely, that the true Isaiah wrote the first half, and a false Isaiah, his equal in native genius, wrote the other. The more toned-down style of the latter half, resulting, as I believe, from its being, first, written in Isaiah's extreme old age, and secondly, composed not for public delivery, but for study in the prophetic colleges, gave some faint colour to the assumption of a different authorship. But it was soon found that this dichotomy could not endure a close and accurate examination. The words used, the peculiarities of style, the metaphors, the sentiments, were in the main identical in the two portions. It soon became plain, that unless large portions of the first thirty-nine chapters were taken away from Isaiah, the whole must be restored to him; moreover, there are parts of the last twenty-seven chapters plainly written before the exile, parts written in a mountainous country, parts which speak of the city and temple as still standing. These must be taken away from the Pseudo-Isaiah. Hence the present state of German thought is as follows:—

The book is a mere collection of fragments, of all dates, written by a confused horde of nameless personages, many of them mere imitators, whose effusions have been patched together upon no other principle than that of filling up the skins of parchment. And yet this *olla podrida*, this hotch-potch, in which are jumbled together the fragments of writers of every age, from Jonah to Ezra, is the book in which Hebrew genius reaches the summit alike of strength and beauty: never elsewhere is the union so clear of the rarest native gifts and the most consummate skill. Never is the line of beauty overstepped, never does the writer fail in reaching it. As Ewald from time to time cuts it into tiny pieces, he is never weary of lamenting that these noble fragments are all that we possess of a writer so vigorous and yet so polished, so strong and yet so beautiful. This, then, is the first trial of your credulity. The subjective critics require you to believe that a union of native force and perfect judgment peculiar to Isaiah, and found in no other prophet, is maintained throughout a long miscellany of fugitive pieces put together upon absolutely no principle whatsoever.

Let us next proceed to the details.

The first twelve chapters are genuine, and undoubtedly written by Isaiah (Knobel, Bleek), but disfigured by glosses, transpositions, interpolations, &c. &c., so that every critic is justified in rejecting anything in the way of his pet theory. Thus Roorda says that chs. i–v. were written by Micah, Gesenius denies the authenticity of ch. vii. 1–16, Koppe, Vater, Rosenmüller reject chs. xi., xii., and Ewald ch. xii.

The next section, chs. xiii–xxvii., are mere 'flying leaves' (Ewald), put together without regard to date or matter, of which ch. xiii. and the first twenty-three verses of ch. xiv. were written by the 'great unknown' at Babylon (Knobel), or at all events by a nameless prophet just about the time when Cyrus took that city (Rosenm., Justi, Bleek). As for the next four verses (ch. xiv. 24–27), they are a fragment of a long prophecy of Isaiah against Assyria (Ewald, Gesenius). The two next chapters (chs. xv., xvi.) were written by Jonah (Hitzig), or if not, then Jeremiah wrote them (Koppe, Augusti, Bertholdt), or if not, then perhaps Isaiah borrowed them, but added the epilogue, ch. xvi. 13, 14 (Ewald), which however is absurd, for the epilogue was written during the Babylonian exile (Bleek). As Jonah lived long before Isaiah, and Jeremiah long afterwards, and as their style and manner are totally distinct, it is hard to invent the reasons which justify so diverse a judgment.

No one at present has interfered with the two next chapters, but ch. xix., of which Egypt is the subject, was written by Onias, who built the temple at Leontopolis in that country (Hitzig). It mentions that men fished in the Nile both with hooks and nets, and that papyrus reeds grew there; facts which plainly could be known only by one who had resided a long time in the immediate neighbourhood of that river!

The first ten verses of ch. xxi. were written by the 'great unknown' (Bleek); the rest, to the end of ch. xxii., are probably Isaiah's.

The twenty-third chapter was written by Jeremiah (Movers), or by a scholar of Isaiah (Ewald), but at all events in the time of Jeremiah (Bleek).

The twenty-fourth and three following chapters —chapters of the most exquisite beauty — were written by an exiled Ephraimite living in Assyria after Nineveh had fallen, and when the Egyptians had begun to be troublesome (Hitzig), though it is hard to see how they could be troublesome to an Ephraimite living at Nineveh. Therefore Gesenius, Umbreit, Knobel, deny that it refers to Nineveh, and say that it is a prophecy of the fall of Babylon, written at the time when Judah went into captivity. But Ewald places it in the time of Cambyses' expedition against Egypt, whilst Vatke prefers the era of the Maccabees. Other discrepancies might be added: I will mention but one more. As these chapters contain a repetition of the prophecy found in ch. ii., namely, 'in this mountain shall Jehovah of hosts make unto all people a feast of fat things,' and as that mountain can properly be only Jerusalem, Bleek ascribes the three chapters to a Jew who lived at Jerusalem in Josiah's time.

The next six chapters (chs. xxviii–xxxiii.) are probably genuine (Knobel); but Koppe doubts about ch. xxx. 1–26, and Ewald ascribes ch. xxxiii. to a scholar of Isaiah's.

The next two chapters (chs. xxxiv., xxxv.), were written early in the exile (Bleek); they were written in the middle of the exile (Knobel); they were written at the end of the exile by the 'great unknown' (Gesenius, Hitzig); they were written during the exile by a distinct author from the 'great unknown' (Ewald, Umbreit).

The last four chapters of the first portion of Isaiah (chs. xxxvi–xxxix.) are a mere historical annex (Knobel), but abbreviated probably from a genuine historical work of Isaiah (Bleek): no, they are entirely spurious (Hendewerk, Hitzig). They were written by a late chronicler, when legend had taken the place of history.

Thus, then, subjective criticism, in order to wrest

the last twenty-seven chapters from the true Isaiah, has been compelled, by the searching examination which its simpler theory has undergone, to mangle the prophet's matchless work into a series of fragments, all singularly beautiful, all bearing the impress of a master mind, all instinct with the presence of rare genius. I see in this nothing that needs serious refutation, but only that Nemesis, that just retribution, which necessarily overtakes those who argue not for truth but for such a foregone conclusion as that every prediction was necessarily subsequent to the date of the event foretold.

Let us proceed to the last twenty-seven chapters. These form too decidedly a whole to be easily capable of similar dismemberment, yet only the first sixteen chapters are now confidently ascribed to the Pseudo-Isaiah. Excepting the prophecy of the capture of Babylon by Cyrus, these chapters contain nothing particularly indicative of their date. Directly you come to anything distinctive, it is impossible to hold any longer that it was all written at one time at Babylon. Gesenius maintained, as long as he lived, and Hitzig still argues for the unity of the authorship, but then they are forced to grant that much of it was written in Palestine, and so too Knobel said that the work could have been put into its present form only at a time considerably later than the return of the Jews from exile. He honestly owned, too, that he could not explain how it came to pass that a work composed at such a time could ever have been ascribed to the true Isaiah. But Ewald denies the oneness of its authorship, as I have shown at length in the note attached to page 295. So Bertholdt said that chs. lii. 13–liii. 12, lvi. 9–lvii. 21, lix., lxiii. 7–lxiv. 12, lxv., lxvi., belong to a date anterior to the attack of the Persians upon Babylon; chs. xl–xlvi., l–lii. 12, to a time subsequent to it; chs. xlvii., xlviii. were written during the siege of Babylon, and chs. liv–lvi. 8, lviii., lx–lxii. after the capture of the city. Knobel, who seemed to hold the oneness of the authorship, yet argued that chs. xl–xlviii. were written during the first siege of Babylon, chs. xlix–lxii. during the period when Cyrus was making war upon Crœsus, and the last four chapters after his victory. Gesenius, on the contrary, thought that the later chapters were written first: while De Wette stood alone in holding that these last twenty-seven chapters were written by one man at one time, namely, the first time of Cyrus, whenever that may have been.

As for the chapters plainly written in a mountainous country (chs. lvi. 9–lvii. 11), some hold with Bleek that Isaiah wrote them, some that it was an ancient prophet who lived in Manasseh's reign, some that the 'great unknown' was their author, after the return from exile. This theory requires the monstrous supposition, opposed to every tittle of historical evidence, that the Jews under Ezra and Nehemiah offered human sacrifices to Moloch. Yet without this supposition it is impossible to see how De Wette, Gesenius, Hitzig, could maintain that these chapters were the work of one author, unless that author were the true Isaiah[c].

Plainly, therefore, subjective criticism has nothing to offer us, on the very ground where it boasts its greatest triumph, but a farrago of disjointed conjectures. And the same is true of it everywhere. Instances beyond number could be brought forward showing its entire want of cohesiveness. I will content myself with mentioning but one more.

Ask it for another of its strong points, and it would tell you that it had wrested Deuteronomy from Moses as thoroughly as it has robbed Isaiah of all but some twelve chapters. You learn from it most extraordinary information about Deuteronomy. It is a very late book, never quoted till the time of Jeremiah, probably a pious fraud palmed off by him and the good high priest Hilkiah upon the too credulous Josiah, and so on. Ewald, however, holds a theory that soon after Samuel's time there was a period of extraordinary literary activity, when, upon the basis of certain ' Books of Origins ' and ' Books of Covenants,' a series of apocryphal narratives were put forth, of which the Pentateuch, Joshua, Judges, the Books of Samuel, and parts of Kings remain to this day. Having, then, no particular bias against Deuteronomy, he finds in his ' History of the Jews ' eight references

[c] These assertions may easily be verified by any one who will consult the Introductions (Einleitungen) of De Wette, and Bleek ; or that of Keil, recently translated into English, and published by Clark, Edinburgh. Knobel also gives a very full account of the guesses and conjectures which form the staple of German negative theology in his valuable work ' Der Prophetismus der Hebräer,' Breslau, 1837, of which I have made considerable use.

to this book in Joshua, more than twelve in Judges, several in Samuel, in the early Psalms, and so on. Never was judgment more opposed to all that the mass of the negative critics say upon the subject.

Plainly, therefore, the attack made upon the Bible has had no such measure of success as to justify its assumption that prophecy has no supernatural element. Still, I can scarcely hope that the negative critics will pay any attention to the arguments which I have endeavoured to offer, in proof that the Old Testament is no human utterance but a message from God. My object will have been fully gained if I have been able to confirm the faith of any who believe, and to remove difficulties out of the way of any who doubt. The prophets are, I know, often regarded as very difficult to understand: I shall not have laboured in vain if I have aided any in seeing how their work led up to and was a preparation for Christ.

CHRIST CHURCH, OXFORD,
Oct. 1869.

PREFACE
TO THE SECOND EDITION.

IN this edition I have made a few verbal corrections, and added an Index. I have also omitted the note on Genesis, as not belonging properly to my subject.

CANTERBURY,
August, 1871.

CONTENTS.

LECTURE I.

PROPHECY A PREPARATION FOR CHRIST.

Romans xv. 4.

Whatsoever things were written aforetime were written for our learning, that we through patience and comfort of the Scriptures might have hope.

LECTURE II.

THE PROPER IDEA AND MEANING OF PROPHECY.

Hebrews i. 1, 2.

God, Who at sundry times and in divers manners spake in time past unto the fathers by the prophets, hath in these last days spoken unto us by His Son.

LECTURE III.

SAMUEL, THE RESTORER OF PROPHECY.

Acts iii. 24.

Yea, and all the prophets from Samuel and those that follow after, as many as have spoken, have likewise foretold of these days.

LECTURE IV.

PART I.

THE SCHOOLS OF THE PROPHETS.

1 Samuel xix. 19, 20.

It was told Saul, saying, Behold, David is at Naioth in Ramah. And Saul sent messengers to take David: and when they saw the company of the prophets prophesying, and Samuel standing as appointed over them, the Spirit of God was upon the messengers of Saul, and they also prophesied.

LECTURE IV.

PART II.

THE ORDINARY LIFE AND DUTIES OF THE PROPHETS.

Hebrews xi. 37.

They were stoned, they were sawn asunder, were tempted, were slain with the sword: they wandered about in sheepskins and goatskins; being destitute, afflicted, tormented.

LECTURE V.

THE COMMENCEMENT OF WRITTEN PROPHECY.

Ephesians ii. 20.

Built upon the foundation of the apostles and prophets.

LECTURE VI.

THE FOUNDATION OF TRUTH LAID BY THE PROPHETS JONAH, JOEL, AND HOSEA.

Acts xxvi. 22, 23.

Saying none other things than those which the prophets and Moses did say should come: that Christ should suffer, and that He should be the first that should rise from the dead, and should shew light unto the people, and to the Gentiles.

LECTURE VII.

SPECIFIC PROPHECIES OF CHRIST IN HOSEA, AMOS, ISAIAH, AND MICAH.

Acts x. 43.

To Him give all the prophets witness, that through His Name whosoever believeth in Him shall receive remission of sins.

LECTURE VIII.

THE PROPHECIES OF ISAIAH.

Acts viii. 34, 35.

I pray thee, of whom speaketh the prophet this? of himself, or of some other man? Then Philip opened his mouth, and began at the same scripture, and preached unto him Jesus.

LECTURE IX.

THE JEWISH INTERPRETATION OF PROPHECY AT VARIANCE WITH THAT TAUGHT BY CHRIST AND HIS APOSTLES.

Matthew xxii. 42.

What think ye of Christ?

LECTURE I.

PROPHECY A PREPARATION FOR CHRIST.

Whatsoever things were written aforetime were written for our learning, that we through patience and comfort of the Scriptures might have hope.—ROM. XV. 4.

ST. PAUL claims in these words for the Scriptures of the Old Testament a special quality distinct from those possessed by ordinary books. They were written, he says, not for temporary use; not for one age and one people, but for all time : and yet for a limited purpose. Their object is not to divert and amuse; not even to instruct or give information upon any of the thousand and one things that concern our temporal state. Incidentally they may give us most valuable information, and the purest enjoyment : but they were written 'that we might have hope.' Even this again is limited. In the original Greek it is not hope generally; not the bright anticipation of joy in life, nor even an indefinite expectation of peace in death. St. Paul's words are, *might have the hope*, τὴν ἐλπίδα ἔχωμεν[a].

[a] The Vatican Codex reads, 'that we through the patience and the consolation of the Scriptures might have *the hope of the consolation*,' τὴν ἐλπίδα τῆς παρακλήσεως. The added words are probably an explanatory gloss, but they give the right sense. 'The consolation of Israel' emphatically was the Advent of the Messiah ; and

It is definitely some special expectation, to which those Jewish Scriptures have encouraged men to look forward: some special promise given in them, by virtue of which they thus instruct and comfort all mankind.

Now this claim, to be the instructors not of one people only, nor at one time only, but of all people at all times, is no ordinary matter. We are most of us so used to the proposition affirmed by St. Paul, that probably it does not strike us with the force which so remarkable a phenomenon would exert upon us, if we were brought face to face with it for the first time. For the assertion is this, that in a considerable number of short treatises, several of them themselves compiled from more ancient documents[b], written by the men of one nation, but at distant intervals, under very different states of outward circumstance and inward development,

what St. Paul affirms of the Old Testament Scriptures generally— ὅσα προεγράφη—is, that directly or indirectly they were all prophetic, all looked forward to and prepared for Christ. Similarly, all believers now look forward. St. Paul's words are applicable to the Christian Scriptures quite as thoroughly as to the Jewish: for they also are for our learning, that we by the exercise of that patience, necessarily implied in the fact that we have not as yet the full possession of the promise, and by the comfort given us by the strong conviction of our faith that Christ will come again, may have hope — *the* hope — that as Christ has come once to open the way of salvation for man, so He will come again to perfect His work.

[b] It is certain that the books of Chronicles were thus compiled, and probably most of the Historical books. Many scholars have also held that Moses made use of the primitive records of the House of Abraham in composing Genesis. The Book of Psalms too, though not a compilation, is a collection of national poetry from the time of Israel's greatest glory down to the return of the exiles from Babylon.

there is a unity of purpose, common in a greater or less degree to them all; and that this purpose was not anything national, not anything contemporaneous with the writers, nor even fully understood by them, but was something future, and for the weal or woe of all mankind. The hope of the whole world—the way of universal restoration—is set before us in the writings of a people, of no great power or influence, limited in number, possessed of many high qualities, but narrow-minded, prejudiced against foreigners, devoid of all cosmopolitan tendencies, not versatile enough to win any large amount of favour, as a matter of fact generally disliked, held usually in subjection by some of the neighbouring powers, but restless and intractable as subjects, and not to be depended upon as friends and allies. These writings possess vigour and beauty, but in so moderate a degree, that few even of those who believe them to be inspired will take the trouble of studying them in the original language: and that language though profound and sublime is intractable: it adds no fresh beauty to the thoughts, though it expresses those thoughts with a fulness and depth which no translation can entirely convey. Now, had the Greeks with their versatile talents, their dialectic skill, and their flexible, copious, and exact language, had writers like Plato been the teachers of all mankind, truth's universal exponents, we could have understood it. But no! The fact agrees with what St. Paul affirmed eighteen centuries ago: these Jewish writers are the great teachers of the world.

Add to their works the writings of a few more

Jews; some fishermen, a tax-gatherer, a physician of Antioch[c], and a citizen of Tarsus, and you have a book with few external charms, which does not allure its readers by its beauty, of one part of which the language is so alien from our studies that even of the clergy few know the letters of its alphabet, while of the other part the Greek[d] is so unpolished that your fastidious student, who prefers his style to his soul, shuns its perusal; yet this book is in every house, is read daily by countless multitudes, is said by these multitudes to give them strength for the struggle of life, and comfort under its sorrows. It is translated into all languages, and poured forth from the press by millions[e], is the subject of daily debate and controversy, and divides nations into hostile parties according as they take one view or another of its meaning, so that even the gender[f] of

[c] Luke by birth was of a family of Antioch, and by profession a physician. Euseb. Hist. Eccl. iii. 4.

[d] Nevertheless, the hand of Providence is very clearly seen in the production of a language so peculiarly fitted for the conveyance of the truths of revelation, and for translation into other languages, as the Greek of the New Testament. Dr. Pusey has pointed this out with his usual force. 'The Septuagint, the dialect which, uniting the depth of Hebrew with the intellectual precision of the Greek language, was to be the vehicle of the revelation of the Gospel, the Greek of Alexandria modified by the Old Testament, were productions of the peculiar character of the third empire in Alexander and his successors.' Daniel the Prophet, p. 148.

[e] The British and Foreign Bible Society alone circulates copies of the Scriptures in 169 languages, and 172 versions: since its foundation no less than fifty millions of Bibles or portions of Bibles have been printed for its sole use. The Society for the Promotion of Christian Knowledge also annually circulates a vast number of Bibles and Testaments, and has had several translations of the Scriptures made into other languages.

[f] It is one of the many archaisms of the language of the Pentateuch that it has only one pronoun for the third person sing. in all

a pronoun becomes in it a matter of earnest debate. A bad translation of this book exercises a depressing influence upon a nation's advance in civilization: a good translation is one of the great levers in a nation's rise. By translating this book Luther moulded the German language into shape and consistency, and made it a fit vehicle for expressing the thoughts of those great writers whose names are now everywhere as household words. Our own translation so elevated and noble, however deficient it may be in exactness, is the mainstay of our language, the means whereby its purity is maintained at home and abroad, and the bond which unites our colonists to their mother-land. Nor is this all. In proportion as men study this book and act upon it, they become more just, more temperate, more self-denying, more willing to labour for the good of others: while its neglect leads to luxury, to

---

genders, namely, הוא, *hu* = *he, she, it*. The Massorites, in the same ignorant way in which they have everywhere endeavoured to reduce the grammar and pronunciation of the Hebrew to the standard of one particular time, give this pronoun a different sound according as it is masculine or feminine. The unhappy result of their labours, in many respects so valuable, has been that they have succeeded only too well in obliterating the traces of change and growth in Hebrew, and given colour to the notion that the language of Abraham and Moses remained without alteration or development till the days of Ezra. As a matter of fact the consonants alone are genuine, and the work of the Massorites, between the sixth and tenth centuries after Christ, was simply a modernizing of the Hebrew text, though a modernizing of it according to a fixed standard handed down by tradition in the Jewish schools. The pronoun then in Gen. iii. 15 proves nothing, nor is it of much weight that the Massorites vocalize it as masculine: the matter is really settled by the verb, which is masculine, and can be nothing else. It is probable, moreover, that the *ipsa conteret* of the Vulgate is itself a mistake, not supported by the best manuscripts.

self-indulgence, to the loosening of the reins of our passions, to national weakness and private infamy. Destroy this book with its 'enthusiasm for humanity,' and no one can even suggest any other influence capable of counterbalancing the materialism of life, and of checking the tendency of increased wealth, and larger command over the powers of nature[g], to pleasure and an effeminate luxury. Destroy this book, and the poverty which grows more deep and dark and desperate as the wealth of the nation in the aggregate increases, will have nothing to give it consolation; nothing to alleviate it with lessons of patience; nothing to ennoble and strengthen it by faith in a future world, where the cruel inequalities of our present social state will exist no more (Luke xvi. 25). Destroy this book, and the bond between rich and poor is gone. There is nothing henceforward to speak to both alike of a God Who is no respecter of persons; Whom rich and poor must both obey, and Who will surely succour the poor who trust in Him. The suffering Christ, the Man of Sorrows, the cross meekly borne leading onwards to the immortal crown, nought of this will there be to comfort the afflicted. The glorified Christ, coming with all power as Judge of quick and dead, and in that judgment putting the poor into His own place (Matt. xxv. 40, 45), nought of this will there be to bid the rich man seek out the poor, and minister to him. To eat and drink and die, that

[g] The rapid advance of physical science in the present day by the increased power it has given us over nature, has opened to us a thousand sources of pleasure and convenience unknown even in the last century. A man of ordinary means has no longer to do battle with life, but finds nature well-nigh subdued to his service.

will be man's all. Among the mass of mankind,—and we must remember that the object of religion is to find a motive power that will influence not one or two extraordinary minds, but the great mass of ordinary people;—among the mass of mankind, a man is in the main just, sober, industrious, temperate, chaste, in exact proportion as he studies and values his Bible. So general, in short, is its influence, that the very student of physical science takes more interest in his facts and theories in proportion as they seem to bear upon some statement of Holy Scripture, or upon some gloss currently put upon its words; and many a so-called scientific treatise is in reality a theological argument.

Spoken then primarily of the Old Testament, St. Paul's words have proved true of the whole body of the sacred Scriptures. 'They were written for our learning:' and the whole atmosphere of English thought still in the middle of this nineteenth century, is saturated with their teaching. The very bitterness with which they are attacked is an unconscious testimony to their importance. If they were powerless, without influence; if men could even shake themselves personally free from their influence, they would then be regarded with philosophic indifference; with that calmness with which thinking men profess to study the problems of human life. Now it would be contrary to the whole tenor of the Bible to expect such a state of calm: to expect a time in which there would not be strong opposition to Christianity: in which it would not have an up-hill fight, and men be compelled to win their way to its peace and blessedness by a severe struggle (Matt. xi. 12). It would be contrary too to the whole tenor of the Bible[b] to expect that even in the Church the fierce contest of passion will cease; that it will not be rent by opposing parties, and weakened in doing its Master's work far more by schisms within than by any and all opposition from without (Matt. x. 21, 22; xiii. 25, 47). But that sword of which our Lord spake is still wielded as trenchantly as ever. With unabated earnestness we still contend against one another and against the world. Our religious opinions or our irreligious, our faith or our scepticism, hold the foremost, the dearest place in our minds. None but the tame and feeble and irresolute are indifferent in the strife. Christianity is not dead nor dying. It is not yet a stagnant pool of moribund and worn-out theories; the spirit of life still broods over its waters, and quickens it with energy, with activity, with power. Strange that it should be so! Strange, humanly speaking! Strange, unless there be in the Bible something more than human, some direct speaking and utterance of God! How could the words of a Galilæan peasant, and the few fishermen with whom He consorted, thus for eighteen centuries be a law to the civilized world, if they were merely human? And why should scientific men, in this advanced and advancing age, care to look so constantly behind them, and busy themselves with the enquiry whether every statement in a Jewish cosmogony written many thousand years ago, agrees exactly and literally with their theories, if that cosmogony was a mere specula-

---

[h] Such a state of blessedness is promised (Isa. xi. 9), but only as the result of the universal propagation of Christianity, and its final triumph over all mankind.

tion? We do not quarrel over the egg, in which Brahm created himself, and then floated majestically over the waters during a period of countless ages, till finally growing tired of his narrow quarters, he parted it asunder, and formed the sky and the earth from its divided portions[i]. We have no counter theories with which to explain, defend, or attack that egg. Nothing in the world depends upon it. In India itself no one cares for it. But a great deal does depend upon the first chapter of Genesis; and it is a note of the value of Holy Scripture that, written as that record was for an entirely different purpose[k], it yet excites so great and sustained an interest in a matter completely subsidiary to its main object.

My business however lies with St. Paul's words in their primary sense. With the New Testament,—with the influence of the Bible as a whole,—I am only so far concerned as it justifies the Apostle's assertion, that the scriptures of the Old Testament had collectively and individually a higher, a nobler, and a more permanent purpose than the instruction of those to whom they were originally addressed. If the preparation in the Old Testament had led on to nothing, if Christianity had been no whit greater than Judaism, if after temporary successes it had proved incompatible with continued and abiding progress in morality and true civilization, if Christian nations had stagnated, and fallen behind others in good government, in laws, in industry, in power, in

[i] Hindu Institutes, or Laws of Manu, Book i. 9-13.

[k] In revelation man in his relation to God is the one object of interest, and thus in Gen. i. we learn that the end and purpose of the natural creation was man, while in Gen. ii. we have the further lesson that man from the first stood in a moral relation to his Creator.

the love of truth, in the pure and ardent quest of knowledge, and in whatever else ennobles our nature, if progress in all that is just and true and lovely and of good report became possible only as men broke away from Christianity, and if its corrupt forms tended to human excellence and human happiness more than an exacter conformity to what is taught in Scripture, and was held in primitive times,—if this were so, then the argument from prophecy would fall powerless upon our ears. The more extraordinary the preparation, the greater evidently must be the result to justify that preparation. If the result be a failure, we could not believe that the Divine Providence had ushered it into the world with more than ordinary care and forethought. Man's works constantly do thus fail. That which is begun with arrogance and ostentation generally results in a mean and disastrous issue. For the most part, great things with men arise out of modest and small beginnings. It cannot be so with God. He is the perfect Worker, and all that He works must be in harmony and proportion.

It must however be borne in mind that the Holy Scriptures themselves declare that sin, misery, poverty, death, and with them irreligion, profanity, unbelief, are not to cease till Christ's second advent. It is possible, then, to claim of Christianity that which it expressly refuses to give. What it does profess to give is the one true probation of the soul, the one true means by which sins may be forgiven, and regenerate and renewed man be made capable of eternal happiness. Why there should be this probation for man, I cannot tell, nor why it should be so difficult.

But I know as a fact that it is difficult; difficult for myself, difficult for others: and the teaching of our Lord agrees with what we know and feel to be the case. He too does not tell us why there is a probation: the Bible never tells us what are our relations to other intelligent beings, nor what the exact place which this our world holds in the vast plan of the universe. It tells us only how in this state of things in which we do actually find ourselves we may so live as not to miss the object for which God placed us here. And it never leads us to expect that in attaining to this object we are to have a comfortable, easy course. Rather if we are to win the everlasting life, it warns us that in this life we must be content to strive, and labour, and forego. The favour of numbers, the popular acclaim—these are not the notes which Christ gave of success. He spake of a narrow way, whose entrance but few find. He spake of many called, and but few chosen. He even spake despondingly, as if there were doubt of the very permanence of religion. 'When the Son of Man cometh will He still find *the* faith on earth?' ἆρα εὑρήσει τὴν πίστιν; (Luke xviii. 8). Why this is so, God only knows. In the Manichæism of my heart I would that it were otherwise; the entrance wider, the way easier, and more frequented. But doubtless God doeth all things well, and our difficulties arise from our ignorance, because we see the present only, and that but dimly, while the past and the future are alike concealed from our view.

But the Bible must be judged according to its own principles and assertions, and with reference to the state of things in which as a matter of fact we find ourselves. Philosophers may conceive of a world without sin and sorrow and unbelief, of man as a virtuous, gentle, intellectual being, of a religion that involves no probation, and of a state of things, in which all, without struggle and without failure, attain to the highest perfection of which their nature is capable; and there by all means let them have their ideal Bible, and their ideal Church. But we inhabit no Utopia, and if in this world, such as it is, the Church has succeeded in doing the work marked out for it by the prophets in the Old Testament, and by Christ and His apostles in the New; and if this work be in close relation to the actual constitution of things as they now exist; then Christianity does justify the extraordinary preparation made for it.

And who can deny its success? It has been, I grant, far more limited than one could have wished. It has but a limited influence even in Christian nations, and Christian nations are but limited in extent. Unbelief, like sin and sorrow, exists everywhere around us; is more universal, more prevalent than faith. But all that this means is, that religion is in exact analogy with and in relation to the general state of things upon earth. It is not a special difficulty with Christianity, but belongs to the province of natural religion, and to the enquiry, Why the state of all things upon earth is just what it is? The solution of this difficulty belongs, I believe, to that time, and to that time only, when we shall no longer see as in a riddle, but face to face, and know as also we are known. Till that time I grant that it is faith only which can make us feel that God doeth all things well: and to faith I am content to leave it, because reason also tells me that it is a childish and ridiculous folly to endeavour to explain a proposition of which we know not the data. Till we learn the past and the future, we cannot understand the present. But while I grant the existence of the awful mystery which shrouds life, still, judging of Christianity in relation both to the actual state of things in which we find ourselves, and to what the Bible itself says of the difficulties in the way of attaining to, and holding the truth, I ask again, Who can deny its success? Attacks upon it from without there will be, and, what is far worse, corruptions within. These corruptions weaken its influence, prevent its increase, and shock our moral sense far more than any attacks from without. There have been times when the immorality and the doctrinal corruptions of the professors of Christianity degraded the Church to so great an extent that its speedy fall seemed inevitable. But God has ever again infused life into its decaying members. Its last stage of decay has ever been also the time of a new birth; reformation has followed close upon the heels of doctrinal corruption; and Christianity still lives, is strong, and fruitful in holy deeds. It alone possesses the power of influencing men largely and generally. It still speaks mightily to the conscience. After every period of decay, it revives to fresh power. After every attack, it springs up with renewed energy. The very blows aimed against it serve but to quicken and animate it. 'Troubled on every side, it is not distressed: perplexed, it is not in despair: persecuted, it is not forsaken: cast down, it is not destroyed.' Its one assurance of life is that it bears about in the body the dying of the Lord Jesus: that it teaches a suffering Christ, and is content to suffer with Him (2 Cor. iv. 8–10).

Nor must it be forgotten that the power of Christianity ever increases in proportion as nations advance in all that most ennobles our nature. Where men are ignorant, immoral, coarse, dull, degraded; where bad government and false doctrine unite in depressing the moral state of the people; where not religion but superstition sways the public mind, there the conscience being darkened, the influence of Christianity is but nominal. But give men good government, good laws; let them freely search and examine God's word for themselves; let knowledge of every kind be diffused; let truth be more loved; and with increasing purity of life and greater freedom of mental action, that nation will also steadily advance towards a more spiritual and more earnest faith. Faith is strongest where the light is brightest, and where life is the purest. The man who believes that the Bible is God's word ought not to fear for it the most searching examination. It is a sickly faith that would seek evasion and concealment. But there is also a sickly utopianism that cannot bear difficulties, and runs away from instead of facing the problems of life. Of neither of these did our Lord speak when He declared that the kingdom of heaven suffereth violence, and must be seized by force.

The preparation then made for the Gospel in the Old Testament has not failed in having a result worthy of it; and therefore we may fairly require that the evidence which prophecy offers in support of the claims of our Lord to be God incarnate in the flesh for man's salvation, should be examined impartially. The existence, the nature, the power of Christianity are all phenomena which cannot be lightly passed over. To reject its claims without examining the evidence it produces in their behalf is, in view of these phenomena, unscientific. At the same time, I am aware that the very magnitude of the thesis to be proved alarms many. The Bible claims no less than to be a message from God to the soul. It claims to speak to all men everywhere with authority, only indeed upon one subject, but that the one great and momentous subject which most deeply concerns us all. In the text, St. Paul tells us that it was given to teach us the Christian hope, the hope of a Saviour. Our Lord more exactly defines its object as our 'eternal life,' ζωὴ αἰώνιος (John v. 39). It tells us then that which no other book tells us: that which we could know in no other way unless God did tell it us in some supernatural manner, namely, what are the relations between God and the soul, how the soul can approach God, be made holy so as to be fit for His presence, and be united to Him. These are high claims, and the fact is not at variance with them. The Book is a great teacher. Kant himself concedes, that 'if the Gospel had not previously taught men the universal moral laws, reason would not have been able yet (that is, in the short period between Plato and ourselves—a couple of thousand years or so) to have attained to so perfect an insight into them[1].' Important as is

[1] Kant to Jacobi in Jacobi's Werke, iii. 523, quoted by Luthardt. p. 160.

this testimony from a man who endeavoured to build up a system of morality upon the reason only, yet the strength of the Gospel does not lie in its pure moral teaching. It lies in that part of it which is directly supernatural. It is in the manifestation of God in the flesh; it is in the work of the Emmanuel, the God-man, that its extraordinary power consists. Take this away—the miracle which is the very centre and core of Christianity—and the rest, though not without value, is yet comparatively of so small value, that it would be scarcely worth a struggle. The power, the might, the life of the Christian world would be gone.

With so great a thesis to prove, it is necessary that the proof should be strong. And naturally the more convincing evidences are those which are usually called *internal*. Our Lord claims to be so much more than a mere historical character, that a mere historical proof falls below the exigencies of the case. It is valuable, indispensable; but not enough. We do not regard our Lord as a teacher in the same way as Socrates and Sakya-muni[m], but as belonging altogether to a higher and diviner sphere. And thus the most convincing evidence of all is our Lord's own character. The more we study that simple but marvellous delineation of Him given in the Gospels, the more certain we feel of His unapproachable perfectness: that no man ever spake as He spake, or taught as He taught, or wrought as He wrought[n]. And

---

[m] See Appendix, Note A.

[n] I would especially recommend a work entitled 'The Jesus of the Evangelists,' by the Rev. C. A. Row, 1868. For fulness of thought, and terseness and accuracy of reasoning, I do not know its

next I should place the evidence of the Epistles of St. Paul. The man who can read them, and not be convinced both of the greatness and the searching and critical character of St. Paul's intellect, and also of his entire, thorough, and profound belief in the truth of every word he wrote or spoke, must have a mind strangely constituted, and strongly biassed. And another powerful though less concentrated proof is that which will be the subject of these Lectures; the proof, namely, which the Old Testament offers to the truth of the New by the fulness and exactness of the preparation made for it, and the wonderful harmony, under vast external differences, which exists between the two dispensations.

To treat so great a subject worthily would require powers far greater than I can bring to the cause of God's truth: to treat it fully would require many volumes, and much time and study. I can but touch the subject slightly and generally, and chiefly I shall confine myself to the nature of the preparation made under the Jewish covenant for Christianity: content if I can remove any difficulties out of the way of those who doubt, and confirm the faith of the devout believer. That faith will, I believe, be best built up by the close study of the Bible itself. If it be God's book, it will speak best in God's behalf. And what

equal. No man can read it without being convinced, I should imagine, not merely of our Lord's historical existence, which is what Mr. Row undertakes to prove against Strauss, &c, but also of His unapproachable perfectness. As a usual rule, it is in myths that we find attempts at describing a perfect character: our Lord is perfect in a way entirely distinct from any and every ideal of perfection that the fancy ever suggested, and with such proofs of historical certainty that the more they are examined, the more convinced we are that the Gospels are simple narratives of fact.

other proof can you offer to the great mass of mankind? Christianity is no heritage of the rich, the studious, the learned : it is common property, belonging as much to the cottage and the village as to the cloister and the university. Its proof therefore cannot consist in elaborate arguments, such as those only have the time to study, who are set free from the cares and the manifold business of life. It must carry its proof with it, and such a proof as working men can understand : such a proof as makes faith possible to the unlearned. And such a proof, felt even where not consciously understood, I believe to be the unity and consistency of the Bible itself, and the wonderful way in which its many treatises form one book, and all combine in setting before men one and the same way provided by God for man's restoration. In the Bible men find the same plan of salvation gradually and steadily unfolded. It grows more plain, more clear and definite as speaker after speaker arises with words from God. No one ever contradicts the past, but each adds his own measure of truth to that already given. And finally 'It is finished :'—the message of God to the soul is completed under such circumstances, and with so great an outpouring of Divine light, as infinitely to excel, while nevertheless it fulfils and exactly corresponds to all the previous declarations of the prophets. Finally, in this message thus perfect and complete men find what they need; it supplies a want, a craving in their own natures. They feel themselves the better and happier for it, and believe not because of other men's words, not because of arguments and proof and evidence, but because they have found for themselves that Jesus is the Christ. Call it, if you will, fanaticism º, but as a matter of fact it is this internal conviction which supports and upholds the true Christian. It is man's own heart at last, taught by the Holy Ghost, which convinces him that he needs a Saviour, and that Jesus of Nazareth both can and will save him.

Nevertheless, if reason contradicted faith; if we had to do violence to our intellect; if after careful and candid consideration we felt that the proof was insufficient, the evidence doubtful, or upon the whole against us, I doubt whether the faith of an educated man, used to weigh and balance testimony, could endure the trial. Our inward conviction, that which springs from faith, can overcome difficulties, provided that the balance of proof in the main incline largely and decidedly in its favour. And thus if the Bible were at variance with itself; if the books of the Old Testament marked out some one way, and some another, for man's recovery: if its principles were contrary to what our Lord sets before us as holy, just, and true: if its lessons and teaching, confessedly and necessarily inferior to our Lord's, did not tend in the same direction, and lead men onwards to Him, in Whom the Spirit dwelt, not by measure but fully:—if this were so, the power of the Bible would be gone. It would carry on its very face its own refutation, and there could be neither peace nor joy in believing, if belief arrayed our intellectual faculties in battle

---

º Though called fanaticism by those outside the faith, it is nevertheless the proof which St. Paul asserts is possessed by all Christians, 2 Cor. xiii. 5. The translation *reprobates* for ἀδόκιμοι rather obscures the sense. It more correctly means 'not abiding the proof,' and so not genuine, real Christians.

against our moral faculties. Far different is the case. And yet it is very extraordinary that this discrepancy does not exist among the books of the Bible;— extraordinary and incredible from the sceptic's point of view. For what is the Bible regarded as he regards it? It is a mere casual collection of the most heterogeneous treatises possible: laws, poems, biographies, sermons, histories, of which few are genuine, and those vilely interpolated. It is the remains of a once far larger Jewish literature, preserved by mere haphazard, dealt with by forgers at their list, but by forgers and interpolators who had not the slightest intention of preparing the way for Christianity. Yet these are the books which the Jews valued as God's most precious gift to them (Rom. iii. 2): these the books which they everywhere carried with them, and of which they made translations into whatever was their current tongue: these the books which they thought assured to them the heritage of the world. If these books were what sceptics assert them to be, is it possible that the Jews could have regarded them with this profound respect? Of these too it is that St. Paul affirms that they were written for the teaching of all mankind: that they all have one and the same high purpose, and an eternal value. St. Paul's view involves a miracle. Unless they had a supernatural element, the Scriptures could not thus be the universal teachers. But in proof of this assertion and the miracle it involves, there is a vast and wonderful mass of evidence, so thorough, perfect, and complete, as in all ages to have satisfied the most intellectual and earnest minds. And finally, these are the books under whose teaching the

Christian world has outstripped, not only in morality, but also in science, the farthest progress of olden time; and tested as they have been by eighteen centuries of the most varied experience, they still possess authority over many of the most critical, judicious, and acute thinkers of the present day. Perpetually attacked, subjected for centuries to a bitter, minute, and searching criticism, they still survive. Man has done his worst to destroy them. Each new phase of scepticism boasts that at length it has won a final victory; but still they speak to man with ever renewed power. 'This is the Lord's doing, and it is marvellous in our eyes.'

Treat the Bible as an ordinary book; take from it the guiding hand of inspiration, the heavenly light of revelation; regard it as a merely national literature, the chance combination of a number of myths, legends, forgeries, fabrications, interpolations, mixed up with a few genuine poems, sermons, histories, and the like, and you have—in the face of these facts—the most extraordinary, the most unaccountable phenomenon upon the face of the earth. That such a Bible,—the Bible of the neologian,—or the Bible in any way except as the Word of God, could stand the test of criticism for a single month, or exert on any one average mind a holy and strengthening influence, I for my part regard as an absurdity too great to be believed.

St. Paul then affirms the prophetic character of the whole of the Old Testament Scriptures. All these writings combine, and were intended to combine, into a concordant body of teaching, given to man to set before him one and the same great truth. For they were given, first, to prepare for the Advent of man's Deliverer: and secondly, to bear witness to, and be the proof of His mission after He had come. But this preparation for Christ again was twofold. It was necessary first of all to make preparation for the external part of His manifestation. If a Deliverer was to come, if that Deliverer was to take upon Him man's nature, He must come of some lineage, must be born in some place, must have witnesses to record what He said and did, must find on earth such a state of things as would permit of His giving the requisite proof of His mission, and of His performing such acts as were necessary for the carrying out of the Divine purpose. And secondly, there must be such a state of mental and moral culture, as would enable men to understand His teaching, and comprehend whatever ideas were involved in the plan of man's restoration.

As regards the first part of the preparation, evidently our Lord could not have come in times like, for instance, the present. How could He have wrought His miracles, and taught His lessons, and gathered people round Him by thousands, and have wandered from place to place always with a more or less numerous following, unless there had been far greater freedom of personal action than is possessed by us now? And again: how could He have died, the just, the innocent, the spotless, unless the times had been rough and arbitrary? Wherever excessive personal liberty exists, wherever each man has to maintain his own rights, while the law is weak, and its action irregular, there the hand of authority endeavours to repress any dangers which seem to threaten itself by violent reprisals. And thus the state of Judæa, restless under the Roman yoke, with its native government all but powerless, while its conquerors were alike unwilling and unable to interfere much with domestic matters, was admirably suited for the work of our Lord's ministry. But this was but one of many conditions equally indispensable: and necessarily much of the Bible is concerned with this external preparation. We see from the time of Abraham all the outward circumstances of our Saviour's mission gradually growing into shape. And it is this which gives its interest to the historical portions of the Bible. Starting with the successive covenants made by God with all mankind in Adam and Noah, it rapidly lessens its field of vision. Nation after nation is dropped out of the programme. Ever it is a narrower stream of history[p]. You have advanced but a short way in the narrative before it is limited to the fortunes of a childless old man, dwelling in his black camel's-hair tent beneath the lofty terebinths of Mamre. But that old man is the ancestor of Christ, and from him a nation springs whose habitation is a land peculiarly adapted for the Saviour's mission, whose institutions all bear close reference to Him, whose ritual sets forth His doctrines, whose heroes are His types, whose fortunes for good and evil are all so controlled as best serve His purposes, and whose sons are the first recipients and disciples and propagators of the new faith. The historical

---

[p] As up to Christ it was an ever narrowing stream, until it all centered in Him, so after Christ the stream is ever widening, till the knowledge of the Lord shall at length cover the earth as the waters cover the sea.

parts of the Bible all relate to this the closing scene of Israel's drama; and so exactly is this limiting principle adhered to, that no sooner have the ten tribes forfeited all part in the noble office of preparing for the Messiah, than they disappear entirely from Holy Scripture. In the prophets subsequent to Hosea, Israel becomes a symbol for wider mercies than those which belonged to the seed of Abraham after the flesh. The purpose of the Bible is not historical. Its history is strictly subservient to the covenant of grace.

But essential as was this portion of the preparation, it nevertheless holds but the lower and inferior place. Prophecy had, secondly, the nobler work of preparing for Christ's teaching. Look at that teaching. Consider how spiritual it is, raised how high above the teaching of any other sage whatsoever. How perfect too in all its parts: not a medley, from which you may cull here and there some of wisdom's scattered pearls, while the rest is mere common verbiage, the expression of loose, inaccurate, ordinary thought. Upon our Master's words the best, the wisest, the most intellectual of men for eighteen centuries have pondered, and found in them a strength and sweetness such as no other words possess. If you bear this in mind, you can then understand something of the greatness of the task imposed upon the prophets. They had to prepare men's minds for that teaching. If when Christ came the Jews had been in so low a state intellectually and morally that they could not have understood Christ, how could His Church have been formed? Whence could He have gathered disciples? Who would have recorded His lessons for us? Whence could the St. Paul have arisen to give us their doctrinal exposition? Whence the St. John to raise the veil from their spiritual and mystic import? That nation could not have been in a low state of mental development whose fishermen and tax-gatherers were capable of understanding and recording the interpretation put upon the Old Testament by our Lord; of seeing our Lord's acts in the light of prophecy, and prophecy as illuminated by those acts. As I shall show hereafter, the Jewish scribes and teachers had not attained to the true meaning of the prophecies. The apostles had been brought up under a recognized interpretation very different from what our Saviour taught. Yet their mental state was such as enabled them to grasp, slowly I grant and unwillingly, nevertheless in due time firmly and fully this new and Christian interpretation of the Old Testament. But while thus the Jews had been educated to such a degree as gave them great aptitude for understanding religious teaching, the nature of the Talmud [q] forbids our conceding them much power of originating doctrine. It is not an elevated or spiritual work, and its strength lies rather in minute

---

[q] The strength of the Talmud lies in what is technically called *Halachah*, the pathway or course of life, in other words *morals*. It never places its morality however upon a scientific basis as Aristotle did in his Ethics, but is full of sensible and sententious remarks; yet even in morals the point of many of its treatises is How you can best break the real intent of God's law while keeping the letter of it. Its weakness is its *Haggada*, its queer tales and narratives, not always of the most innocent description, and rivalling in wildness and monstrosity many of the tales in the Arabian Nights. Something of this tendency of the Jewish mind may be seen in the Book of Tobit. The morals of the book are excellent, but the stories of the fish's liver, and of the love of an evil spirit for Sara, belong to the wildest class of legends.

details, than in those great principles which rouse in us the fire of a noble enthusiasm. And yet it is the literature of a people great in teaching, and if we cannot give them a high place in philosophy, still in morality — practical morality — their system was far more pure and excellent than that of many nations capable of reasoning upon it with more dialectic skill. Prophecy had done its work. It laid the foundation upon which to build, but the builder was Christ. Christ is the great teacher of mankind: but it was Jews, Jews of the middle and lower classes, who carried the great Teacher's words to the Gentile world, and thereby fulfilled that high office and destiny which the prophets had not hesitated to claim for the Jewish nation. 'The law shall go forth of Zion, and the word of the Lord from Jerusalem' (Micah iv. 2).

And still prophecy speaks to us. For its other great purpose was to bear witness to the truths of Christianity. Man's works are for some limited object. They have their use and then pass away. One half of that which we call progress is the removal of what was once sound and good, but is now obsolete, worn out, and decayed. Just as the generations of men pass away, and leave their places for the young and strong to fill, so do their works pass away. But God changeth not, and His doings are not subject to time, do not grow old, do not become obsolete, nor need restoration and renewal. And thus His Word 'shall stand for ever' (Isaiah xl. 8, 1 Peter i. 25). Necessarily using human language, and clothing its eternal truths in the ideas current in each writer's time^r, it has also to fulfil an impossible condition—impossible for man, and possible only for God—namely, that it must belong to all generations, and speak forcibly to men in every stage and degree of culture and civilization. The more I reflect upon the conditions of the problem, the more extraordinary it seems to me that the Bible should still be a living book. And what is more, not the New Testament only, but also the Old Testament still fulfils this most difficult condition. It is no more obsolete than the words of our Lord and His apostles. It still has its use: still has its lessons for poor and rich, and the testimony of the Saviour to its power still finds an echo in our hearts. 'Search the Scriptures; for in them ye think ye have eternal life: and they are they which testify of Me ... Had ye believed Moses, ye would have believed Me: for he wrote of Me' (John v. 39, 46). It still bears witness to all the

---

^r It is an amusing absurdity of the present day, that some students of physical science speak as if God's Word ought to have used scientific, instead of popular language, that is, it ought to have used the phraseology of the nineteenth century. For scientific language is itself but an approximation to an exacter phraseology, just as science is but an approximation to truth. What is scientific language now will be unscientific a century hence. Speaking to men, the Bible must use human words, and, what is worse, human ideas. The best of these words and ideas fall infinitely short of the Divine realities (2 Cor. iv. 7, xii. 4), and are but shadows of the truth. No words short of those used by heavenly intelligences (if they use words) could have adequately expressed the truth, and if so expressed men could not have understood it. God has deigned therefore to clothe His revelation in such words as men generally can understand, and each writer uses the phraseology of his own period, but we are warned against the folly of supposing that we can see the whole truth as long as we are here in the flesh (Ex. xxxiii. 20, 23, 1 Cor. xiii. 9, 12).

great principles of Christianity, and those principles are the best, the truest, the sole firm foundation for whatever is good in man; upon them all the better part of modern civilization rests, and they alone are its preservatives, and resist and correct the tendency of every form of civilization to exhaustion and decay. I do not know whether modern civilization may or may not have a decline as well as a progress, a fall as well as an uprise: but if it fall, it will be because Christianity has been overpowered, and unbelief taken its place, and let loose the base herd of human passions from their foul den. But wherever Christ's Church shall still exist—for it ever will somewhere exist with Christ present in it, according to His promise (Matt. xxviii. 20)—there will be purity, chastity, temperance, self-restraint, the willingness to suffer, the spirit that 'counts all things but loss so that it may win Christ.' And these things it is which save not the soul only, but society, according to the deeper meaning of the promise, that if there be but ten righteous men in a city, God will not destroy it for those ten's sake (Gen. xviii. 32).

" To all the great principles then of Christianity the Old Testament bears witness, as well as to the facts of our Lord's life and the nature of His person and offices. Gradually, by a long course of teaching, the prophets led men on till they were fit for Christ: so fit that when Christ came the news of His mission was rapidly carried throughout the world, and found acceptance in every city. Even in the Gentile world, at all the great centres of human activity, devout men had been gathered from among the heathen in readiness for Christ. They were not proselytes, had not submitted to the burdensome ceremonial of Judaism, but they had learned from the Jewish scriptures the doctrines of God's unity, His justice, His mercy, His omnipresence, His spiritual nature. Without being Jews they went on the Sabbath to the synagogue to hear the words of the prophets read there. And these were the men who almost universally accepted Christianity, and who, added to the believing Jews, gave the nascent Church a strength and influence it could not, humanly speaking, have otherwise gained among the Gentiles. These were the men who made Antioch the second mother of the faith, who gave there to Christianity its name, freed it from all that was local and temporary in Judaism, and taught and commended it to the Gentile world. And they were the fruits of prophecy. In them the prophets had won the heathen as an inheritance for Christ.

In fact, Christianity could neither have so quickly won its way to general acceptance, nor have occupied now so firm and sure a position, had there not been this marvellous preparation for it, carried on so steadily through so long a period of time, and still testifying so clearly to its divine origin. That preparation began with the primæval promise made to the woman in the hour of the first great earthly sorrow. From that day onward one purpose, and one only, is ever kept in view in God's dealings with His fallen creatures. The promise was that man, worsted in his first encounter with his spiritual adversary, should crush that adversary's head by means of one of the same nature as himself, emphatically the woman's seed. That promise contained in outline the whole of prophecy. Of that promise the Gospel is the one fulfilment. From the day on which Eve was comforted by it, all God's dealings in grace;—for the Bible has nothing to do with God's dealings except as far as they belong to the covenant of grace; it is not a book of natural religion, but of supernatural;—but all God's dealings with man in grace, which are the proper object-matter of the Bible, relate to the performance of that promise. They are God's means for raising ruined man, not only to that height from which he fell, but to a far more glorious and perfect state even than that to which Adam would have attained, had he kept the terms of the first covenant (Rom. v. 15–21).

From this short sketch of the office of prophecy it will be manifest that it is by no means to be confounded with prediction. It was but a part of the office of the prophets to foretell certain necessary facts and particulars with respect to Christ. It was necessary that the preparatory dispensation should give certain sure signs by which the Messiah when He came might be identified. It was also necessary to keep alive in men a confident belief that the promise of a Deliverer would be fulfilled. Lastly, as the time of that fulfilment approached, it was necessary that the minds of men should be roused to a lively expectation that 'the latter days' had at length arrived. But this was not the whole office of the prophets, and the proof which the Old Testament offers to the truth of the New is something far larger and broader than even that extraordinary series of predictions so exactly fulfilled in our Lord and in His Church. Time however will not permit me to enter upon so wide a subject to-day, but in my next lecture I shall endeavour to show what is the true idea of prophecy, and what was the proper office and mission of the prophet.

LECTURE II.

THE PROPER IDEA AND MEANING OF PROPHECY.

God, Who at sundry times and in divers manners spake in time past unto the fathers by the prophets, hath in these last days spoken unto us by His Son.—
HEB. i. 1, 2.

THE Apostle in these words distinguishes between the manner of God's revelation in the Old and in the New Testament. In both God speaks: and the word used of this speaking is a kind and homely word (λαλέω), agreeing well with the informal[a] way in

[a] It is, however, really this informal manner in which the truth is given that renders the study of the Bible so rich in results. No other book could be dwelt upon word by word, and sentence by sentence, all our lives through, as we dwell upon the Bible, to find ever not only the dear old familiar long-treasured truth, but some new aspect or meaning or application of it. There is always a mine in it, not of new doctrine, but of fuller instruction in the deeper significance of the truths entrusted to the Church's keeping. Each age too of the Church collectively finds in the Bible what exactly answers to its needs. And thus it is not a mere record, nor a body of dead formulæ and definitions of doctrine, but is fraught with power, and with that faculty of adaptation which living bodies possess. Experience justifies what is said of it in Heb. iv. 12: 'The word of God is quick, i.e. living, ζῶν, and active, ἐνεργής,' capable of doing work, as living bodies alone are capable. Men may ridicule our respect for the Bible, may call it bibliolatry and book-worship; but the question really is whether what is said in Heb. iv. 12 is true. If the Bible possess a living energy such as no other book possesses, does not reason require us to treat it differently from mere ordinary books?

which the truth is given, not in set definitions, but so as to arrest our attention and interest us, and dwell upon our memories. But though the revelation is made in this informal way, nevertheless it is God who speaks, not *by*, as our translation renders it, but equally *in* the prophets and *in* the Son (ἐν τοῖς προφήταις—ἐν υἱῷ). The prophets were not mere messengers, to whom a definite form of words was entrusted: they spake freely, and fully, but yet not of themselves. They had some share in what they taught. There is no book in which the personality of each writer is more plainly marked than in the Bible. Each retains, alike in things great and small, his own individuality, his favourite modes of expression, even his peculiarities. But however great the freedom of the messengers, it was nevertheless God's message which they spake. And they knew it to be His. They ever ascribed it to Him, and declared that their words were not their own, but God's; not the working of their own minds, but something that came to them from without[b].

The difference, then, between revelation in Christ and in the prophets is not that the words of the One are more God's words than those of the others. To

---

[b] In the Hebrew text there is considerable diversity of expression in the manner in which the prophets refer all that is spoken to Jehovah. Thus Isaiah, while constantly saying that it is Jehovah who speaks (Isa. i. 2, 10. 18, &c), yet does not use an introductory formula in the regular way in which Jeremiah and Ezekiel prefix one to their several prophecies. Once or twice he speaks of a vision, or a word which he *saw*, a phrase peculiar to himself, to Obadiah, and Habakkuk, though evidently in popular use long afterwards (Ez. xii. 27, xiii. 6–8, Zech. x. 2). The usual title of

mark how thoroughly they both stand upon the same footing, the Apostle does not hesitate to use language from which perhaps we might have shrunk. We should have said, perhaps, that Christ spake of Himself, of His own fulness: that being God as well as man He spake as God. The Apostle, of set purpose, says, 'God spake in the prophets, and in the Son.' We must not then draw distinctions between the Old Testament and the New, as though they differed in authority, or in the nature and extent of their inspiration. Where God speaks, man's business is to obey. The distinction which the Apostle draws is in the manner of the revelation, the different way in which it was given, not in the degree of it. In the Old Testament it was partial, gradual, progressive; in the New, it is full, perfect, final, complete. We look forward to no further revelation. Not that we possess all truth. 'We shall know as fully as we are known' only in the beatific vision; but we possess

---

his prophecies is *massâ*, an ambiguous word signifying a *sentence*, *decision*, authoritative *decree*, in which sense Isaiah used it, and also a *burden*. This ambiguity led to ridicule and profanity on the part of the wits of Jerusalem (Jer. xxiii. 33-38), but nevertheless the word continued in use in its proper sense of a sentence passed by God, especially upon Gentile nations (Nah. i. 1, Hab. i. 1, Zech. ix. 1), though not confined to them (Zech. xii. 1, Mal. i. 1). Isaiah also says that Jehovah spake *by* him (Isa. xx. 2). Jeremiah constantly uses two formulæ, the first, 'The word of Jehovah was *unto* me' (c. ii. 1, &c.), and a stronger form, 'The word that was *upon* Jeremiah' (c. xxv. 1, &c.), implying the duty on his part to speak it, and suggesting also the reluctance against which he had so often to struggle (c. xv. 18, xx. 7, 8, 9). Ezekiel's constant phrase is, 'The word of Jehovah was *unto* me,' and this is the usual formula with the rest (Hos. i 1, Joel i. 1, &c). It must be noticed that it is always *Jehovah*, the covenant God, not *Elohim*, God simply, who speaks. It is the God of grace, not of nature.

all that necessary knowledge of our relations to God in Christ, and of our hopes for a future world, which was the proper object-matter of a revelation; all, namely, which the conditions of our probation in this world involved, if that indispensable probation was to be also merciful and just.

Revelation, then, in the Old Testament was, first, *in many parts or portions*, πολυμερῶς, not 'at sundry times' only; that is but a small part of the meaning. What the Apostle says is that it was an imperfect revelation, given in bits; now a little, and then a little, with long intervals during which no addition was made to the heritage of truth. The attitude of the saints of old was that of expectation; 'they searched, and searched diligently what time, or what manner of time the Spirit of Christ that was in them did signify, when testifying to them of Christ's sufferings (1 Pet. i. 11).' And thus they themselves constantly spake of 'latter days,' and of a 'new covenant;' whereas in the New Testament we read of the 'fulness of time,' and of a 'faith once for all delivered to the saints.'

Ours, too, is an attitude of expectation. 'We wait for the second coming of the Lord Jesus Christ.' But we wait for no new truth: we believe in no development of old truths. The truths of Holy Scripture, by its very faculty of life (Heb. iv. 12), adapt themselves to each succeeding age, and portions often long neglected, or but partially understood, break forth with new energy when circumstances call for their application. Of other portions it is only by careful study and diligent and oft-repeated examination, that the Church at length attains to their full meaning, and due relation to other truths. But a new article of the faith, by its very novelty, stands self-condemned. The Church's duty is, not to invent new dogmas, but to defend and maintain in its integrity the whole truth entrusted to its charge. Our duty is to study the inspired records, so carefully and with prayer, that by the Holy Spirit's aid we may comprehend, as adequately as our limited powers will permit, the unsearchable riches of the truth as revealed in Jesus Christ our Lord.

And next the truth was given 'in divers manners;' there is a varied ministry in the Old Testament, both of angels[c] and of men. And to men God spake variously, to Moses face to face, to others in dreams and visions; to some it may have seemed as the welling up of their own hearts, while to others it was an express message, which they delivered in God's name. When Moses gave his two histories of creation, he must have been recording absolute revelations, made to some of the patriarchs, in the first of which (Gen. i-ii. 3) man appears as the final crown simply of creation, its lord and master, whereas in the second (Gen. ii. 4–iii. 24) he appears as a being in covenant with God, using his freedom for his ruin, yet with that promise of restoration made him, which all the rest of the Bible is occupied in fulfilling. But in the account of the flood he gives the narrative of an eye-witness (see for instance Gen. vii. 19); and so also the history of Joseph (Gen. xxxvii–l, omitting Gen. xxxviii, inserted to keep the history of Judah, to whom now belonged the birthright, synchronological with that of Joseph) bears many internal proofs

---

[c] Especially in the time of the Judges.

of having been compiled from contemporary records, or even from a narrative composed by Joseph himself. Subsequently Moses recorded revelations made to himself, facts of history witnessed by himself, and predictions of the future, for Israel's warning and guidance. There is moreover a rich diversity of manner in which the truth is given: and constantly words, called forth by some temporary occurrence, rise up to an eternal significance. When David was celebrating the glories of Solomon's wide-spread dominion, his language, not perhaps altogether without his being conscious of it himself, swelled onwards to the universal reign of Christ. When in other psalms, and in the prophets, the saints poured out their sorrows, God's hand mysteriously rested upon them, and caused them to foreshow the deeper mystery of Christ's passion: so to foreshow it, that those who read felt that the words meant more than mere private grief. And then there were the types and shadows and figures of the law: and many symbolical acts both in the ritual and in the history of the nation, and typical personages, of all of which we know that the Jews regarded them as intended to convey doctrinal truths. It is no peculiarity of St. Paul that he finds Christian verities in Sarah and Hagar, and in the passage of the Red Sea, and in the smitten Rock. But we never interpret the New Testament in this way. It is not a book of type and allegory, but one whose teaching is explicit, definite, and complete. And it is so because we have in Christ 'the brightness of God's glory,' the ἀπαύγασμα, the pure light, that is, of God, unveiled, shining in absolute clearness, limited not in itself, but in us, by our narrowness, held but in part by us, because infinitely larger than we can hold. And thus, surrounded by the clear daylight, our business now is to endeavour thoroughly to understand what is revealed: for all necessary knowledge has been already given us; we have no new revelation to expect. It will be by the enlargement of our faculties that we shall attain to that entire insight into all truth, which will perfect the bliss of the beatific vision (1 John iii. 2).

But though thus the revelation of Christ in the Old Testament was first, partial, and secondly, bestowed in many different ways, yet absolutely the prophet was one in whom God spake. He was God's representative, whose business it was chiefly to speak, but often also to act for God. And plainly this is something far wider than the mere foretelling of future events. Prediction is part of prophecy: for as the past and the future are both present to God, one in whom God spake would be raised above the limits of time, provided that this elevation were needed by that particular portion of God's truth which he was commissioned to deliver. But if, as often was the case with the prophets, their office related to the present state of God's Church, no prediction would be spoken by them. Prediction, like miracle, was rare: nevertheless Isaiah declares that on fit and proper occasions prediction is an essential element of prophecy. In those noble chapters in which he so utterly overthrew idolatry, and proved the necessary unity of God's nature, he speaks thus; 'Tell ye and bring them near (that set up the wood of their graven image, and pray unto a god that cannot save): Who hath declared this from ancient time? Who hath told it from that time? Have not I, Jehovah? and there is no God else beside Me! A just God and a Saviour: there is none beside Me! (ch. xlv. 21).' And again; 'I am God, and there is none like Me, declaring the end from the beginning, and from ancient times the things that are not yet done! saying, My counsel shall stand, and I will do all My pleasure (ch. xlvi. 9, 10).' For plainly as God's knowledge is not limited like man's knowledge, so His words cannot be limited like man's words. Nor does the difficulty really lie in the possession by the prophets of this superhuman element. It lies farther back in the existence of the supernatural at all. If there be a God; if that God be more than a blind force; if He can will and do; if being thus a personal God He deign to have relations with man, His chief creature here on earth; if these relations involve His bestowal upon man of such knowledge as, being necessary for man's restoration, could yet in no other way be bestowed except by a message from God, the bearers of that message must have some proof to give that they really are God's messengers; and no proof can be sufficient except it be supernatural. The two supernatural proofs offered in the Bible are miracle and prediction. Any proofs but these would fall infinitely below the exigencies of the case.

For you would have men, who professed to bring words from God, words upon which man's everlasting salvation depended, and yet these men would have no proof to offer that their words were more than common words. Without prescience of the future, without power over the present, they could do nothing to justify the belief that what they said was anything better than hopes and aspirations dictated by their own hearts. Nay more: Christ spake as never man spake. He declares too that for those who are of God His words would be enough: for 'he that is of God heareth God's words (John viii. 47).' He further says, that if God had not spoken[d], if there had been no revelation, as there would have been no covenant of grace, no possibility of salvation, so also there would have been no such thing as sin. Man would have been in the same state as the cattle (John xv. 22). Yet, in spite of this, unless Christ had performed miracles, there would have been, He tells us, no obligation to examine into His claims, and no sin in rejecting Him. 'If I had not done among them the works which none other man did, they had not had sin (Ib. xv. 24).'

God spake then in the prophets: and necessarily His speaking in man must be something more perfect than mere human speaking; and being itself a miracle, it requires the supernatural proofs of prediction and miracle. And yet it is possible that

[d] In God's speaking we must nevertheless include the light of nature. God speaks in the conscience, and the fact that man possesses the faculty of distinguishing between right and wrong involves the duty of choosing what is right. A being set between right and wrong, and endowed with the power of distinguishing between them, is bound to do so. Bound to whom? What follows if he choose evil? If he resist conscience? Bound, I answer, to Him Who gave him a conscience, and Who enabled him to distinguish between good and evil. A being so endowed must be liable to a future judgment. If not, man is a blunder, a mistake in creation: he has the false semblance of qualities which serve for no useful purpose. As for happiness, instincts would not merely have sufficed, but have better provided for human happiness than conscience does.

the wonderful series of absolute predictions respecting the person and offices of the Saviour may have led in many minds to too complete an identification of prophecy with the foretelling of future events. Let us then examine what the Bible says of the prophet's office: for this too exclusive consideration of fulfilled prediction, while it rightly appreciates the great value of the Old Testament in bearing witness to us of Christ, yet makes us perhaps put too much out of sight the influence exerted by prophecy upon the Jews, its preparation for Christ's spiritual teaching, and the testimony it bears to many cardinal truths both of Christianity and also of natural religion.

Let us begin then with the names applied to the prophet in the Hebrew Scriptures. Of these the first is *Roëh*, a Seer. With two exceptions this name is applied only to Samuel; of these the first is in 2 Sam. xv. 27, where David asks the high priest Zadok, whether he is not a seer: while the second is found in the Book of Chronicles (2 Chr. xvi. 7, 10), a work compiled at a date subsequent to the return from Babylon, when the language was no longer spoken or written in its original exactness and purity. Isaiah also uses the term in the plural: 'This is a rebellious people, which say to the seers[e], See not, and to the prophets, Prophesy not unto us right things (ch. xxx. 10).' Nowhere

---

[e] The meaning of Isaiah is, that neither in their worldly matters nor in things spiritual would they listen to upright advice. The seers to whom they went on matters of business, the prophets to whom they went on matters of conscience, were both to combine in flattering and cajoling them. Still many of the seers may have been impostors, and false claimants to supernatural powers.

else does the word occur except with reference to Samuel.

From the narrative in Samuel we learn that the people were in the habit of consulting the prophets upon occasions of difficulty, and according to the reading in the Septuagint the term Seer was the popular name[f] assigned to them when so consulted. The Hebrew text makes the term Seer an archaic name for the prophet: the more probable reading of the Septuagint makes it not merely archaic, but also colloquial. In any case the term has nothing to do with prophecy in its proper sense. Even the large majority of those who, as belonging to the prophetic order, were called Nabhis, prophets, were not inspired[g]; and though the term inspiration, or its equivalents, is used in a far wider sense in the Old Testament than we might have expected[h], yet there is no reason for supposing that the Seers had any special Divine help whatsoever in resolving the difficulties of the people. Samuel, when consulted by Saul, did give him a divinely-inspired answer, but it was because the occasion was a great one; for the raw youth, who came with his half-shekel to enquire about his father's lost asses, was to be Israel's first king. Undisciplined as he was, unbroken to the yoke, and, as it proved, destined to fail in his probation, he yet possessed alike

---

[f] The LXX in 1 Sam. ix. 9, read העם for היום, the difference being simply the junction of the two central letters. The sense however is much altered, namely, 'for the people formerly used to call the prophet the seer.' The difference however in the letters would be much greater in the ancient or Samaritan method of writing, and thus the diversity of reading is probably subsequent to the Babylonian captivity.

[g] See Lecture III.   [h] See Appendix, Note B.

great personal and great mental endowments, and by his soldierlike conduct he did much in raising Israel to the dignity of an independent nation. But we have no reason for supposing that Zadok was inspired, or that the seers generally, as a class, were inspired. Even Hanani, who is mentioned in Chronicles as a seer, though undoubtedly also a prophet[1], may have really been a seer in the proper sense of the term, and Asa's rough treatment of him may have arisen from his venturing to transgress his usual office. It may be doubted whether Asa would have dared to imprison one generally regarded as a prophet.

But though not inspired, the seers were men of acute understanding, and probably often of better education than the mass of the people. By the exercise of a practised intelligence they solved difficulties which passed the comprehension of the rude countrymen around them. Their advice possibly was usually good in itself: but its success was due even more perhaps to the renewed energy which it breathed into the enquirer. Many even of these seers may have been impostors, if not consciously, yet unconsciously, and have claimed for themselves more than was their due. Even among us in Christian England there are all sorts of pretenders to spiritualistic

---

[1] He was a prophet, because his reproval of Asa, and the sentence passed upon him, are recorded as true prophetic acts. But it would not follow from 2 Chr. xix. 2, as unwary readers might suppose. Seer (in Hebrew Chozeh) belongs there to Jehu, who is thus described as above his father in dignity. He was a Chozeh, his father a Roëh. In Hebrew, people are described by their own name, and that of their father, and commentators not remembering this, sometimes ascribe to the father what undoubtedly belongs to the son; for though our version is ambiguous, the Hebrew is not. Thus, hen, Jehu Hananison is the Chozeh, and not Hanani.

powers, all sorts of books published which profess to divine the future. And, what is more extraordinary, there are even people who believe in them. But such pretensions can never endure the test of time. And so as regards these seers, the fact that the very name so entirely disappears suggests the idea that it became discreditable[k]. Seers in Samuel's days there were probably plenty: but the word of the Lord was rare, 'It was precious in those days: there was no open vision (1 Sam. iii. 1).' If seers had been equally rare, there would have been no popular name for them; nor would Saul's man-servant have known so exactly what was the method of consulting them. If it was customary to ask advice, and make a return in presents of food and half-shekels, there would be plenty, we may be sure, ready to receive the gifts.

Still at best we can only conjecture what the functions of the seers were. Like so much in Holy Scripture, we learn about them only incidentally, by reason of the providential occurrence which brought Saul to Samuel. No account is given of them, nor was intended to be given: but we may perhaps infer,

---

[k] Like most appellations it was an honourable one at first. For if Roëh does not occur till Samuel's days, other words from the same root do. Thus mar'eh, a vision, is found in Gen. xlvi. 2, 'God spake to Israel in the *visions* of the night,' and in Num. xii. 6, 'If there be a Nabhi among you, I Jehovah will make myself known unto him in a *vision*.' Here then it is spoken of as the usual form of revelation, yet as something infinitely lower than that which Moses enjoyed. The verb also is of frequent occurrence, as in Gen. xii. 7. One to whom a mar'eh was vouchsafed, would rightly be called roëh. Visions do not however appear to have been the ordinary way in which God revealed Himself to the greater prophets, Elijah, Elisha, Isaiah, Jeremiah, &c, though Ezekiel's vision of the dry bones is the most instructive of that great writer's lessons.

from the manner in which the name is applied to Samuel, that he was often thus consulted. Every real prophet would be thus beset. Instead of taking the trouble of deliberating for themselves, and doing their best, all feeble, slothful, and superstitious people would try to get the prophets to help them out of their difficulties. But in Samuel's time there was some excuse for it. The miserable state of the land after the utter defeat of Israel at Ebenezer (1 Sam. iv. 1, 10), made the people need, not the advice only but the encouragement, of the wise and thoughtful man who raised up the nation once again from its utter prostration to a renewed life. As he travelled on circuit year by year round the land, not merely judicial matters, but difficulties of every kind were probably laid before him. But again, we have no reason to suppose that either his answers as a Roëh, or his decisions as a Judge, were inspired[1]. As one established to be Jehovah's prophet he was by Divine right the temporal ruler of the country. He ruled well and firmly: he was a just, upright, able, and active man: he was more. God's gifts of grace were

---

[1] The gift of inspiration rested permanently on Moses, yet not for all and every, but only for fitting purposes. We find him even thankfully accepting the advice of his father-in-law, Jethro, upon a matter of the highest though only temporal consequence (Ex. xviii. 13—26). We are not to suppose, therefore, that in judging the people even he had any supernatural aid. So of the Apostles, St. Paul wrote at least three epistles to the Corinthians, one of which is not in our canon, being probably lost, because it was not inspired (1 Cor. v. 9). So again, it is by no means certain that he was right in going up to Jerusalem after the many warnings he had of what awaited him (Acts xx. 23, xxi. 11): the warnings were perhaps given him to prevent the great loss which the Church would sustain by his imprisonment. But he was an intrepid, determined man: was he also obedient?

largely possessed and used by him. One so holy, so pure in word and deed, was well worthy that under the extraordinary circumstances of the Jewish dispensation, the higher gift of Divine knowledge should rest upon him, to be used on all fitting and proper occasions. But miracle and prophecy were ever too sparingly given to justify us in supposing that the Roëh, the seer, possessed anything more than ordinary but practised acuteness. He must not be confounded with the prophet [m].

In the authorized version the term *seer* repeatedly occurs elsewhere, but it is the translation of an entirely different word. When we read in the same verse (1 Chron. xxix. 29) of 'Samuel the seer, and Nathan the prophet, and Gad the seer,' it would not suggest itself to an English reader, that the three terms are

[m] The Bible never does confound these entirely different gifts in Samuel. When Saul goes to consult him about his asses, it is incidentally mentioned that the vulgar view of the prophet was that he was a person to be consulted in the ordinary difficulties of life. It is quite possible that Samuel may have been even called Seer from this one occurrence. For the choice of Saul as king, and the valiant achievement (1 Sam. xi.) which made all Israel feel that he was king in very deed, must have made the whole land ring with every incident in his appointment. I incline however to the other view, that Samuel did give the people advice in their troubles. But this was a very different thing from those weighty matters in which 'Jehovah was with him,' and for which 'Jehovah appeared to him in Shiloh.' As Moses was the founder, so was Samuel the restorer of Israel; and it was, in this grand work that 'all Israel from Dan even to Beersheba knew that Samuel was established to be Jehovah's prophet (1 Sam. iii. 19–21).' Even the heathen could see that the two things were essentially distinct: for so we read of Oedipus,

ἀνδρῶν σε πρῶτον ἔν τε συμφοραῖς βίου
κρίνοντες, ἔν τε δαιμόνων συναλλαγαῖς.

Oed. Tyr. 33, 34.

essentially dissimilar[n]. Samuel is the *Roëh*, the man who can see, whose eyes are open, and who therefore is consulted in all the more important circumstances of human life. Gad is *Chozeh*, the gazer, one who sees visions, not the acute intelligent man, possessed of insight in matters of worldly business, but the tranced man who gazes with dazed eyes upon the verities of the spiritual world. This term is as distinctly modern, as that of Roëh is archaic. The usual term for a prophecy was Massa[o], a *sentence*, but also meaning a *burden*, and so usually rendered in our version. 'Remember how that when I and thou rode together after Ahab, Jehovah *burdened this burden* upon him,' but more correctly *passed this sentence* (2 Kings ix. 25). Subsequently a prophecy was called a *vision*, a term apparently brought into general use by Isaiah[p], and probably having in his writings a distinct reference to the glorious spectacle (ch. vi.) by which he was inaugurated into his office.

[n] Ewald (History of Israel, vol. i. 189 note, ed. Martineau) affirms that these words are not intended to convey different ideas, as is clear from 2 Chron. xii. 15, xiii. 22. I believe on the contrary that every word has its own proper idea, and its several history. Still, I grant that the word *Chozeh*, applied to Gad, came in popular language to be used as almost identical with *Nabhi* prophet, though its idea and origin are distinct. Mr. Martineau's translation, however, of *Chozeh* as *viewer*, is unfortunate. To view implies careful, exact examination. To view a vision is impossible. The real equivalent of Chozeh is *gazer*. Ewald's references do not touch the word Roëh. In a different place, in his Propheten d. A. Bundes i. 27 note, ed. 2, Ewald regards the three names Roëh, Nabhi, and Chozeh as distinct in idea, and as marking three progressive stages in the development of Hebrew prophecy.

[o] See note to page 33.

[p] Before Isaiah's time it occurs only in the 'open vision,' literally, 'the vision bursting forth' of 1 Sam. iii. 1, and in Psalm lxxxix. 19, and Prov xxix. 18.

By the simpler visions of the almond rod and the seething caldron Jeremiah (ch. i. 11, 13) was summoned to be Jehovah's prophet, and Ezekiel (ch. i. 4–28) by the chariot of the cherubim, and the four living creatures. And thus the thought of a vision became inseparably connected with the prophetic office. By a vision the prophet was appointed: and the word was applied collectively to the whole body or mass of a prophet's writings (Isa. i. 1, Obad. 1, Nah. i. 1, and 2 Chron. xxxii. 32), because in that inaugural vision all the rest, all God's subsequent revelations to him, virtually were contained.

This term, then, Chozeh, the seer, however different in derivation, became in time equivalent to the word 'prophet.' It meant the man who had been summoned to speak for God by a vision such as those of Isaiah, and Jeremiah, and Ezekiel. It does not follow that Gad had seen such a vision; it was simply a title first applied to the prophet in Isaiah's time because of the magnificent spectacle which he had witnessed, and which subsequently lost its special meaning, and was used of all the prophets indiscriminately[q]. And then, lastly, there is the one proper term for the prophet, *Nabhi*. Its derivation is from a root signifying 'to bubble up like a fountain[r].'

---

[q] This indiscriminate use of it however is confined to the Books of Chronicles. By his contemporaries I do not doubt but that Gad was called Nabhi.

[r] Ewald, Proph. d. A. B. i. 7, ed. 2, explains Nabhi as meaning a *loud clear speaker*. But he draws his explanation from the Arabic. This use of Arabic I have long rejected as utterly unscientific, and as having done more to corrupt Hebrew and to confuse Hebrew scholars than anything besides. Who would dream of settling the meaning of an Anglo-Saxon word by its present signification in English, or

But this overflowing fulness is not the prophet's own. The verb never occurs either in the Hebrew, the Syriac, or the Chaldee in the active voice. Like *vaticinor* in Latin, and μαντεύομαι in Greek, it is properly a passive, and as a passive[s] it is constantly used in the Scriptures both of the writings and of the oral teachings of the prophets. It was by compulsion that the message burst forth from their lips. So the word implies; and Jeremiah declares that such was literally the case with him. In deep distress at the supposed failure of his efforts, disappointed of his hopes, with wounded feelings at the mockery and derision which daily attended his preaching, surrounded by false prophets to whom the people willingly gave ear, he wickedly rebelled against God, and determined to cast his high office from him. 'Then I said, I will not make mention of Him, nor speak any more in His name.' But Jeremiah's rebellion was as vain as Jonah's flight. 'His word,' he says, 'was in my heart, shut up in my bones: and I was weary with forbearing, and I could not stay (Jer. xx. 9).' The prophet therefore neither regarded himself, nor was regarded by others as entirely a free agent. His freedom was not absolutely overpowered;

interpret the laws of the ten tables by French or Italian? There is a connection between Himyaritic Arabic and Hebrew sufficiently near to be of use: between the Arabic dialect which Mohammed adopted and Hebrew there is just such a false show of semblance as suffices to lead all those who use it utterly wrong.

[s] The passive in Hebrew is called *Nifal*. As an instance of the use of the verb in Nifal we may quote Amos iii. 8 :—

'The lion hath roared: who will not fear?
The Lord Jehovah hath spoken: who will not prophesy?'

i.e. who will not be compelled to pour forth. Our version, as usual, translates the vowels of the name of God, and leaves the consonants, which alone are genuine, untranslated.

but there was a bit in his mouth, and to be restive and struggle against it only brought grief and suffering upon himself.

The verb is also used in the reflective[t] voice, *he acted the prophet*. In this way it is spoken of the seventy elders, and of Eldad and Medad in the camp (Num. xi. 25–27); of the music and dancing of the sons of the prophets (1 Sam. x. 5); of Saul's participation in their religious exercises (1 Sam. x. 6, 10, 13); of the excited cries and contortions of the prophets of Baal (1 Kings xviii. 29); of the prophets who prophesied lies at Jerusalem (Jer. xiv. 14); and of those at Samaria who professed to be inspired by Baal (Jer. xxiii. 13). So, too, it is the word employed by Ahab, who probably regarded with something like contempt the wish of Jehoshaphat to know Jehovah's will (1 Kings xxii. 8, 18). Occasionally therefore it is used in a good sense, though scarcely ever of real prophecy. The seventy elders were regularly appointed to their high office of being deputies for Moses in the administration of justice, by having a share of the spirit that rested upon him communicated to them[u] (Num. xi. 17). It was God's gift, but it was the gift of government; just as it was God's spirit that rested upon Bezaleel, but it was the gift of artistic skill. Twice however it approaches the character of real prophecy. Thus it is said that Eliezer acted the prophet as to the

[t] This is called in Hebrew the Hithpahel. It means, to give one's self out as, or profess one's self, a prophet, to play the prophet.

[u] When first communicated there was evidently however a certain amount of excitement and agitation on their part, showing itself in unpremeditated and perhaps partially incoherent utterances, chiefly probably of praise.

wrecking of Jehoshaphat's navy (2 Chron. xx. 37)[x]; but the use of the verb suggests that Eliezer brought a prophetic message merely to Jehoshaphat; that he came in the character of a prophet, but was not himself inspired. And finally, in the vision of the dry bones (Ezek. xxxvii. 4, 9, 10, 12), Ezekiel is commanded—not to prophesy to the dry bones, and to the wind, as our version renders it, but—to *act as a prophet*. It was a vision, not a real occurrence. The vision was a revelation, and though Ezekiel seemed to himself to take part in it, and to give commands in the character of a prophet, this really was part of the vision, and not an actual fact. And the Hebrew, with that wonderful accuracy which marks every part alike of the Old and New Testaments in the original tongues, notes the distinction. It says that Ezekiel seemed to himself to take part in this vision, to be summoned to act in a prophetic capacity, and as such to utter God's commands.

Everywhere else the distinction between the real prophetic gift (Nifal), and the mere acting the prophet (Hithpahel) is so clearly marked that none can mistake it. The music and dancing of the sons of the prophets formed part of their regular education, and very probably were carried on, as dancing is in the East now, with an intense and enthusiastic

---

[x] The Books of Chronicles however, the latest in date of the Hebrew Scriptures, being composed when Chaldee and not Hebrew was the vulgar tongue, are not so exact in language as the rest, and therefore if any one considers that Eliezer was himself a prophet, all I can say is that he may have been, but he may not. If he was an independent prophet, then the use of the Hithpahel is a Chaldaism: for the Chaldee, having no Nifal, uses the Hithpahel as a simple passive.

excitement, such as seemed to pass the bounds of nature, while really it did not. But as a general rule, everywhere except in the four places ⁷ I have mentioned, the word is used absolutely in a bad sense, of a false and wicked sham, a blasphemous pretence. The distinction is so plain that it is noticed at least once in our version—'Every man that maketh himself a prophet (Jer. xxix. 26).' The Hebrew tells us that the prophets who prophesied lies at Jerusalem, and the Baal prophets at Samaria, and those who leaped on Baal's altar, while Elijah derided their folly, were not prophets made by God, but men who made themselves prophets. So, too, in Ahab's mouth the word was a confession of his unbelief. Neither the four hundred Jehovah-prophets, who bade him go and prosper, nor Micaiah, who warned him that he would go and die, were in his view men instinct with a higher power, but men who practised an art for their own gain.

But the word is even used in a worse sense. When Saul had failed in his probation, and fallen from God, and hardened himself in crime, it is said that 'an evil spirit of God came upon Saul, and he prophesied in the midst of the house (1 Sam. xviii. 10).' Really the word means that he imitated the prophetic excitement, and raved, and roamed about in a moody frantic state, miserable no doubt as bad men are; but instead of repenting he let jealousy take possession of him, and twice in his phrenzy cast his javelin at David. There was no doubt, a certain degree of

---

⁷ These four are (1) The seventy elders; (2) The sons of the prophets; (3) Eliezer's mission to Jehoshaphat; (4) Ezekiel's vision of the dry bones.

madness in his state: and to this day the Orientals regard madness as something divine. Even in the true prophets there was occasionally this labouring and excitement of spirit, such as made Elisha call for a minstrel to soothe his troubled feelings before he would prophesy in the presence of a son of Ahab. And so when a son—a disciple—of the prophets came as Elisha's messenger to anoint Jehu, the captains, struck by his strangely abrupt and hasty manner, describe him to Jehu as a madman:—'Wherefore came this mad fellow to thee? (2 Kings ix. 11)' So too in the Book of Jeremiah, madness and this acting the prophet are coupled together in the contemptuous letter of the false prophet Shemaiah, wherein, writing from Babylon, he urges the deputy high priest (Pâkîd) Zephaniah to punish and imprison Jeremiah. 'Jehovah,' he says, 'has made thee priest, that thou shouldest put in prison and into the stocks every man that is mad and maketh himself a prophet (Jer. xxix. 26).' By this use of the word he asserted that Jeremiah's claims to be a prophet were untrue[z].

[z] Ewald, Proph. d. A. B. i. 13, describes madness as the melancholy side of prophecy, resulting from the prophet not being able to control the strong emotions arising from the violence with which the Divine truth urges itself upon him, and hurries his whole nature along. Having thus lost his balance, he becomes either a fanatic or a dreamer. In proof of this he refers to Hos. ix 7, where 'the inspired man' is described as 'mad,' or rather as going backwards and forwards, in a state of great excitement. But such excitement would imply no madness. The prophet is speaking of the days of Israel's visitation, when the Assyrian host would crush the ten tribes with the sword. The nabhi, who had long preached repentance and foretold the coming ruin, would now be a 'fool,' having no more counsel to give, no more words of wisdom, no more salutary advice to utter. And 'the inspired man' might well roam

And thus, then, there is no looseness or inaccuracy in the Bible itself as to this great gift of Divine inspiration. The seventy elders, and Eldad and Medad, had a gift, but not that of prophecy. The sons of the prophets had no supernatural aid in their music and dancing. Saul, the false prophets at Jerusalem, the Baal priests of Samaria, raved no doubt; but of prophecy there is not a word. So exact is the Scripture, that Moses does not wish that the Lord's people had even such a gift as that of Eldad and Medad. He does not wish them either to claim what they did not possess, or to be all appointed officers and rulers in Israel. There would not have been room for all to be rulers. What he wishes is, that they were all true, genuine prophets, such as he was himself. 'Would God that all Jehovah's people were Nabhis!'

As regards this word *Nabhi*, the first place where it occurs is Gen. xx. 7, where Abimelech is warned in a dream to restore Sarah to Abraham, 'for he is a nabhi, and he shall pray for thee.' The word in this ancient book [a] is thus used in a distinct sense

---

about, horror-stricken at the miserable end of his country. There is in fact a plain allusion in the word to Deut. xxviii. 34, where it is said that the sight of the horrors committed by an invading army would produce this feeling in the minds of the conquered Israelites. The word does not imply the loss of reason, but only a frantic state of excitement. See 1 Sam. xxi. 14, 15, 2 Kings ix. 11, Jer. xxix. 26 Even if David's terror had made him temporarily deranged, the word itself does not prove it.

[a] Owing possibly to the Massorites having done their best to carry out a uniform system of grammar and pronunciation throughout the Bible, people entertain the vague idea that the language of the Pentateuch differs but slightly from that of Isaiah and other later writers. The exact opposite is the case. Not only is there an absence of several distinctions of gender which came into use afterwards, but as a usual rule the words employed are different.

from any that it ever had in later times[b]. It means one under God's special protection, one holding a closer than ordinary relation with God, and whose prayers therefore are acceptable. It may suggest the idea that Abraham bore a sort of sacred character; but his paying tithes to Melchizedek shows that such was not the case to any large extent. And certainly the history never sets him before us as one who had any message from God to the Canaanites[c]. He

[a] I became gradually more and more aware of this in writing my Syriac Thesaurus. I there found that the Syriac word is constantly represented by one word in the Pentateuch, and by another in later books. Ewald, whose view is that the historical books of the Old Testament have been recast an indefinite number of times, yet fully grants this fact so destructive of his theories. Speaking of 'the great book of the primitive history,' and of 'the great book of the kings (Judges, Ruth, Samuel, Kings)' he says: 'Although both are equally made up of passages by the most diverse writers, yet on the whole each is distinguished by a peculiar cast of language. Many fresh words and expressions become favourites here, and supplant their equivalents in the primitive history; others that are thoroughly in vogue here are designedly avoided in the primitive history, and evidently from a historical consciousness that they were not in use in the earliest times; but the most remarkable and pervading characteristic is that words of common life, which never occur to the pen of any single relator of the primitive history, find an unquestioned reception here.'—Hist. Israel, i. 133. In the face of this he affirms that the basis of the Pentateuch is in the main two historical works (helped out by a multitude of others), the first *the Book of Covenants*, written in Samuel's time, and parts of which are incorporated in *Judges*; and *the Book of Origins*, which covers the whole space from Gen. i. to the building of Solomon's temple, and of which parts are incorporated in *1 Kings*. Both works, then, had a common basis: how could the language be kept distinct?

[b] The passage quoted from Ps. cv. 15, is a remarkable corroboration of this. Tradition had evidently preserved the fact that the patriarchs had been called prophets, at a time when such a meaning of the term had long disappeared from the ordinary language.

[c] Abraham, taking with him a powerful clan (Gen. xiv. 14), left the probably more thickly peopled Ur of the Chaldees, and subse-

taught his own household religiously, as every upright head of a family would now, but he had no commission to speak in God's name, and reveal His will. Once, and once only besides, is there a similar use of the word in Holy Scripture. 'Touch not my anointed, and do my prophets no harm (Ps. cv. 15).' The prophets here referred to are the twelve patriarchs, men not inspired, but living in closer than ordinary relations to God, as admitted into covenant with Him.

The next place in which the word *Nabhi* occurs is one that throws singular light upon its meaning, and which will sufficiently settle its true sense. 'Jehovah said unto Moses, See, I have made thee a God, Elohim, to Pharaoh, and Aaron thy brother shall be thy prophet (Ex. vii. 1).' Now Aaron had no message of his own to deliver. He was not even a man fit to be trusted apart from Moses (Ex. xxxii. 1–6). His duty was to find words with which to explain to the people the will of Moses, according to what we read in the parallel place, 'Aaron shall be thy spokesman unto the people (literally, shall speak

quently Haran, to wander in the southern districts of Palestine, a region by no means of great fertility, and where the population was sparse. We find the Amorites there confederate with him, and a priest-king blessing him in the name of 'the most high God,' and receiving tithes of him (Gen. xiv. 13, 19, 20). We gather from this that though the Canaanites in many of the more fertile parts were grossly voluptuous, yet that they still possessed some knowledge of the true God, and were not tainted in the country districts with the sins which brought down chastisement on the cities of the plain (Gen. xv. 16). Abraham then wandered in the wildernesses of southern Palestine to preserve his clan from corruption, just as afterwards Israel was shut up in Goshen that it might remain pure. The time for the regeneration of the world had not yet come, and Israel was only being trained for effecting it.

for thee to the people): and he shall be to thee instead of a mouth, and thou shalt be to him instead of God (Ex. iv. 16).' Now God and man are so infinitely remote in their own proper natures, that without a mediator or interpreter it would not be possible for them to hold any communication with one another. God's will, and whatever knowledge He may be pleased to give us of heavenly things, must be brought down to human ideas and narrowed to the smallness of human words, before we can possibly understand them. To suppose that human words and human ideas can be adequate exponents of divine truths in their full perfectness is simply absurd. As certainly as a vessel can hold no more than its own measure, so certainly no being can understand anything higher than itself. The animals have no power of understanding those qualities in which man transcends the limits of their nature: man has no power of understanding those qualities in which angels excel us[d]: the very angels and archangels have no power

[d] We must suppose that St. Paul himself understood the revelations made to him in 2 Cor. xii; and also that there was nothing unlawful or unfit to communicate to other saints in the things of which the angels conversed with him. But if St. Paul understood those revelations only by supernatural help, the law which prevented his communicating them to others (2 Cor. xii. 4) must have been the law of man's nature. The revelations probably did relate to those things into which men often so earnestly try to penetrate—the mysteries of Christ's future kingdom and of the world to come. Now if St. Paul had endeavoured to bring down these paradisiacal ideas to the level of human language, he would necessarily have been misunderstood, and the Church would have been injured and not benefited by having revelations made to it beyond the bounds of its present capacities. Hence it is a note of the Canonical Scriptures that they are silent upon these mysteries. The nearest approach to an exposition of them is in Rev. xx, and early councils very strongly condemned what looks like a not unreasonable exposition of St. John's words.

of comprehending God's infinities. For the finite, however large, can never comprehend the Infinite. If then any knowledge of heavenly things was to be given to man, there must be a mediator between God and man. The very centre of Christianity is that such a Mediator has been given; one in Whom the infinite, incomprehensible, unapproachable God became one with finite man. In this God-man, the Immanuel, Whom Isaiah describes as God's especial sign, there was this meeting of heaven and earth, by means of which the truths of heaven could be communicated to man. 'God spake in the Son:' it became possible to express in human ideas and human words, not perfect knowledge, but such knowledge of divine things as was necessary for man's salvation. And such as Christ was in His fulness, such were the prophets in their degree. I bade you before remark that the Apostle uses the same word of them as of our blessed Lord. And now I ask you to observe how, in the very first place in which the word 'prophet' is used in its proper sense, we have just the same truths set before us. We should shrink from the language twice used, that any one man should be a God to another. But it is God Who speaks it. And how deep the mystery! Moses as God, Pharaoh as sinful man, cannot approach one another. There must be a mediator. The prophet is that mediator. Until the true Mediator came, the prophet was His representative. When the true Mediator had come there were prophets no more. There are no mediators now between heaven and earth. Christ is the one point of junction, the one bridge which makes a pathway over the abyss, and unites the Infinite and the finite. The last representative prophet was John the Baptist. The προφήτης of St. Paul's epistles, the προφήτης of the early Church, was something quite different. His business was to preach, to speak for God by urging upon the consciences of the people acknowledged truths. He had no new truth to declare; bore no message from God but that once for all entrusted to the Church's keeping.

Under the Old Testament, then, the prophet was the mediator, whose business it was in his measure to do that which Christ did fully and finally for His Church. For the whole theory of the Bible is that man needs a certain amount of information as to his soul, its relations to God, and to eternity. This knowledge must be conveyed to man through some such medium as will enable him to understand it. It cannot be perfect knowledge, because man is incapable of understanding perfect knowledge. It would be no use giving man even angelic knowledge: for man is not merely 'an earthen vessel' (2 Cor. iv. 7), but a very small vessel; the utmost knowledge therefore of which he is capable is but little, and that little must be in relation to himself, and such as suits his feeble powers. God then chose men as the mediators to convey to man in a human way, as being the only way in which he could possibly understand it, such knowledge as was both necessary and sufficient. Sufficient it must be, or it were no good giving it at all. But the amount of truth given was limited by man's needs. There is all that he requires, but nothing more: nothing given to satisfy our curiosity, or even our thirst after knowledge. Yet God of His mercy has given us this limited measure of truth in such a way that we seem never to reach the bottom of it. The more we read, the more full of meaning the Bible seems to be: and as men grow in grace it does unfold to them more and more of God's ways, and they do see more clearly in it God's mysteries of love, and read it with deeper awe and reverence, as it speaks to them with more power, and becomes day by day more thoroughly the law by which they live, and the comfort which sustains them in this troubled world. Still, we are not to read it for knowledge' sake merely, but for use. It has been given to us to enable us to walk in that narrow pathway whereby we may attain to those mansions of perfection where knowledge also will be ours, for 'we shall know even as also we are known (1 Cor. xiii. 12).'

I know that by many these mansions are regarded as but an unsubstantial hope; and each advance in science, each growth in knowledge, as it reveals to us more and more of those perfect laws by which the Creator works, is supposed to remove that Creator from us, and to leave us laws only without a lawgiver, and earth only without a heaven. But however perfect the knowledge of our bodies may become, there is ever something beyond, something which physical science cannot grasp, because it lies not within its province; and still do the secret cravings of our nature prompt the question, Has this earthly body, constructed so curiously and admirably, any unearthly inhabitant? Is life mere chymical action and nothing more? Are these so-called mental workings within it simply the result of organization, and therefore not mental but corporeal? Are there truths that lie safe within the heart of man, because placed there by God? or are they, not truths, but unsubstantial mockeries?

The answer to these questions cannot be given by physical science; it belongs to other studies, studies such as those in which Plato of old excelled, who, by the examination of the workings of the human mind, deduced the conclusion that there was in man something immortal. The very first lesson about man in the Bible is that he was made out of the dust of the ground. We start with this; every part of man's bodily organization is physical: and science, by giving a more exact meaning to the language of Scripture, does but enable us with deeper insight to join in the Psalmist's words, 'I will praise Thee, for I am fearfully and wonderfully made' (Ps. cxxxix. 14). But it gives no answer to the question, Is the universal belief of mankind in the existence of a God the result of a Divine impress upon the human mind? Is it a breach of my nature to deny that God exists, and that He has relations with me? Are those other words of the Bible true which speak of man as made in God's image and likeness? (Gen. i. 26). Now verities such as these the Bible never attempts to prove. It never strays off into philosophy or metaphysical science, any more than it does into physical science. Wherever any allusion is made to these branches of knowledge, it is for some moral purpose. The existence of a God, His unity and perfectness; the existence of a soul, its immortality and spiritual nature,—these cardinal truths are taught by the very constitution of the human mind, and by its irresistible promptings. The Bible does but state them clearly, purely, adequately: it does not prove, but asserts them. It asserts them as self-evident truths. Apart from religion they may be but probabilities: yet even as the probabilities of our nature, they become the law of our nature—the law of our higher and spiritual, though not of our physical nature. The groundwork of the Bible is the tacit assumption that there is a difference between right and wrong, that answering to this difference there is in man a conscience, above man a God, and before man a judgment. It assumes this, and the prophet's message related simply to man's duty to God; it told him of his present probation, of his future hopes, of God's love, of an opened way of mercy, of sins forgiven, of man reconciled to his Maker, and admitted to an eternal happiness. The prophet in these things was God's spokesman.

Now there are two things in the Mosaic record entirely in accordance with what I have here said, and which will both themselves be better understood if viewed in connection with the prophet's office, and also throw much light upon it. The one is the nature of the government of the Jews as established by Moses, the other is his celebrated prediction of God raising up unto them a prophet like unto himself.

The idea of the government established by Moses was that of Jehovah's direct autocracy. The Jews were fenced off from all other people, and were to live under a special providence, with Jehovah as their king. The actual administrator of the government was to be chosen by Him, and was to have His direct aid and counsel. The ordinary means provided for this by Moses was the Urim and Thummim; and the priest was the appointed person by whom Jehovah's will was to be made known. But Moses himself made no use of the Urim and Thummim.

It was intended for use only when there was no prophet: and thus when, after Samuel's days, God was pleased to bestow the gift of prophecy more abundantly, we read of it no more. David is the last person mentioned as thus consulting God, and Abiathar the last priest who spake in God's name by means of the ephod^e. The priest therefore with the Urim and Thummim was confessedly something inferior to the prophet. Probably nothing more could be learned by it than Yea and Nay. And while it is quite possible that Moses may have expected that the priests would perform many of those duties which as a matter of fact they neglected—I mean the spiritual duties of their office, teaching, and preaching, and instructing the people, and warning them of their sins, and urging upon them the necessity of a godly life;—while the priests seem to have attached

^e Thus David 'enquired of Jehovah' not only when fleeing from Saul (1 Sam. xxiii. 9), but in his wars with the Philistines after he was made king (2 Sam. v. 19, 23, 1 Chron. xiv. 10, 14). From 1 Sam. xxviii. 6, however, it appears that we must not infer that the term 'enquired of Jehovah' necessarily implied making use of the ephod, so that it is quite possible that Nathan, or some other prophet, may have given David the instructions recorded in 2 Sam. v. 19, 23. Passages certainly referring to the Urim and Thummim are Judges xx. 27, 1 Sam. xxii. 10, 15, xxviii. 6, 2 Sam. ii. 1, xvi. 23, 1 Chron. x. 14, xiii. 3, and probably 2 Sam. xxi. 1. We observe in these passages that it is accounted as a sin to Saul that he made no use of the Urim and Thummim; that is, being the first king, he deliberately rejected that means whereby the will of Jehovah as their civil ruler had been previously made known. David's restoration of the ark to its place, and his frequent use of it and of the ephod, mark his determination to rule as Jehovah's representative. Nevertheless gradually he abandoned the use of it, and in the rebellion of Absalom he absolutely declined the presence, not only of the ark, but of Zadok and Abiathar (2 Sam. xv. 24-29). Whatever his reason may have been, he refused to make use of the Urim and Thummim in that unnatural war.

themselves too much to their ritual duties, and to have neglected the weightier matters of their office, still, even from the first, the prophet stood on a far higher elevation than the priest. Moses was as high above Aaron as Isaiah was above Azariah, the high priest of the house of Zadok (2 Chron. xxxi. 10) in Hezekiah's days; as high above Aaron as Jeremiah was above Seraiah and Zephaniah, the high priests in Zedekiah's days (Jer. lii. 24); as high above Aaron as the spiritual must ever be above ritual. And the prophets, with their earnest preaching and teaching, their incessant admonition of the people, their stern and unwavering denunciations of sin, their attacks upon idolatry, their warnings that sacrifices and sabbaths, fastings and festivals, might be an abomination, and that to trust in the temple—to trust in anything but in a cleansed heart and a contrite spirit—might be to trust in lying words (Jer. vii. 4);—they in all this were the worthy followers of Moses. They had not necessarily civil power. Samuel possessed it; and we read that in his days the possession of the spiritual illumination of the Nabhi carried with it the right to the government of the state[f]. But when the people determined to have a king, they separated the two things for ever, and Samuel long protested

---

[f] This is implied in 1 Sam. iii. 20. It seems, from the example of Eli, that, when there was no prophet, the high priest was invested with the temporal power, possibly because he alone could consult Jehovah by means of the Urim. As the ark is often associated with the Urim, the people probably took it and Eli's sons with them to battle for the purpose of obtaining auguries (1 Sam. iv. 4); but immediately that it became plain that the prophetic inspiration rested upon Samuel, the priests with the Urim retired into their proper office, and Samuel, as Nabhi, became also Shophet or Judge.

against the change, because he saw that henceforward the true representative of Jehovah, the true administrator of the theocratic government, would be deprived of his right place. But even then the prophets had the right, and usually the power, to dethrone kings, and bestow the crown upon others (1 Kings xi. 31, &c.). And though shorn, from the days of Saul, of the civil power, yet in all other respects they were the successors of Moses ; only so far from excelling that great spokesman for God, Holy Scripture clearly points out the particulars in which the rest of the prophets fell short of the full powers possessed by the first and greatest of their order (Num. xii. 6-8, Heb. iii. 5).

The prophet then was the representative of God under the theocratic government, the vizier, or deputy, whose business it was to speak in God's name. And in the Book of Judges, the civil governors, who were also God's representatives, hold a sort of prophetic position. Deborah indeed judged Israel because she was a prophetess, and the warrior Barak obeyed her. Her successors were men chosen, as we should say, providentially, yet some by direct commission, by the agency of angels, as Gideon and Samson. But their gift was in the main that of government and military skill. And thus, as not having the highest gift, that of speaking God's truth, they are not called prophets, and we read of angels, spiritual messengers from Jehovah, more frequently than of prophets in the interval between Moses and Samuel [g]. Yet neither

---

[g] The only prophet mentioned in the Book of Judges besides Deborah was the nameless man who preached repentance just before

Joshua, nor Othniel, nor Gideon, nor Jephthah, nor Samson seem to have used the Urim and Thummim: apparently it was used only when God had no representative, no one who had the right either to speak or to act in His name (cf. Judges xx. 18, 23, 28). 'The Spirit of Jehovah,' we read, 'came upon Othniel, and he judged Israel (Judges iii. 10);' 'The Spirit of Jehovah came upon Gideon, and he gathered the people for battle (Ib. vi. 34);' 'The Spirit of Jehovah came upon Jephthah (Ib. xi. 29).' And four times the same phrase is used of Samson[h] (Ib. xiii. 25, xiv. 6, 19, xv. 14). The impulse to perform those actions necessary for the preservation of Israel's nationality came

---

Gideon was summoned to Israel's rescue (Judges vi. 8-10). Here then the higher and spiritual duty of preaching was separated from that of government, even more completely than in the case of Barak.

[h] A difficulty may perhaps often have been felt with reference to the high praise given to the heroes of the Book of Judges, which may be resolved probably by bearing in mind two considerations. The first, that God's Spirit, resting upon men like Jephthah and Samson, did not remove them out of the level of their own age. They are both freely numbered with God's saints in Heb. xi. 32, and were doubtless worthy of the high rank given them, and yet may have attained to a far lower degree of holiness absolutely than the saints of the New Testament or of Christian times. They must be judged relatively to their own times, for God's Spirit is never revolutionary: the settled order of things goes on in what seems a natural sequence of cause and effect, and the saints are liable to all the prejudices and common errors of their own age, nor can they advance more than a certain limit beyond it. And secondly, the gift of the Spirit, either for government or for declaring the truth, did not interfere with a man's individual probation. God's gifts do not take away our responsibility, but only increase it. In the Book of Jeremiah we have a deeply interesting account of the struggles that went on in the prophet's mind before finally grace was triumphant. But see Note B in the Appendix.

upon them from without, from God, quite as much as the impulse which compelled the prophets to proclaim certain truths. And this was an essential part of the theocracy. It was God's direct government: and for that government it was necessary that certain acts should be done, or it could not have been carried on. But those who spake for God held a still higher place than the civil governors. For though certain even of their acts might have a typical meaning, yet primarily the Judges had their commission for temporal and present purposes only, for the good government of the Israelites and the preservation of their national existence. The prophets had further to prepare for Christ, and continually to raise the nation to a higher state of morality, of knowledge, and of fitness for the spiritual truths of the Gospel.

And thus, then, we come to the second point, the prediction namely of Moses, twice referred to in the Acts (iii. 22, vii. 37): 'The Lord thy God will raise up unto thee a Prophet from the midst of thee, of thy brethren, like unto me; unto Him ye shall hearken[i]

---

[i] Ewald (Hist. Israel, i. 125, note 3) denies that this passage was originally Messianic, and asserts that it became so only through the influence of Deut. xxxiv. 10–12. But this latter place asserts, what is undeniable, that no prophet ever did rise up in Israel like unto Moses, and if, as probably was the case, it was added by Ezra, it gives his deliberate judgment, that during the whole era of prophecy the promise made by Moses had not been fulfilled. Further, it shows that the Jews did look forward to the coming of a prophet, who should occupy a place similar to that held by Moses in the wilderness. But, as not unfrequently is his custom, what Ewald denies in one place he virtually grants in another. Thus he says, that 'the eternal truths were nowhere so clearly and firmly held as in Israel, and consequently the strong consciousness could not but prevail there that their

(Deut. xviii. 15).' Now we have already seen that the prophet was, generally, the mediator between God and man; and specifically, that under the theocracy he was God's deputy, and endowed also with the civil power until the people, by the appointment of a king, separated their state government from the direct control of Jehovah. Now both these powers, the power of speaking for God, and the power of acting for God ʲ, existed in Moses in a far fuller manner than

community must advance to some more perfect state, to something nearer the ideal of human striving. But these Messianic hopes were no invention of the prophets: they inherited them as an old and settled property' (Proph. d. A. B. i. 29, ed. 2). But from whom did they inherit them? How did Israel first gain these eternal truths? Whence came this certainty that Israel was to bestow upon all mankind a perfect blessedness, and itself enjoy an imperishable existence? Well! the great part which Moses had in endowing Israel with these high hopes—hopes destined to be fulfilled—is undeniable, and Ewald does not deny it. The whole is granted, but the parts must be denied. The Jews always did look forward for some one to come, though their ideas were often modified by present circumstances. It was Moses who made them thus look forward. This is granted. But Moses must not be allowed to say anything special. Explain everything special away, and the haze that remains will do no harm. It is not enough for faith, and therefore may be left alone. But is such a method of exposition sound and reasonable?

ʲ I ought rather to have said 'for *Jehovah.*' In His covenant relations to Israel the name of the Deity is Jehovah. Not Elohim, the God of nature, but Jehovah, the God of grace, was the king of the covenant people; and doubtless by this name is meant our Lord Jesus Christ. So in the Te Deum, addressing Christ we say, 'We acknowledge Thee to be the Lord,' i. e. Jehovah. And thus, while the 'Word of God' is a phrase constantly used in the New Testament, where God's mercies are coextensive with all nature (Mark xvi. 15), it is not used more than half-a-dozen times in the Old Testament; nor do the prophets speak in the name of God, but of Jehovah. As for the real pronunciation of this name, while Jehovah is certainly wrong, I am fully convinced that Jahveh is not right. Its use is to me a mere in any of his successors. The distinction is declared by Jehovah Himself. We read in the Book of Numbers (xii. 5–8), that when Aaron and Miriam reproached Moses for having married a Cushite wife, and Moses meekly bore their reproaches, Jehovah came suddenly down in the pillar of the cloud, and summoning the offenders into His presence, reproved them thus: 'Hear now My words: If there be a prophet among you, I Jehovah will make Myself known unto him in a vision, and will speak unto him in a dream. My servant Moses is not so, who is faithful in all My house. With him will I speak mouth to mouth, even apparently, and not in dark speeches; and the similitude of Jehovah shall he behold.' Now, not only does it follow from this that inspiration was a permanent and abiding influence upon Moses, an occasional and temporary gift to the rest, but it shows us why Moses had this higher gift. He held a position such as no one besides ever held. In all God's house—in His Church —it was his to order and command as he would, though only as the steward, the servant, while Christ is the Son[k]. That which Moses did by appointment,

---

affectation of an unattainable exactness. The true sound of the name was pronounced only once a year while the temple stood, on the great day when the High Priest entered the Holy of Holies. Had it been recoverable, it would have been found out before the nineteenth century. All the arguments for the name being Jahveh start with the incredible assumption that the vocalization of the Massorites represents the original pronunciation. It is very useful, very clever, very systematic, but that it gives us the actual pronunciation used by Moses is not only not proved, but is contrary to the evidence.

[k] Even the Son is not absolute master. He is heir of all, and His rights come to Him by nature, not by gift. Yet as Son He can neither

by a delegated authority, that Christ does by right of His nature; and in His own house, for 'the Church is Christ's body (Eph. i. 23),' in which His will, as being the will of the Head, reaches to and controls every part. But the Jewish Church stood in no such relation to Moses. It belonged to Jehovah, and Moses was His slave.

The changed institutions of our time make us lose much of the force of this comparison between Christ and Moses. Used to the idea of predial slavery, and to the degraded condition of the slave as set before us by the political economists of Greece, who in their inhuman materialism regarded him only as ἔμψυχον ὄργανον, an implement endowed with life, differing from the plough or mattock in much the same way as the ox differed from them;—used to see this detestable idea pushed to its base but legitimate consequences by the trading avarice of Christian nations, aided no doubt by the fact that the slave in modern days is one of a different race and colour, marked off by physical inferiorities from his master, and not therefore appealing to his sympathies in the same way as if he had been in the main his master's like and equal;—used thus to negro and predial slavery, we carry our horrible notions into the Bible, and imagine that the Hebrew slave held an analogous condition. When we turn to oriental commentaries,

---

do nor say anything as of Himself. For the former, see Christ's words in John v. 19; for the latter, John xii. 49. Yet in this there is a mystery, though not past solving, when we reflect that the Son is the χαρακτήρ (Heb. i. 3), in Whom the Father's ineffable will finds outward form and expression.

we find altogether a different feeling. We read, for instance, in an Exposition of the Prodigal Son[1], that in the household there are three grades of dependence, first that of the son, next that of the slave, last of all that of the hired freeman, 'the mean white' of modern days; and it is noted as a mark of humility in the repentant prodigal, that he asked only for the lowest place. However this may be, we certainly find two things in the Bible; first, the entire recognition of the religious equality of the slave. He was to be admitted to the covenant (Gen. xvii. 12, 13), the Sabbath (Ex. xx. 10), the passover (Ib. xii. 44), the feast of weeks (Deut. xvi. 11), and tabernacles (Ib. xvi. 14), on just the same footing as his master. And further we find, that if there was no son, then the slave stood next. He was heir to the property; on him devolved the tribal chieftainship[m]; and if there were daughters, husbands were chosen for them from the slaves[n]. In the clan the head slave stood in all respects next in rank to the chief and his sons.

The same thing happens in oriental countries now. The great officers of state, its prime ministers and

---

[1] Cod. Bodl. Or. 624, fol. 670. See also Ex. xii. 45.

[m] Thus Eliezer of Damascus, a slave born in his house, was Abraham's steward, the next in rank to him in the tribe, and till a son was born the heir to all his wealth and power. This office of steward is exactly parallel to that held by Moses in Israel towards Jehovah, Israel's king.

[n] Thus Sheshan gives his daughter in marriage to an Egyptian slave named Jarha (1 Chron. ii. 34). By so doing he prevented his landed possessions and chieftainship from being absorbed in those of some other princely house.

treasurers, begin life often as slaves. And thus we can understand the meaning of that peculiar title given in so remarkable a manner to Moses, by virtue of which he holds a place in revelation inferior only to that held by our Lord. He is Jehovah's servant; literally translated, *Jehovah's slave;* translated according to the sense, Jehovah's prime minister, His vicegerent and vizier. Now Moses never appropriates this honourable distinction to himself[o]. It is first found in the narrative of his death, by whomsoever written, and whensoever added to the history. 'So Moses the servant of Jehovah died in the land of Moab (Deut. xxxiv. 5).' It is subsequently given him in the Books of Joshua (seven times), of Kings (1 Kings viii. 53, 56), of Chronicles (2 Chron. i. 3, xxiv. 6), in the Psalms (cv. 26), and in Malachi (iv. 4). He is called the servant of Elohim in Chronicles (1 Chron. vi. 49, 2 Chron xxiv. 9), in Nehemiah (x. 29), in Daniel (ix. 11), and finally in Revelation (xv. 3), the substitution of the term Elohim being probably occasioned by that superstitious reverence for the

---

[o] Moses records in the place quoted above (Num. xii. 7), that Jehovah called him *My servant Moses;* but so he records that Jehovah spake in similar terms of Caleb, *My servant Caleb* (Num. xiv. 24). It seems, therefore, that the name was not given to Moses because of God thus addressing him, for then it would have equally been applied to Caleb. It was given to him because he did as a fact hold a peculiar place in God's dealings with mankind. Unless this too is borne in mind, and the relation in which Moses, Jehovah's servant, and Christ His son, stand to one another, it will be impossible to understand the place held by Jehovah's servant in the last twenty-seven chapters of Isaiah. The LXX had a true appreciation of the importance of the name when they applied an analogous term, παῖς, to Abraham (Gen. xviii. 17).

name Jehovah, which gradually grew up among the Jews, which made them unwilling to utter it, which has further led to its being usually translated *Lord* in our version, and which makes us at this day pronounce it with vowels belonging to another word. Jehovah is a name made up of the consonants of one word, and the vowels of another[p].

Moses, then, emphatically is Jehovah's servant: and the name is virtually peculiar to him. It is true that Joshua, that is, Jesus[q], is so styled once, in the narrative of his death (Josh. xxiv. 29); and rightly. He was the finisher of Moses' work, and the type of the true Jesus. And once, and once only, is it found again, in Isa. xlii. 19, in a passage strongly Messianic. Why there used, and what it means, I have elsewhere fully discussed[r].

Moses therefore ruled Jehovah's house as that servant who, in the familia, the household of slaves, represented the master, and was invested with his authority. Less than the son, greater than any besides, nearer to the master, yet not one with him in nature as is the son, he is the steward, armed with all

[p] The Jews read it by the vowels alone, that is, they read it either Elohim, *God*, or Adonaẏ, *Lord*, according as it had the vowels of one or the other. Usually it has the vowels of Adonaẏ, the first *a* being a schva, or auxiliary vowel merely, like the *a* inserted by us in 'baptism,' pronounced baptisa'm, or baptisem. The words might thus be written, J'hovah, 'donay. The word *Lord* in our version is a translation, not of *J'hovah*, which is distinctly a proper or personal name, but of *'donay*.

[q] Joshua is always called Jesus in the LXX and in the New Testament (Heb. iv. 8). There is very great doubt about the correctness of the Massoretic punctuation Joshua and Jehoshua. The Massorites themselves twice punctuate the name Jeshua = Jesus, namely, in Ezra ii. 2, iii. 2.

[r] In my 'Messianic Interpretation of the Prophet Isaiah.'

the master's power, and entitled to lay down the law, yet not by any plenary or inherent right, but by virtue of his office. In this respect Moses holds a place distinct from any prophet beside; and our Lord was a prophet like unto Moses. There is no such complete analogy between our Lord and the ordinary prophet. The ordinary prophet did but deliver another's message. But Moses was a legislator—the bringer in of a dispensation. So also was our Lord. On Moses the spirit of prophecy rested without measure (Num. xii. 8): so it did on Christ (John iii. 34). Jehovah knew Moses face to face (Ex. xxxiii. 11, Deut. xxxiv. 10): 'the only begotten Son, which is in the bosom of the Father, hath declared that God Whom no man hath seen at any time (John i. 18).' No prophet was like unto Moses in the signs and wonders which Jehovah sent him to do (Deut. xxxiv. 11): Christ wrought works which none other man did (John xv. 24). But that which Moses did by an authority delegated to him, that Christ as the Son did by His own inherent power.

But if Christ and Moses stand in this relation to one another, then necessarily must Moses give the outline of the whole Gospel. The most ancient writer in the Bible, by the peculiar position which he holds, must in some way or other be commensurate with Him in Whom revelation reaches its last and ultimate perfection. And this absolutely is the case. Moses does mark out the whole programme [a] of God's scheme for

---

[a] Ewald (Hist. Israel, i. 101) well points out that the support for the furthest prophetic outlook, or, in other words, for the Messianic expectations as they existed in their fullest development in the writings of the

man's restoration. All the rest of the Bible is but the gradual filling up of the plan of redemption sketched in the Pentateuch. We have the outline of it in the narrative of man's original intimacy and communion with God, followed by the account of his fall, and the promise of a Deliverer. Of this Deliverer Moses next sets before us many notable predictions, as that of Shiloh (Gen. xlix. 10), of the Star (Num. xxiv. 17), and of the Prophet like unto himself (Deut. xviii. 15, 18). He farther gives us many remarkable types of Him; but chief of all, the entire scheme of the Levitical law, the whole burnt-offering, the sin-offering, the thank-offering, the passover, the scape-goat, the Tabernacle with its various parts, all looked forward to, and were fulfilled in Christ. It is not merely the fathers, who often set forth their evangelical import with wonderful force[t]; St. Paul equally rests his teaching upon the Pentateuch. So too constantly does our Lord, Who even affirms that not one iota of it may really pass away. Lastly, in the Epistle to the Hebrews we have an authoritative exposition of many of its chief particulars. The prophets link the two together. On the mount of Transfiguration Elias unites Moses to Christ.

And thus then the prophet belonged specifically to the theocratic government. That government might

greater prophets, is to be found in Genesis. He quotes Gen. xii. 1–3, xviii. 18, 19, xxii. 16–18, xxvi. 4, xxviii. 14. Of these he says in his way, 'Few finer presentiments would be found to be declared by the real great prophets of the ninth and eighth centuries before Christ.'

[t] See, for instance, the noble sermon of S. Cyril on Luke ii. 25, in my Translation of S. Cyril's Commentary on St. Luke, Oxford, 1859, p. 24.

be administered by men on whom the Spirit of Jehovah rested for action only as statesmen or soldiers. Its highest administrator was the prophet, who could speak and command in Jehovah's name, as well as act for Him. And of this government Moses was the founder. He, in all the grandeur of his viceregal office, as the very representative of Jehovah, gave the chosen people the law which was to train them for Christ: farther, in type and symbol he marked out the nature of the true manifestation of God upon earth, and the office of the true Mediator, Who is the real point of union between God and man, the real Way of access to God, the true Restorer of man's fallen nature. And upon Moses other prophets followed, not equal to him in greatness, but carrying on his work, unfolding to clearer view the truths he had veiled in symbol, and preparing the world for the last prophet; the prophet like unto Moses as being a legislator, but the legislator of a perfect and final law; like unto Moses as being the founder of a Church, yet that Church not local nor temporary, but catholic, and with the promise that it shall endure till Christ come again: a prophet not like unto Moses, in that His is no delegated authority, no vicegerency, but in His own right, by right of nature as the Son, He governs and commands in His own house.

And in Him all the wants of our nature are supplied, the breach between heaven and earth repaired, man raised from his fallen state, the veil which had shut out heaven from earth torn asunder, access granted us unto God, and earth and heaven in Him made one; just as in Him, the Emmanuel, God and man became one. He is the Mediator of the New Covenant, God's final dispensation; for there can be no higher and better Mediator than Christ. And if to Him gave all the prophets witness, His words are to us the final and sufficient proof of all our heavenly hopes. 'Lord,' we say with Peter, 'Lord, to whom shall we go, save unto Thee? For Thou, Thou only, hast the words of eternal life.'

LECTURE III.

SAMUEL, THE RESTORER OF PROPHECY.

Yea, and all the prophets from Samuel and those that follow after, as many as have spoken, have likewise foretold of these days.—ACTS iii. 24.

ST. PETER in these words points out that prophecy had in Samuel a new beginning. As I have before observed, the theocratic government was carried on in the time of the Judges not so much by prophets as by heroes. God's spirit rested upon mighty men of valour for government and military enterprise, without which the nation could not have been preserved. In two instances only do we read of prophets (Judges iv. 4, vi. 8); in every other case the commands of Jehovah, as Israel's king, were given either by the priest with the Urim (Judges xx. 27), or by angels (Judges ii. 1, v. 23, vi. 11, &c., xiii. 3, &c.). But with Samuel there began a new order of things. On the one hand prophecy became a regular institution, placed upon a settled basis; and on the other it wrought within a narrower circle, and for a long time in a far humbler way, than when, as in Moses, it gave a powerful nation its laws alike in things human and divine. Not merely in Samuel's days was a final severance made between those two functions of speaking for Jehovah and acting for Jehovah, which had hitherto been combined in the prophet; but even in speaking for God his words were confined within a more limited range. Great as was Samuel, he had no new truth to declare to mankind, no light to throw upon old truths [a]. Moses had marked out the whole limits of Gospel truth; and several centuries passed after Samuel before the prophets began to fill up the outline. Whatever was given of fuller knowledge was in the Psalms. Whatever kindling up there was of Messianic hope was connected with the family and throne of David, the hero-king. Yet Samuel's was no mean calling. His office was to preserve the truth as taught by Moses, and to work for holiness, for spirituality (1 Sam. xv. 22), for a higher moral elevation on the part of the people, and for a fuller appreciation of those primary truths upon which all real civilization rests; such truths as the unity and spirituality of God, the union in Him of mercy and justice, and the certainty that evil deeds must, because of God's justice, bring a heavy retribution upon the offender. These were the truths that Moses had taught; and Samuel was to restore them and invest them with new power over the hearts of the people.

Now it will be impossible to understand the nature of Samuel's office as the Restorer, and in one sense even the Founder, of prophecy, unless we take a glance at the history of his times. He stands then in the middle, between the fall of the great landowners who had exercised an irregular authority during the days

[a] The only Messianic prediction connected with Samuel was that of a faithful high priest to walk before God's anointed for ever (1 Sam. ii. 35). But as God's anointed was the king, the words had a primary reference to the new relations between the priesthood and the temporal power.

of the Judges, and the new birth of the nation after its crushing defeat at Ebenezer, when, under those two able warriors, Saul and David, the youthful energies of the nation had that grand development which made Israel for a time the most powerful monarchy in the East. Now in the Book of Judges we find no traces of progress except in one, and that a very necessary way, namely, the union of the people into one nation. When it left Egypt, not only were there those tribal jealousies and differences which finally divided the nation into two hostile kingdoms, but there were great diversities among the people themselves, and nothing but the extraordinary vigour of Moses' mind could have held together so motley a multitude, and have stamped one character upon them. For we trace clearly the presence in Israel of those three classes so generally to be met with in every ancient history. There were first the great nobles, personally descended from Jacob, whose genealogies you find in the Books of Numbers and Chronicles. Men certainly few in numbers, as those genealogies teach us, and possessed of great power and vast landed estates. Even these nobles were not all of equal rank. The chiefs of Dan and Naphtali, of Gad and Asher, descended from slave mothers, and therefore of impure blood, did not stand upon the same elevation as the chiefs of Judah and Ephraim. Even Leah's last two sons, Issachar and Zebulun, born after a long period of barrenness, never attained to the high dignity possessed by the first four. Of these Judah held the foremost place in the camp (Num. ii. 3), and ultimately prevailed over his brethren (1 Chron. v. 2); and the whole nation in the third period of its history bore his name. In the second line in the camp Reuben's banner was foremost (Num. ii. 10), while in Genesis we read that it was Simeon and Levi, the two other sons of Leah, the first of the high-born wives, who were able with their dependants to conquer the Canaanite city of Shechem[b], and add the mass of its population to their clans. To Joseph, the elder son of the second highborn wife, belonged the birthright (1 Chron. v. 2); from Benjamin, her other son, the nation chose its first king. And in short, with some notable exceptions, such as that of Samson[c], it was the nobles of pure blood who gave Israel its heroes and its kings.

And next there were the retainers, who formed the strength of these noble houses. The idea that all the Israelites who came out of Egypt were descended from Jacob is so contrary to every text of Holy Writ, that it passes comprehension how it could ever have arisen: even though the truth is obscured in our version by the translation 'little ones' for a word[d] which the

---

[b] Though Jacob was afraid of the consequences of this deed (Gen. xxxiv. 30), and justly condemned the violence and cruelty with which Simeon and Levi had acted (Ib. xlix. 5–7), he nevertheless felt considerable pride in the exploit itself (Ib. xlviii. 22).

[c] Barak probably belonged to the tribe of Naphtali, though acting under the orders of Deborah, who dwelt in Mount Ephraim. What is more important is that we find Ephraim claiming supremacy over even the two princely Manassites, Gideon (Judges viii. 1) and Jephthah (Ib. xii. 1).

[d] This word, in Hebrew טף *taph*, correctly answers to the word *household*; thus, in 2 Chron. xxxi. 18, the taphs of the priests are said to consist of their wives, their sons, and their daughters: and so when, Ib xx. 13. the men of Judah brought their taphs to pray in the temple, Gesenius points out that it means their who'e households, excepting only the head. So too we read that 'Joseph nourished his father, and his brethren, and the whole house of his father according to the taph,' i.e. according to the number of the whole household, Gen. xlvii. 12. So Pharaoh was willing to let the Israelites go, but they must leave their taphs, their households, behind, Ex. x. 10, 11. So when the

Septuagint correctly renders *household* and *clan* (οἰκία and συγγένεια). For we have already seen that the fundamental law of circumcision was that every slave, whether born in the house or bought with money, was to be circumcised (Gen. xvii. 12, 13): thereby he became a member of the covenant just as fully as his master. But Abraham could equip 318 trained servants born in his house, and take them with him to battle. He must have left other servants at home to guard the women and children, the flocks and cattle. You would scarcely find three hundred active young men in a clan of three thousand souls, and yet Abraham grew far more great and powerful than he was at the early period here described (viz. Gen. xiv). So too of Isaac. Not only did he inherit all that Abraham possessed, except the probably large gifts bestowed upon Ishmael and the sons of Keturah (Gen. xxv. 5, 6), but we read that he so grew in wealth, that Abimelech the Philistine king of Gerar bade him depart: 'for,' said he, 'thou art much mightier than we'[e] (Ib. xxvi. 16).'

Gadites and Reubenites built cities for their taphs, Num. xxxii. 16, 24, 26, it does not mean for small children, but for their households. While forty thousand of the men numbered in Num. xxvi. went over Jordan to the conquest of Canaan, more than sixty thousand stayed behind; but probably most of these were armed retainers, and the taph did not strictly include such, but only the domestic slaves: see Ex. xii. 37, where the taphs are not numbered among the six hundred thousand men who left Egypt. In Num. xxxi. 17, 18 the taphs are described as consisting partly of males, who were all to be put to death, and partly of women, some married and some virgins. The translation 'women children' is erroneous. In other places a distinction is made between the women and the taph; see Deut. xx. 14, xxix. 11, Josh. i. 14, &c. In such places the children and domestic slaves are meant.

[e] This verse seems to me to solve the difficulty which some have felt as to the presence of Philistines in Canaan at this remote period. Caphtor, i.e. Crete, was their original home (Amos ix. 7), and an early body of immigrants had founded this kingdom of Gerar in the south of Palestine.

To this again must be added the numerous retainers brought back by Jacob from Mesopotamia. Though unable to cope with Esau, who came against him with four hundred men, it was not so much perhaps because of inferiority of numbers, as because his men were untrained, while Esau had with him the hardy mountaineers of Seir. His present to Esau was that of a mighty prince, and proves the greatness of his wealth. But further, we read of Jacob being accompanied from Padan-Aram by his brethren. They it was who piled up the hill of Galeed (Gen. xxxi. 46, 54). Now, strictly speaking, brother he had none but Esau, and these brethren can scarcely have been aught else than confederates, who had migrated with him from Mesopotamia, and who were doubtless absorbed into the twelve tribes. But independently of this, we read that after Isaac's death, when Esau and Jacob had divided his wealth between them, 'their riches were more than that they might dwell together; and the land wherein they were strangers could not bear them because of their cattle (Gen. xxxvi. 7).' And so Esau seized upon Mount Seir, and reduced

They were however comparatively few, and finally were conquered or absorbed by the Canaanites. When, centuries afterwards, Israel entered Canaan, we read at first nothing about Philistines, and Judah conquered Gaza, Askelon, and Ekron without trouble. But either the opportunity afforded by the troubles consequent upon the invasion of Palestine by Israel, or internal agitations in Crete, induced large numbers of Philistines to seek once again a land well known to them by tradition as once occupied by their countrymen, and thus as early as Judges iii. 3 we read of the five lords of the Philistines. From three of these cities they must have expelled the men of Judah, and powerful by sea and land they became Israel's most dangerous enemies, till they were conquered by David, who so respected their valour as to form of them his bodyguard (2 Sam. viii. 18). To what exact date Judges iii. 3 belongs is uncertain.

the Horites there to subjection (Deut. ii. 12), while Jacob abode in Canaan.

Now 'the gifts and calling of God are without repentance (Rom. xi. 29);' and I have yet to find the place in Holy Scripture which deprives these men, admitted by express command to the covenant, of their covenant-rights. Equally, I have still to find the place where we are told that the ground opened and swallowed them up; or that they perished by fire, or pestilence, or famine f. I am quite sure that the great chiefs would not have put them to death, because in them consisted their power. I should as soon expect to find the 'patres majorum gentium' at Rome putting their clients to death, or the captain of a Scottish clan putting his clan to death, as any of the chiefs mentioned in the first chapter of Numbers putting their housoholds to death g. What good would

---

f All those commentators who make elaborate calculations to prove the possibility of the six hundred thousand men at the Exodus being Jacob's lineal descendants, do by some sleight-of-hand manage to exclude all these men from the covenant, to which, both by the original law of circumcision and by subsequent enactments (e. g. Exod. xii. 44), they were expressly admitted. But fairness requires that we should know by what process they were excluded, at what date it took place, and what became of them.

g The history of Joseph may seem at first sight to militate against what is so absolutely certain from every other part of Genesis, namely, that Abraham, Isaac, and Jacob were the chiefs of powerful clans. But in so very brief a narrative, the silence of Holy Scripture is not so significant as the pregnant hints which from time to time it drops, and by which we are able to form some idea of the patriarchs in their worldly aspect. They are not set before us as human history would delineate them, but as men of God, the founders of the Jewish Church, and the forefathers of Christ. Now Joseph's history is full of religious instruction. He is the very model of suffering meekly borne for conscience' sake: he is the visible example of that working of God which brings good out of evil: he is the proof of God's goodness, Who though He the vast territories which Caleb gave to his daughter Achsah, her southland, and her upper and nether springs, have done her, if neither she nor Othniel had had dependants to till them? What good would Hebron have been to Caleb, if he had had to till it with his own hands? The lineal descendants of the patriarchs always strike me in reading the Bible as remarkably few.

These clans, then, formed the great strength of Israel, both in Goshen and in the Holy Land. At the head of some such body of retainers the sons of Ephraim made that expedition into the land of Palestine which ended so disastrously in their slaughter (1 Chron. vii. 21, viii. 13). No less powerful was the other son of Joseph; for we find that Jair,

long try His people will yet surely visit and save: he is the sign of God's providence, so overruling men's good and evil, as to bring about His great designs. Intent upon this, the history puts out of view all those particulars upon which worldly history would descant at large. Of course twelve sacks of corn would not do much to maintain a numerous tribe, but probably the great mass of the servants were dispersed seeking pasturage for the cattle. Most probably too Jacob's sons went down only to open trade, and make arrangements for the future. There was thus ground for Joseph treating them as spies. There is no reason to doubt but that when they were settled in so vast a region as Goshen, their numbers stood in some relation to the country assigned them. Even the great chiefs were not all born of Jacob. How could Othniel the son of Kenaz be the younger brother of Caleb the son of Jephunneh in any other way than by adoption? Caleb however himself is called a Kenezite in Josh. xiv. 14, and, from the manner in which he is spoken of in Josh. xv. 13, it is plain that he himself did not belong to the tribe of Judah by birth. Apparently the Kenezites were incorporated with Israel at the Exodus, and Caleb and Othniel, the chiefs of two several portions of the tribe, were reckoned as descendants of Judah, and as brothers; but in the official genealogy (1 Chron. iv. 13, 15) no attempt is made to connect them either with Judah or with one another by actual relationship. They were brothers only in the sense in which Jacob's confederates were his brothers.

accounted to belong to Manasseh (Num. xxxii. 41), because his grandfather Hezron, a son of Judah, had married a daughter of Machir, the son of Manasseh,— we find that this Jair possessed in Gilead, as the representative of Machir's daughter, no less than twenty-three villages (1 Chron. ii. 22), and himself extended his rule over thirty-seven more (ver. 23). No wonder that another Jair of the same house judged Israel for twenty-two years, and that men long remembered his wealth and his magnificence, and talked of his thirty sons riding upon thirty ass colts, and living in feudal style each in his own city[h] (Judges x. 3, 4).

Now these retainers grew gradually out of the taph, or household. As I have shown, the position of a slave was not accounted dishonourable, and in course of time those born in the house attained apparently to a certain amount of independence, and regarded their lord rather as their chief than as their owner. When Abraham and the patriarchs bought slaves (Gen. xvii. 12), they would probably be employed at first in domestic service, or in tending the cattle, but their children would enjoy greater freedom; and, finally, in a land so large as Goshen, would acquire a higher position and greater rights. The liberal spirit which had secured for the purchased slave admission to the covenant and equality in religious matters, could not stop there. Civil rights must in time follow, and personal freedom. But the

[h] In Judges xii. there are several other instances of this sort of barbaric grandeur, coupled with polygamy upon a large scale; a thing which is always sure in the long run to lead to the decay of those families which indulge in it.

connection between them and the great chiefs apparently was never dissolved; and the lineal descendants of the patriarchs, whose genealogies are so carefully given in the Books of Numbers and of Chronicles, depended for their power and influence upon the number of the men who formed their clan, or family [1], as it is called in Num. xxvi. 5 sqq.

[1] The word rendered family, *mishpachah*, means one of the larger divisions into which the tribe was distributed, and which bore the name of one of the sons or grandsons of the patriarch after whom the whole tribe was called. Thus the 43,730 men of the tribe of Reuben formed only four families (Num. xxvi. 5, 6), which were subdivided into houses (*ib.* i. 2). The chiefs of these houses were important men, and are called 'chief fathers' in Num. xxxi. 26, and 'heads of the fathers' in Josh. xiv. 1, which latter is the more exact translation of the Hebrew words. From 2 Chron. v. 2 we gather that while each tribe and each house had its chief, the family had none. The same also follows from Num. xxxvi. 1, where the spokesmen for the family (not the families, as in our version) of the Gileadites are the chiefs of its houses. In Josh. vii. 17, 18, in the history of Achan, we find the tribe of Judah thus divided into families, houses, and individuals. Now as the tribe of Judah consisted of 76,500 men, divided into four or at most five families, each subdivided apparently into about the same number of houses, the whole number of each house must have been large, but by the individuals— those brought man by man—plainly are meant, not the retainers, but those only of pure blood—the nobles actually descended from Jacob, and who would be few. It is necessary to remember this meaning of family. When Saul speaks of his family as the least of all the families of Benjamin (1 Sam. ix. 21), it does not follow that Kish was not a powerful chieftain—Gibeah apparently belonged to him,—but that as Benjamin was but a small tribe, so the division of it to which Saul belonged was not that which held the foremost rank. No doubt each house looked to its Mishpachah for aid, and the Mishpachah to the whole tribe: in which probably some one family bore the preponderance, possibly because the tribal chief usually belonged to it. In Saul's history we find an undesigned corroboration of the narrative in Judges xx. xxi. Benjamin, according to Num. xxvi. 38-40, was divided into six or seven families—probably the latter number. But Saul's family, that of Matri, is not one of them. Doubtless when the tribe was reduced to six hundred men, several of the old families were obliterated, and in course of time new ones took their place.

But besides these armed retainers, the glory and strength of the great houses, there was also a mixed multitude (Ex. xii. 38, Num. xi. 4), a *plebs* as it was called in Latin, but in Hebrew *Ereb*. In Goshen it had formed the lowest class, and probably had consisted of Arabs chiefly, who had been forced in times of famine or trouble to leave the wilderness[j] of Sinai, and seek refuge in the Egyptian border-land, where they had been compelled to own the superior power of Israel. But at the Exodus there must have been Egyptians, too, who threw in their lot with Moses. For Moses had mighty truths to preach, such as God's unity, His spiritual nature, His holiness. Brief as is the narrative, it tells of Egyptians who feared the word of Jehovah (Ex. ix. 20). Such would not have been content to remain behind; for religion is too powerful a motive to let men endure having their conscientious convictions trampled under foot: and as certainly as it was a struggle for religion between Moses and Pharaoh, so certainly would all those who hated the debased worship of animals in Egypt, and

---

[j] There could not be a greater mistake than to judge of the fertility of the wilderness of Sinai in the time of Moses by its present barrenness, the result, partly of the large mining operations once carried on there, when the wood was consumed for smelting the ore, and partly of the ravages of the Arabs since the days of Mohammed. In the Bible we always read of it as a populous region, inhabited chiefly by the powerful tribe of Amalek, but also by the Madianites, with whose chief Moses sought refuge. But just as famines had caused Abraham, Isaac, and Jacob to go down into Egypt, so probably the same cause led to many small Semitic tribes seeking a refuge there with the more powerful Israelites, who had been settled in Goshen by the Pharaohs, and fostered and protected by Joseph, Pharaoh's vicegerent. So, in the march through the wilderness, the Kenites and Kenezites joined Israel. Mr. Tristram and the Rev. F. W. Holland have abundantly proved that the wilderness of Sinai was once a thickly-wooded and well-watered region.

the grovelling superstitions prevalent there, ally themselves to one who proclaimed truths of such marvellous purity as those for which Moses and Israel strove.

Occasionally the chief of an Arab tribe, or an Egyptian of noble rank, may have been adopted into the princely houses; but the great mass of the Ereb were men of inferior rank. What were their precise position and legal rights we cannot exactly tell, but certainly they had no landed property assigned them. You never find a small landed proprietor in the early history of Israel. You find men like Micah in Mount Ephraim with his house of gods, and rich enough to hire a Levite for his domestic priest. You find Nabal in Carmel, owning sheep and goats by thousands. You find Barzillai providing a king and his army with sustenance while he lay at Mahanaim. Even Ziba, a servant of the house of Saul, has his fifteen sons and his twenty servants. Still more significant is the picture of Boaz, a mighty man of wealth, surrounded by his retainers, and living in rustic opulence at Bethlehem. The idea that the Israelites were, by the terms of the Mosaic law, a nation of small proprietors[k], is opposed to everything that we read of in

---

[k] Certainly what the daughters of Zelophehad were so anxious to secure was not a miserable acre or two apiece, but some such princely territory as their cousin carried as dower to Hezron (Num. xxvii. 1, 1 Chron. ii. 21, 22). The whole thing is made clear by the instructive genealogy in 1 Chron. ii. 50-55, where cities and clans are reckoned as sons. Compare also 1 Chron. viii. 29 with ix. 35. It is quite plain that Gibeon in these two places was the property of Jehiel. Really, too, it follows from the law as given in Num. xxvi. 53-56. The land was to be divided among the 601,730 men mentioned there, 'according to the number of names. To many thou shalt make his inheritance much, and to few thou shalt make his inheritance small: *to each shall*

the Bible. The Mosaic divisions were into tribes, families, and houses.

But, further, we are not to suppose that this plebs or Ereb had any share in the covenant[1]. In Goshen their connection with Israel was probably a very loose one, but at the Exodus they would be compelled by the need of protection to attach themselves to one or other of the tribes, and with this closer amalgamation a higher position would also gradually be won by them. But it would not be till after the conquest of Canaan that they would fully rank as Israelites[m].

his inheritance be given according to those that were numbered of him.' Surely these words must mean that it was the chiefs who had the land, and that their share was greater or less according to the number of their retainers. Of course they would hold it for their clan, and would make allotments to them, but on what terms is uncertain. In the reign of Solomon the power of the great houses seems to have been crushed, and the land subdivided into smaller portions. As much is implied in the phrase 'dwelling every man under his vine and under his fig-tree (1 Kings iv. 25).' By what steps this change was brought about we are not told, but the fact is certain. Though we still read of the princes (1 Kings xx. 14, 2 Chron. xxx. 24), their power and wealth had greatly declined since the days of David. They had become rather the great officers of the court (Jer. xxxvi. 12), than chieftains living among their own people.

[1] It was simply by confounding these three entirely distinct classes of people, of which the first and second only were members of the covenant, the first by their own right, the second by the fundamental law of the rite of circumcision, that those ingenious arithmetical puzzles were constructed which some short time ago puzzled the unthinking. Those numbers, as of the first-born in the wilderness, really enable any one with a little historical insight to judge of the relative proportions of the three great classes who collectively formed the Israelite nation.

[m] It is quite possible that when Joshua renewed the covenant of circumcision at Gilgal (Josh. v. 2–7), the Ereb was admitted into it. If so, its members would then be attached to some tribe, and henceforth numbered with it. They were not so numbered at the Exodus (Exod. xii. 38), but possibly many of them were included in the census recorded in Num. xxvi.

For by that conquest a still lower class was formed, consisting not merely of the Gibeonites, but also of large remains of the native inhabitants (Judges iii. 5). And the Ereb, dignified by the share they had taken in Israel's wanderings in the wilderness, and in the conquest of Palestine, looked down it may be with contempt on the conquered Amorites, who had become little better than serfs[n]; and so in time they would be regarded even by the true Israelites as their worthy companions and friends.

And thus they formed a very valuable portion of the community. Enjoying personal freedom, and residing principally in the towns as traders, though many of them no doubt still roamed about as nomads—for to the very last there were large tracts of open country where any could pasture their sheep[o]—

---

[n] Many native towns no doubt maintained their independence during the days of the Judges besides Jebus (2 Sam. v. 6-8). In fact, we learn from 2 Sam. xx. 15-22 that a walled town was a troublesome thing to conquer. Many such towns and large properties retained by Canaanites (thus Araunah is even called a king in 2 Sam. xxiv. 23) would probably be absorbed by marriages (Judges iii. 6), but while thus the nation was growing in internal unity, its moral state was being depressed by these marriages to the level of the Ereb, and even of the Canaanites.

[o] The Israelites had always been a people partly agricultural and partly pastoral. Great part of Palestine is a vast table land (the mountain of Matt. v. 1), and much of this apparently was not appropriated, but only the fertile valleys by which it is constantly traversed. Yet even of this Mr. Tristram tells us that 'the whole country south of Hebron, which now is a series of rolling downs, bare, and covered only with turf, testifies every mile or two by its ruined heaps, its olive-presses, wine-vats, and wells, to the density of a past population;' and no doubt the large districts originally given to the chiefs (Josh. xix. 50, xxiv. 33, Judges i. 20, 1 Chron. ii. 23, &c.) were, as population increased, broken up into smaller sections. But a large mass of the people still subsisted by pasturing

being above all things independent, they would temper and moderate the power of the large houses. But their moral condition was probably low, nor had they those grand and noble ideas of the Godhead which marked the true descendants of Abraham. Of these in the main, the Book of Judges speaks, telling us how in successive dangers they delivered Israel from the inroads of the neighbouring nations, and exercised a sort of sovereignty, now in one quarter of the land and now in another. How great was the preponderance of these houses we learn in Gideon's history. When Jehovah's angel came to him, his difficulty in undertaking the command in the war against Midian was the smallness of his father's house. Yet the town of Ophrah belonged to his father Joash ; Gideon, 'the least in his father's house,' had himself ten menservants whom he could take with him to throw down Baal's altar. He does it by night, because 'he feared his father's household' as well as the men of the city ; and when they come to Joash to complain of his son's conduct, Joash puts them off with a bitter jibe at their having a god who could not help himself. The townspeople, then, had a sort of importance, and yet could not cope with even the small proprietor to whom they appertained. And as consisting chiefly of the Ereb, with an admixture of Canaanites, we find them given up to idolatry. It is ever the towns at this era which are the seats of false worship and immorality. It was only gra-

---

their flocks in the wilderness or table land. Thus the powerful house of Rechab could all take to a nomad life at the command of Jehonadab, and Jeremiah speaks as if living in tents was still common in his day (Jer. iv. 20, x. 20).

dually that the higher teaching of the pure Israelites leavened them, and it never leavened them thoroughly. Probably few but pure Israelites went into captivity with Jehoiachin, and returned to found the second temple (Ezra ii. 58–65).

During the days, then, of the Judges, there was no settled form of government, but the rule only of a dominant class, of whom occasionally one here and one there emerged into more general power. Meanwhile the nation was growing in unity; so far there was progress, but we cannot detect many signs of it in any other direction. The extraordinary elevation of Moses' character, which had stamped so deeply upon the minds of his contemporaries such noble truths as that from Jehovah come both love and chastisement (Exod. xx. 5, 6, xxxiv. 6, 7), and that in God a nation finds at once its protection and its code of morality, and that therefore God must alone be king: this influence seemed to lose its hold upon the people as Joshua and the rest who had known Moses passed away. We find instead a race of men valiant, self-reliant, with many rough and youthful virtues, but whose moral state was low, and their capacity for spiritual thoughts limited. Even those to whom Moses must have chiefly looked for carrying on his work, left their religious duties unattended to. Neither priests nor Levites seem after the days of Eleazar and Phinehas to have devoted themselves to the teaching of the people; and the gift of prophecy, though not absolutely withheld, yet exerted itself in no other way than in the preservation of Israel's national existence.

Yet the people never abandoned their conviction

that they were consecrated to Jehovah, and held a special relation to Him. When sin entangled them, and national calamity came as its result, they never doubted but that upon their true repentance Jehovah would come to their succour. They knew that it is sin which separates man from God, and that repentance is not the cry of the lips, but the change of the heart. And thus when they returned to God He accepted them, while the splendid reformations of Hezekiah and Josiah wrought no deliverance, because the heart of the people remained unchanged. We find even some slight traces of Messianic hopes. Jephthah's daughter bewails not her death, but her virginity; as though every Jewish mother hoped that from her might be born the promised Deliverer. They were not untrue then to their calling, and it is even possible that the higher views of the true Israelites were gradually leavening both the mixed multitude who came with them out of Egypt, and the large number of Canaanites who still remained in the land. At all events, when Samuel appears the whole nation is ready to join in the spiritual worship of the one true God.

Now, whence came this deep conviction, even in those coarse times, that there is but one God, and that God requires as His sole true service holiness? If there be one constant tendency in the human heart, it is to make worship a matter of the senses; to express truth by outward sign and symbol. Truths ever crystallize and harden into objective forms, and lose thereby their quickening and penetrating force. How came this one people ever to struggle after spiritual truth, and finally to win it and impart it to all mankind? Whence gained Abraham that better knowledge which made him abandon those gods which Terah worshipped (Josh. xxiv. 2), to serve a God whom no image may represent? Rachel brings with her Laban's teraphim, and yet no canker of idolatry is the result. Excepting Joseph, the patriarchs are not set before us as men free from very deep stains of sin, and when the nation settled in Egypt, it was brought into contact with a people whose idolatry was of the basest kind, who worshipped cats and crocodiles, and animals of every sort, and even vegetables, but who nevertheless possessed a civilization—a culture, as it is the fashion now to call it—very far superior to that of the Hebrews, and such as must have greatly influenced and impressed them. It did in fact so debase them, that a forty years' sojourn among the mountains and wildernesses of Sinai was necessary to free them from the demoralizing influences of Egypt. But, in spite of this, there was on their side a healthy love of truth, and the power of embracing it; and, on the other side, there was Moses, the one man who falls below the level only of Christ, the one man in whom human nature reached its highest glory, and who points onward to Christ, as the perfection of that which Moses sought, but through human infirmity could not reach (Num. xx. 12, 24, xxvii. 14). After Moses we have the picture of a people impressed by his master-mind with indelible convictions, but convictions far higher than their own moral level. It is but too probable that Moses' own grandson[p] was ready to minister before a graven

---

[p] Many scholars consider that the Jews, to save the credit of Moses' family, changed Moses into Manasseh in Judges xviii. 30; the

image, on the excuse, no doubt, that it was but a symbol of the true Deity (Judges xviii. 30). The ephod made by Gideon, in remembrance of the defeat of the Midianites, became a snare both to his own house and to the people generally (Judges viii. 27). Not one of the gods of their heathen neighbours but found worshippers in Israel (Judges x. 6). Plainly the nation was leading a double existence. Whence came its better knowledge? Read through the Book of Judges. You do not find there any men capable of winning spiritual truths for themselves. You do not find men struggling after new ideas, and gradually attaining to them. Measured by their times the Judges were men of whom the world was not worthy. For, mixed up with much that was low and bad, they had an unwavering trust in Jehovah, an honest manly love of truth, and a consciousness that God must be served in holiness, and that repentance means a reformation of life—ideas altogether superior to anything in the times wherein they lived. But they stand upon an infinitely lower level than Moses. Even Samuel and Jeremiah, the two other most perfect characters of Judaism, reached not up to the standard of Moses.

The wisdom of Moses was not the product of Jewish culture, nor was it of Egyptian growth. Trained as was Moses in all the wisdom of the Egyptians, and admitted probably to the priesthood, as Egyptian tradition[q] affirmed, he learned their

change consisting in but one stroke, namely, altering מוישה into מנשה, It is remarkable how entirely the family of Moses disappears from Jewish history.

[q] Manetho's account, as quoted by Josephus, c. Apion. 1. 26 sqq., though grossly distorted, contains much nevertheless in itself

teaching only to hate and condemn it, and at Mount Sinai his purpose was to raise up an eternal barrier between the Israelites and the religion of the country wherein they had so long dwelt. There did this extraordinary man lay broad and deep the foundations of the one true religion, which was in due time to become the right of all mankind (Mark xvi. 15). Still in the Ten Commandments we recognize the most perfect summary of our duty to God and man. Still we worship 'Jehovah, as a God merciful and gracious, long-suffering, abundant in goodness and truth, but that will by no means clear the guilty (Ex. xxxiv. 6, 7).' Still in the types and ceremonies of the law we see the outlines of truths since revealed, and which were ordained of old not to hide and conceal the light already given, but to prepare and lead men on to more light, to new truths, but truths for which the world was not then ready. No jot or tittle of the law has passed away, but all has either been fulfilled in Christ, or lives on in Christianity in more full and perfect significance. Moses was no mere product either of Egyptian wisdom, or of Israelitic striving after spiritual truth. Truth, in the way of nature, is gained by man only after long struggles, and its ultimate exponent is preceded by a long series of men who have ever been advancing nearer and nearer to its reality. No doubt in Moses personally there had been a long striving after God; but there was nothing in the times that went before or that followed after to account for the extraordinary

credible. Cf. Ewald, Hist. Israel, ii. 76. From it we gather that the Exodus was the result of a religious struggle, and that Moses, as he appears also in the Pentateuch, was the bitter opponent of the wisdom of the Egyptian priests.

purity and elevation of his views. No long line of men had preceded him to lead him upwards to the truth. If, as we believe, he was one chosen by God to reveal to mankind the true nature of the Deity, and the right manner in which God must be served, all is easy. God did by him so implant in the chosen people the germs of true religion, that in spite of every difficulty and obstacle it grew and deepened and widened, till at length the time was full and the world ready, and Christ came. If Moses was the mere product of a struggle between Egyptian and Israelitic theology, he is a greater miracle than inspiration itself.

The times of the Judges, then, enable us to form something of a judgment upon the greatness of Moses. Immeasurably do the heroes of those times fall below him. They were in proportion and relation to their times; Moses was great and good absolutely. His standard of truth was perfect, even though personally he once or twice fell below his own standard. And yet the Judges were seekers after God, and wrought too for that complete ascendancy of the Mosaic institutions and views which we find in the days of Samuel. When we think of the long years passed by Israel amid the debasing associations of Egypt, when we think of the vast mixed multitude, which lusted only after sensual pleasures (Num. xi. 4), and of the numerous Canaanitish idolaters, among whom the Israelites freely lived (Judges iii. 5-7), we can estimate the difficulties of the times of Barak, and Gideon, and Jephthah, and Samson, and our wonder is not that the nation fell so low, but that it ever rose again.

It was at a time of the deepest agony and despair

that a new life came to it. For many years the Philistines had been gradually crushing Israel. Even in the days of Joshua the people had not been able to conquer the inhabitants of the plains and of the sea coast, and now, aided probably by new immigrations from Crete, the Philistines had gained a decided superiority[r], against which Samson vainly struggled by detached acts of heroism. At length, at the place subsequently called Ebenezer, the national ruin became complete, and church and state fell in one day. Since the days of Joshua the place where the ark was deposited, and which was therefore the centre of the national religion, had been Shiloh in Mount Ephraim; and the Philistines destroyed Shiloh with such hideous barbarity, that centuries afterwards the heart of the people shuddered at the very mention of the name[s]. They never restored the place. Even Jeroboam, though of the tribe of Ephraim, never ventured to use, as a rival to Jerusalem, a site consecrated by so many centuries of worship. In the Psalms you read many a bitter wail over its fall. So late as the time of Jeremiah, the threat of a similar fate hanging over Jerusalem so stirred the rage of the people that but for the princes they would have put Jeremiah to death. So utter was Shiloh's ruin, that its very site was not known until the last few years[t]. It seems as if the people could not bear any allusion to scenes and remembrances so inexpressibly painful.

[r] Judges xiv. 4.
[s] See Ps. lxxviii. 60-64, Jer. vii. 12, 14, xxvi. 6, 9. There is probably also an allusion to the return of the ark from captivity in Ps. xiv. 7.
[t] It was discovered by E. Robinson: see his Palestine, vol. iii. 302 sqq.; and Wilson, Lands of the Bible, ii. 293 sqq.

But from Shiloh's fall Israel dated its regeneration. There had been brought up there from his infancy a calm, wise, and thoughtful man. A Nazarite like Samson, he was cast nevertheless in a higher and nobler mould. Cut off from the affections of home, he was a daily witness of the supreme power being wielded by a weak and irresolute man, and of the religious sanctuary of the nation being defiled by the immoralities of that high priest's sons. Such a training would have ruined one not possessed of rare and unusual gifts. But he had that rarest gift of early yet not precocious piety: a youthful goodness that was a fit prelude for his religious manhood. But there was also at Shiloh something to make amends for this painful isolation. Eli was at least personally a good man: but of far more consequence for Samuel's mental and spiritual growth were those religious records stored up in the tabernacle. These doubtless were Samuel's study, and from them he learned that great truth which was the inner spring of all his subsequent conduct, namely, that Israel's strength lay in its true religion—that Jehovah was Israel's sole stay and deliverance. Impressed with this truth, he gave his whole heart to teaching it; and Jehovah accepted him as His spokesman. 'All Israel, from Dan even to Beer-sheba, knew that Samuel was established to be a prophet of Jehovah (1 Sam. iii. 20).' And up to this time God's spokesman was also God's representative. As prophet, Samuel was also the temporal ruler, the Judge, of the nation.

We may be sure that it was against his advice that the ark was taken to battle. People of debased ideas may imagine that success depends upon some holy relic, some consecrated banner, some labarum or oriflamme carried out before a host waging it may be unholy war for lust of power or spoil, or to rob freemen of their rights. Such ideas are natural to man. Among the heathen you always find some ancile, or palladium, or image of the great goddess Diana, upon which their safety depends, and which always plays them false at the hour of need: and heathenism is nothing more than man's selfish instincts narrowed and hardened by contact with the material world till he loses all perception of the truth that in union with God alone is life and deliverance. Now this truth was Israel's real strength, and when the unchaste and unholy sons of Eli took the ark to battle, they put superstition in the place of religion ; and if the ark had not been captured, and the people utterly smitten, the spiritual teaching of Moses would have been so overborne that it is difficult to see how it could have survived the shock. Degraded then to so base a use, the ark not only did not save the people, but was itself taken in battle. And yet at such a crisis, if there had been no interference of God in the nation's behalf, so heavy a chastisement might have been more than the faith of Israel could have borne. Even then in captivity the god of the Philistines falls prostrate and broken before the ark, and it is restored to Israel in such a way as proved Jehovah's power and the deep reverence with which He must be approached. And never afterwards was the ark put to any superstitious use. The people who broke even the brazen serpent to pieces were too spiritual in their views to regard the ark as anything more than a symbol of God's more immediate presence at that spot which He had chosen as the chief seat of His worship.

But while this disastrous battle was being fought at Ebenezer, Samuel was probably busy in removing from Shiloh those precious records, of which afterwards he so well knew how to make use. Some possibly were laid up inside the ark[u], and were restored with it by the Philistines. But however saved, from these records Samuel learned the great lesson that a nation's strength and prosperity come to it not from without but from within; not from what a people have, but from what a people are. Not active trade and victorious armies, but religion and morality are the safeguards of freedom. When faith is lost, virtue soon departs also, and corrupt at its very core, an unbelieving nation soon sinks tamely and meanly into decay. Samuel's great work was to bring about a reformation of the people themselves.

The influences which in modern times raise or depress a nation are far more general and diffused than in times when books and reading scarcely existed. Even now the virtues and mental strength of one man may do much for a nation's good, or by mistaken policy he may guide it into a course whence it may be difficult for it to retrace its steps, and escape ultimate ruin. Yet at every turn he will be checked by other influences, and the reaction, which in the main consists of the combined resistance of units, themselves singly powerless, may prove in the end more powerful than the mightiest intellect of the day. But in old time the individual was well nigh everything. Nations rose and fell according to the characters of their leading men: and so, ancient

[u] See Deut. xxxi. 26.

history is mainly the history of these men, and of the effects which followed upon their working. Such men were Moses, the founder, and Samuel, the restorer, of Israel. Still, you must not suppose that the people went absolutely for nothing—that they had no probation, no part in the nation's fortunes. The Bible sets before us the very opposite principle. God bestows His gifts, but they must be accepted (Deut. xxx. 19, Jer. xxi. 8). His people must be willing in the day of His power (Ps. cx. 3). The nation did accept Moses and Samuel. When subsequently the people fell away, God granted first a Hezekiah, with Isaiah to press home to their consciences the necessity of reformation. He gave next a Josiah, with Jeremiah to aid his efforts. But all was in vain (Jer. viii. 17–20). The influence of a nation's great men may be vastly more at one period than at another, but the issue rests with the nation at large. With us, in modern days, broad principles are at work; and not one but many minds labour together for good or for evil. Of old, the result was more plainly connected with some one mind; but then, as now, a nation's uprise or decay depended finally upon the nation's own choice.

Samuel's lot fell upon times when the instincts of religion prevailed. The testimony of the Book of Judges shows that the people had not lost their conviction that Jehovah was their Deliverer. When then the national existence seemed crushed at Ebenezer, they came to Samuel, as Jehovah's prophet, for aid and comfort. As such all Israel had recognized him in the days of Eli, and now they turned to him as their sole hope. Brief as is the history of his doings we learn from it three things. The first, that he urged upon the people the necessity of putting away their idols (1 Sam. vii. 3). Now this had a moral, as well as a religious significance. Idol worship was but another form of wantonness. Turn where you will, the worship of false gods is the worship of human passion. In honour of the gods men did that which they would have blushed to do as men, but which nevertheless they wished to. The god served only as an excuse to silence conscience. The worship of Jehovah was not a sensuous but a spiritual worship. It meant temperance, chastity, self-restraint, justice to others, holiness. The heart must be prepared for Jehovah; and this, at Samuel's exhortation, the people did by fasting, by prayer, by the confession of sins. And God accepted their repentance because it was sincere; and at Ebenezer, the very place where they had been so disastrously overthrown and the ark captured, the yoke of the Philistines was lightened. Though they still had garrisons in Israel (1 Sam. xiii. 3), and prevented the importation and manufacture of arms (ver. 19–22), yet all marauding expeditions ceased in Samuel's days: whether or not Israel was tributary to the Philistines does not plainly appear.

Samuel's first act, then, was to bring about a thorough reformation among the people; his second was to provide for the maintenance of morality and religion, by personally undertaking the regular administration of justice. In profane history we find that Deïoces by this means raised the Medes into a nation. But Samuel did more than Deïoces. Not at one centre only, at Ramah, did he judge the people, but went yearly on circuit to three chief places, Bethel, Gilgal, and Mizpeh (1 Sam. vii. 16). Nor did justice with him subserve the purposes of personal ambition. True to the high theory of the theocracy, as Jehovah's representative he sought only Jehovah's honour. And by his just decisions, and the example of his own unblemished purity, he taught the people themselves to be just, and also united the tribes together into something like one nation (1 Sam. xii. 4).

Now it was in this upright administration of the government that Samuel soon found the need of fit persons to act under him. The people were no doubt very ignorant, and reading and writing[x] were mysteries confined to the descendants of those great scribes, Eleazar and Phinehas. Samuel determined therefore, in the third place, to raise the nation intellectually, as he had already raised it morally; and for this purpose he gathered round him at Naioth, that is, the meadows or open pastures at Ramah, where his own house was situated, a number of young men, whom he trained in reading, writing, and music. As their education was in course of time entrusted to Nabhis, prophets, they were called the sons, that

---

[x] It is a mark of the intellectual superiority of the Semitic races that syllabic writing was known to them at a very early period, while the Egyptians, like the Chinese, never advanced beyond pictorial writing. Ewald, Hist. Israel, i. 51, shows that writing existed among the Semitic nations before we can historically trace it, and though it is uncertain to what Semitic people 'half the civilized world owes this invaluable invention, so much is incontrovertible, that it appears in history as a possession of the Semitic nations long before Moses.' In opposition however to so great an authority I venture to think that the phraseology of Gen. xxiii. 17 belongs to a written document, and therefore that the art of writing existed in Abraham's days.

is, the disciples, of the prophets; and from this modest beginning arose 'the schools of the prophets,' of which we read so much afterwards, especially in the history of the northern kingdom. And thus prophecy now first became a regularly organized national institution.

But let us consider who these Nabhis or prophets were, whom Samuel gathered round him at Ramah to aid him in the work of education. For it is expressly said that 'the word of Jehovah was rare in those days (1 Sam. iii. 1);' and after Deborah and the prophet who preached repentance throughout Israel before Gideon was summoned to the rescue, we read nothing of prophets till Samuel. But the Spirit of Jehovah was not withdrawn. 'When a young lion roared against Samson, the Spirit of Jehovah,' we read, 'came mightily upon him, and he rent the lion as he would have rent a kid (Judges xiv. 6);' and can we suppose that that Spirit, at such a crisis in Israel's history, would be withheld from good and earnest men, thoroughly penetrated with the same truths as Samuel, and joining hand and heart with him in once again giving life to the Mosaic institutions? Had Samuel stood alone he could have effected but little. But other holy men caught from him the pious enthusiasm, and spread it in a wider circle. Now the great characteristic of the prophet is that intense conviction of the truth and necessity of religion which compels him to proclaim its truths to others. On this account there is much in common between the prophet and the preacher. Often the terms are synonymous. Very fittingly, therefore, does our Church require the profession of an inward call before she admits any one into her ministry. 'Do you trust,' she asks, 'that you are moved inwardly by the Holy Ghost to take upon you this Office and Ministration [y]?' Now, as certainly as the Spirit of God rested upon Samson and Saul (1 Sam. xi. 6), and did not make them prophets, but only heroes, so may even the prophetic spirit rest upon men, and yet they may rise no higher than earnest preachers. Who shall deny the gift of the prophetic spirit to Wyclif and Luther, to Wesley and Whitfield, to Wilberforce and Clarkson? Who deny it of old to Augustine and Ambrose, to Basil and Bernard? 'The testimony of Jesus,' we are told, 'is the spirit of prophecy (Rev. xix. 10).' Men bear that testimony now; they bore it of old. But there were four [z] great periods at which this testimony rose to a higher and more directly supernatural level. At these periods God's purposes of mercy towards mankind made the higher gift necessary. Prophets then had not merely truths to preach, but truths to reveal. But because no revelation was made by them or to them, I do not therefore infer that the prophets whom Samuel gathered round him had not the Spirit of Jehovah, and were not true prophets, even though the Divine Spirit wrought within strictly natural limits. So, in

[y] The Ordering of Deacons, Question 1.

[z] These four periods are, (1) the Davidic period, when many Messianic Psalms were composed; (2) the Assyrian period, of which the great glory was Isaiah; (3) the Chaldee period, equally ennobled by Jeremiah; (4) the post-exilic period, when the beautiful Psalms of Degrees were composed, and Zechariah, Haggai, and Malachi flourished. The Mosaic period I regard as something higher than ordinary prophecy. It corresponds to nothing but Christianity. The prophets wrought within the circle of the Mosaic truths; Christ finally made those truths full and perfect, and bestowed them upon all mankind.

the Christian Church, I do not infer that Agabus was more a prophet[a] than the rest, because he was endowed with prescience also. And believing, as I do, that there are even now men 'inwardly moved by the Holy Ghost to take upon them the work of the Ministry,' and yet that this influence does not surpass the bounds of human nature, I recognize in such God's presence, though fully aware of the great difficulty of exactly defining where the influences of the Spirit remain entirely within the limits of man's natural, yet quickened and elevated, powers, and where they rise entirely above them. But when the Word of God so truly ascribes to His Spirit that mighty impulse which made Samson rend the lion, and which nevertheless, in another way, may still be viewed as

---

[a] The prophets in the early Church were men inspired by the Holy Ghost, not to foretell events, but to preach truths. They stood, therefore, next to the apostles, and higher than mere teachers (1 Cor. xii. 28), with whom, however, they are constantly associated (Acts xiii. 1). It was the office of the apostles to rule, of the prophets to preach, of the teachers to instruct and catechize. Upon the apostles the Holy Spirit rested supernaturally for certain special purposes. These were, (1) to bring back all Christ's teaching to their remembrance (John xiv. 26); (2) to guide them to the right understanding of that teaching (Ib. xvi. 13); (3) to tell them the things that were coming (Ib.). St. Paul, moreover, obtained his knowledge of Christ's life and preaching by revelation (Gal. i. 12). But these supernatural gifts were so regulated as not to interfere with their own probation (1 Cor. ix. 27). The faculty of prediction, as in the case of Agabus (Acts xi. 28, xxi. 10, 11), was not involved in the term προφήτης, but belonged to that fulness of charismata which distinguished the early Church. We must further suppose that as the apostles were divinely aided in their own knowledge and understanding of Christ's teaching, so they were guided and assisted by inspiration in their communication of it to the Church. But the prophets of St. Paul's times had not necessarily any such inspiration, but that only which every real Christian has, and which is described in 1 Cor. ii. 10-16.

only a natural impulse, we need feel no hesitation in believing that that same Spirit mightily stirred many hearts, and made them run over with earnest words, when Samuel called God's people to his aid. The error is in circumscribing too narrowly the office and duties of the prophet, when men fear to apply the name to those who, though moved by the Holy Ghost, had yet no revelation to make, no commission to declare new truths in Jehovah's name[b].

At first, indeed, Samuel may have attempted to train his young men himself; but soon I doubt not that he gathered round him as teachers many on whom Jehovah's Spirit rested, as it may rest on men now, and who were irresistibly urged thereby to proclaim the old Mosaic truths of God's unity and spirituality, His justice and mercy, and of light and life and strength to be found alone in Him. And evidently Samuel was anxious that there should be many such men dispersed everywhere throughout the land; and in his circuits he sought such men

---

[b] I wish, in fact, to protest against two errors: the first, that the inspiration of the prophet was unlike anything that happens now. On the contrary, I believe that the Holy Ghost still impels and forces men to preach Christ. But the second seems to me the worse error; namely, the denial of any spiritual gift higher than is vouchsafed now. On the contrary, I believe that on special occasions the great prophets of old were under the influence of a directly supernatural power. No preacher or teacher now is secure from error, but unless the writers of the Holy Scriptures had been thus secured, what reliance could we have placed upon their words? No preacher now has any new Divine truth to reveal; but it was the very office of prophets and apostles to reveal new truths to the Church. While, then, God's gifts now do not surpass the bounds of our natural powers, however much they may quicken them, a further and supernatural gift was bestowed upon a certain small number of persons in old time, but strictly for one special purpose.

out, and, if young, he took them with him, and gave them fuller instruction. Probably he began with one or two youths who seemed more especially fitted for so high a calling; and then his institution grew, and teachers had to be found as well as scholars. But it is chiefly the results which the Bible sets before us. We find there nothing less than a new life rapidly beginning for the nation, so that comparatively but a few years separate the rough and untaught anarchy of the times of the Judges from the learning and order and piety of David's reign[c].

Now there can be little doubt but that Moses had intended the priests and Levites to be the instructors of the people. For this purpose he had raised them above the necessity of labouring for their bread, and had dispersed them among the people. Unfortunately they proved but sorry teachers; and God, in Samuel's days, raised up others to take their place. God has not given to any body of men whatsoever a chartered

---

[c] One instance of this enormous change will suffice. There is much to be learned from the proper names in Holy Scripture. Compounded very frequently of some appellation or other of God, they show us what were the prevailing religious ideas of the time. Now, judged in this way, Saul is half a heathen. He names one son Jonathan = God's gift, in Greek, Theodore; but another is Ish-baal = Baal's hero (1 Chron. viii. 33). Jonathan's son is Merib-baal = Baal's striver. Soon after, feelings so changed that men would not even use the name of Baal, but said instead Bosheth = shame, or disgrace, and, in still later times, abomination (Is. xliv. 19, Dan. xi. 31, xii. 11. Mat. xxiv. 15). But what a world-wide difference a few years had made between the state of feeling which allowed Saul to call his son Baal's hero, and that which could not endure the name of Baal, and substituted for it Ish-bosheth = Shame's hero! It is very true that the Baal of Saul's time was a very different being from the Baal of Ahab and Jezebel; but it was a term too directly connected with idolatry to admit of its use by any right-minded man.

right to lock up heaven, and let His people perish for lack of knowledge. If those who are regularly called, and who are the priests according to the true succession, neglect their duties, their place will very soon be supplied by those who have only the inward call. The prophets essentially were men whose sole claim to teach was this inward call. So entirely was this the case that the men trained in the prophetic colleges were themselves the first to acknowledge the higher gift which summoned Elisha from his farming at Abel-meholah to be their head (2 Kings ii. 15); and which urged Amos to leave his scanty subsistence, as a puncturer of sycamore fruit at Tekoah, to publish to the ten tribes a warning so weighty that, as the high priest testified, 'the land was not able to bear his words (Amos vii. 10).'

From the days when Samuel first gathered a few youths round him at Ramah, the schools of the prophets never seem to have ceased in Israel. We read of them afterwards as flourishing at numerous places, especially among the ten tribes, and of the Nabhis, the prophets trained in them, as existing by hundreds—sometimes nobly dying as martyrs for the truth, like those whom Jezebel persecuted to death, but of whom Obadiah saved a hundred prophets, hiding them by fifty in a cave (1 Kings xviii. 4); at other times ready to lie and flatter, like the four hundred Jehovah-prophets, who bade Ahab go up to Ramoth-gilead and prosper (1 Kings xxii. 5, 6). Evidently they filled a position analogous to that of the clergy in the Christian Church, except that their call was somewhat irregular. For neither did these schools form part of the Mosaic institutions, nor was even education in them necessary before entering upon the prophetic office. They had been raised up to take the place of men who had failed in their duties; but they had no regular charter, nothing to appeal to but an internal impulse; and naturally therefore to the last we find a sharply-defined opposition between them and the priesthood. Of the two sides of the truth they press almost exclusively the need of real, deep, personal religion: of the necessity of external aids to our infirmity they say but little. I do not see how they could have done otherwise. The need of these aids is a deduction of the reason drawing its arguments from experience. The prophets spake from a fervent heart, eager for the end and not calmly examining the means. And so their text ever is, 'Behold, to obey is better than sacrifice;' and their teaching a foreshadowing of His Who taught that the true worship must be 'in spirit and in truth [d].'

Among the men trained in these colleges, there were, I doubt not, thousands who preached the pure spiritual doctrines of the Mosaic economy, and who formed the true core of the nation, and laboured earnestly for that great end for which the Mosaic institutions were given, and which we now enjoy in Christ. But we must not confound these preachers, true prophets though they were, with those few and divinely-gifted men who were speakers for God in a far higher sense, as being directly inspired either

---

[d] So in the New Testament, there is little direct teaching about institutions and ceremonies: it was left to the Church, the great society of believers, to appoint such institutions and ritual as might best help in guarding the truth intrusted to its keeping, and in propagating it throughout the world.

to explain old truths, or to proclaim some new portion of that heavenly knowledge which was to be made perfect in Christ. It is to those who were prophets in the largest sense that we owe the Bible. If the preservation of the several books of the Bible was probably due to the prophetic colleges, the writers themselves were men to whom prophecy was no mere calling or profession. There were Jehovah-prophets by hundreds, doing in the main God's work, as our own clergy do, and who felt that they were inwardly moved to do this work; and here and there we find men who falsely professed to be thus called, because of the dignity or emoluments to be gained by such a profession. And from time to time the Spirit of Jehovah rested upon some one man—not necessarily of greater natural gifts, but of a heart more intensely devoted to God. And this special call was tied down to no institution whatsoever, nor to any class. It might come to an Amos, gaining a scanty living by his own labour; it might come to the young priest Jeremiah, dwelling on his own lands at the priests' town Anathoth; it might come to Zephaniah, a prince of the blood royal, amid the splendours of a court. But it came by no initiation, by no training, by no ordinances of men, but directly from above, from God. And when the call came, it summoned them to trouble, to sorrow, to disappointment. The book spread before them was written within and without ; and the writing ever was lamentations, and mourning, and woe (Ezek. ii. 10). They might be wanted for some special mission, as was Amos, and would afterwards return again to ordinary life. It might be a life-long service. Jeremiah must daily be God's witness during the forty

I

and two years which preceded the fall of Jerusalem. He must forego for ever all share of domestic happiness (Jer. xvi. 2); must abstain from all pleasant [e] company, and dwell lonely and apart (Ib. xv. 17); must take no share in the joys or the sorrows of life (Ib. xvi. 5, 8); and this not to attain to rank and power, not to win those prizes which stir in men an honourable ambition, but to become 'a man of strife, a man of contention; one that every one did curse (Ib. xv. 10).' 'Why,' said he, 'is my pain perpetual, and my wound incurable, which refuseth to be healed? (Ib. xv. 18).' Such was God's call to him; and such was it ever. The prophets were sent to a people whose heart was fat, and their ears heavy, and their eyes shut (Is. vi. 10). Their cry ever is, 'Lord, who hath believed our report? (Ib. liii. 1).' For the false prophet there was reward, honour, emolument; for the true the word was, 'I hate that man. Put him into the prison, and feed him with the bread of affliction, and the water of affliction,' till his words be disproved (1 Kings xxii. 8, 27).

And this was necessary for two reasons. First, as regards the prophet. He was summoned to his office by an internal call. But men deceive themselves too greatly for such a call to be trustworthy if it leads on to wealth and power. At first it did lead to power; Moses and Samuel held their authority by virtue of their prophetic office: and in men of such

---

[e] There is nothing to justify the translation of the A. V. *mockers*. The word really means *those who laugh and are cheerful*. Our version entirely corrupts the sense. Jeremiah, as a prophet, had to abstain from what was right, or at least innocent, and not merely from what was wrong.

extraordinary elevation of character no danger would ensue. But when we find that there were professed prophets who polluted God among His people for such mean gains as 'handfuls of barley and pieces of bread (Ezek. xiii. 19),' to what degradation might not the prophet's name have fallen, if wealth and honour had been its guerdon? The prophet was called to the highest and noblest of all vocations: he was Jehovah's minister. But his earthly lot was scorn and the enmity of the world. He had his reward, but it was not one that allures worldly-minded men. It was a spiritual life hidden in God: and this none can enjoy but the pure in heart.

But still more important was it for the people. The prophet brought them a message from heaven. Upon this message their acceptance with God depended. How were they to know that it was God's message? Remember that there were false prophets as well as true, and that they made great professions of their prophetic power. We read of Zedekiah making him horns of iron as a sign that Ahab should push the Syrians till he had consumed them (1 Kings xxii. 11). We read of Hananiah taking the yoke off Jeremiah's neck and breaking it in token that Nebuchadnezzar's empire should be broken (Jer. xxviii. 10, 11). We read of Shemaiah writing from Babylon, and reproving the high priest for not punishing Jeremiah, and putting a stop to his predictions of woe (Ib. xxix. 24 sqq.). In the last days of the monarchy the false prophets obtained a fearful ascendancy: and that chiefly because the people loved falsehood and hated truth, and therefore themselves corrupted the prophets. We find the first note of this in Isaiah, 'This is a rebellious people, lying children, that will not hear the law of Jehovah, which say to the seers, See not; and to the prophets, Prophesy not unto us right things, speak unto us smooth things, prophesy deceits (Is. xxx. 9, 10).' In severer terms Jeremiah speaks of a fearful alliance of prophets, priests, and people in mutually deceiving and corrupting one another (Jer. v. 30, 31). How then, in such a state of circumstances, could one who truly sought God know who was indeed the bearer of God's message?

He would know it chiefly by the message itself. There is no man who does not at some time or other feel that there is a message from God to his soul: and that that message bids him repent and be holy. He knows that God's message must be a reproof of all that is wicked in him, and a warning that for his wickedness there will be judgment. This is just the message which the true prophets always brought. Not a smooth message, but a rough message of rebuke and expostulation, and of promise only where there had been first repentance. But men deceive themselves. They have ever some excuse, some plea for themselves: and therefore the message must be brought by those who are not merely disinterested, but are actually sufferers by it. Such is still the case now. The highest calls of duty are ever incompatible with worldly profit. And such certainly was the case with the prophets of old. They neither gained nor expected to gain from their labours anything but opposition, abuse, and injury. Read their history through—search in their works for the motives which influenced their conduct; examine what they taught, and the principles which they urged upon others, and you will never find that what they sought was either pleasure or riches, or any worldly, low, mean, unworthy object. They laboured for God, and found in Him their sole reward. And even this very labouring came not to them of their own choice. They sought not the office. 'As for me,' says Jeremiah, 'I have not hastened from being a pastor to follow Thee: neither have I desired the woeful day; Thou knowest (Jer. xvii. 16).' The inspiration came from God, unsought, against their own wills; and they knew that earthly ease, happiness, enjoyment must be foregone. Such were the criteria of the true prophet: a message which did not flatter man, but raised him from earth to God; and himself an example of every earthly good resigned that duty might be done, and God obeyed and found.

Such was the teaching and such the conduct of the men who wrote for us the Old Testament: but to show more clearly their extraordinary excellence I shall in my next lecture explain what was the general nature of the prophetic institutions, the kind of instruction given in their colleges, their mode of life, their ordinary average standard of duty and religion. It is only by contrasting the inspired prophet with his uninspired brethren, that we can see how high he was raised above the usual level of his contemporaries.

LECTURE IV.

PART I.

THE SCHOOLS OF THE PROPHETS.

It was told Saul, saying, Behold, David is at Naioth in Ramah. And Saul sent messengers to take David: and when they saw the company of the prophets prophesying, and Samuel standing as appointed over them, the Spirit of God was upon the messengers of Saul, and they also prophesied.—1 SAM. XIX. 19, 20.

IN my last lecture I endeavoured to give a general outline of the nature of Samuel's times, and of the work which he accomplished. We find ourselves in his days transported into an entirely different state of things from that which had existed before. It was the second great era of Judaism, inferior to the age of Moses, but yet one in which the truths taught by Moses first acquired that ascendancy over the Jewish mind which they never afterwards lost; on the contrary, from Samuel's time they ever grew in strength and clearness, till finally the veil was withdrawn from them in Christ, and apostles and evangelists completed what Moses had begun. I showed somewhat of the difficulties with which Moses had to contend. Though round him he had the heads of the tribes, men impressed with the same truths as

himself, yet the mass of the people were not merely
debased by a long sojourn in Egypt, but were originally of inferior position, retainers[a] merely, who had
learned somewhat of the nature of God from their
chiefs, but probably in a very imperfect manner.
And then there was that base mixed multitude, who

[a] The number of first-born males, as given in Num. iii. 40-43, is
22,273. All the genealogies show that large families were the exception among the Israelites, and not the rule. An average of three
or four sons in a family would be a high one, and thus we cannot be
far wrong in estimating the number of lineal descendants of Jacob
at the Exodus as under eighty thousand. Now Jacob and all his
kindred when they went down to Egypt amounted to 'threescore and
fifteen souls (Acts vii. 14);' but if we add together Jacob's 'brethren'
and the menservants he brought with him from Mesopotamia, the
captives taken at Shechem, and the half of Isaac's possessions, we may
safely conclude that Jacob's whole household amounted to many
thousand persons. In Egypt Joseph was ruler over the whole land,
and his power is proved by the expeditions made by his grandsons
into Palestine. By the time of his death the Israelites in Goshen were
probably more than a hundred thousand strong, since for military
reasons Joseph would do all he could to increase their numbers, so
as to enable them to protect the north-eastern boundary of the kingdom,
where they were posted. Many Semitic tribes may have been incorporated with them in Joseph's days, just as the Kenites and Kenezites
were in the days of Moses. If their chiefs were adopted into the patri-
archal families, as Caleb and Othniel were into that of Judah, even
the eighty thousand spoken of above would not all be lineally descended
from Jacob. Now, multiplied by four, the sixth generation would
make these 75 souls into 76,800, but this implies an average of eight
children, all arriving at full age and marrying. But, as a matter of
fact, we find that Joshua was the twelfth generation from Joseph
(1 Chron. vii. 20-27). It is a vexed question whether the 430 years
mentioned in Exod. xii. 41 are to be reckoned from Abraham's vision,
Gen. xv. 13, or from the descent into Egypt: but one complete
genealogy like that of Joshua has more weight than the shorter genealogies like those of Moses, because it was the rule with the Hebrews
to omit names. Names are omitted even in our Lord's genealogy in
Matt. i. As Ewald observes, the names in the genealogy of Moses
may represent each a century. In four centuries Jacob's lineal descendants might well amount to fourscore thousand men.

were half-heathens in their views; and, after the conquest of Canaan, there was added to all this a large admixture of the native population, whose wanton nature-worships had a powerful attraction for at least all the inferior portion of the mighty multitude who left Egypt.

Even the princes did not always give Moses a hearty support. Aaron and Miriam, and Aaron's sons, on more than one occasion failed him. The chiefs of Reuben, and Korah a prince of Levi, broke out once into open rebellion; but the real difficulty, as is evident everywhere in the history of the wanderings in the wilderness, was with the mass of the people. When, at the end of a year, they reached the borders of Palestine, their cowardice was so great that they refused to enter upon the conquest of the land; and it was not till after that whole generation was dead, and Moses at his head-quarters at Kadesh-barnea had trained up an entirely new generation, invigorated both by his teaching and by the healthy air of the desert, and the hardy mode of life they led there, it was then only that marching upon Canaan by an entirely different route he conquered in person the Amorites of Heshbon and Bashan, and the Midianites, and placed Joshua at the head of a band of hardy warriors, whom nothing could resist. A vast moral and physical change[b] alike had passed over the people, but it was not complete. Perhaps a large proportion of the tribes were necessarily dispersed over the desert during Moses' days, seeking

---

[b] Compare Ex. xiv. 11, 12, xvi. 3, Num. xi. 4-6, xiv. 1-4, with the bravery displayed when Moses started the second time from Kadesh for the conquest of the land, Num. xxi. 24, 35, &c.

pasture for their flocks and herds, though incontestably the whole region then was vastly more fertile than it is at present. But however it be accounted for, evidently the Canaanitish rites had only too great an attraction for the mass of the people, and the times of the Judges are set before us as times of constant lapses into idolatry, and of a by no means elevated moral tone.

But in the days of Samuel we find the worship of Jehovah everywhere firmly established, and from their defeat at Ebenezer the people rise to a more vigorous, a nobler, and a higher life. As the conquest of Canaan by Joshua was really Moses' work, because he had formed and trained the men whom Joshua led, so the victories of Saul and the conquests of David were really Samuel's work, because he had raised the nation to that moral level which made it fit and able to win first independence and then empire. Samuel by his reforms had endowed the nation with a vigorous inner energy, which showed itself outwardly in strong acts. Israel had, I grant, never lost that hardy valour with which it emerged from its thirty-eight years' training in the wilderness [c];

[c] I am quite ready also to grant that David's strength was in part owing to the decisive way in which Judah now entered the confederacy. It had always been the most warlike of the tribes (Num. x. 14, Judges i. 2, xx. 18), but from the time that Othniel drove back the Mesopotamians (Judges iii. 10), we read nothing more of it, except the not very patriotic proceeding in Judges xv. 9-13. Apparently, however, it had enjoyed a period of unchequered prosperity; for when David numbered the people, there were in Judah 500,000 valiant men that drew the sword, and only 800,000 in all the rest of the tribes. Now at the last numbering of the people, in Num. xxvi, the tribe of Judah had consisted of 76,500 men, and the other eleven tribes, omitting Levi, of 525,230 men. I think we may appeal to this as an undesigned

but Samuel had revived in it its early enthusiasm, had filled it with fresh faith in Jehovah, and with a renewed confidence that Israel was Jehovah's people, and that, if it served Him in truth and holiness, He would be its strength and sure defence. This new life not only won for Israel freedom, but dominion over the neighbouring states. It was but too natural for a warrior who had broken the yoke of foreign subjection from off the neck of his own people, to place it, if he could, upon the necks of others. I do not find, however, that the prophets approved of this. Rather they strongly condemned it. When David numbered the people, the prophet Gad reproved him, and bade him choose one of three severe punishments. Why? We do not doubt but that it is absolutely right to number the people. Moses twice numbered the people. All civilized nations number the people. Yes; but David numbered only 'the valiant men that drew the sword,' and he numbered them for a bad purpose—for foreign war and aggression; and the punishments were all of such a kind as to abate this fighting lust. And when David would have built a temple for Jehovah's service, leave is refused him. A man who had 'made great wars, and shed much blood upon the earth,' must resign so pure and elevated a purpose to 'a man of rest (1 Chron. xxii. 8, 9).'

Now we saw in the last lecture the three great

coincidence. In the Book of Judges every other tribe is exposed to constant trouble, but Judah remains tranquil in its southern fastnesses. When it emerges from its obscurity, it has grown so strong that it is well-nigh a match for all the rest. The other tribes had increased in numbers, but not to any great extent. Judah had increased more than sixfold.

means employed by Samuel in producing this marvellous change in Israel, of which David's empire, and the learning and culture prevalent in his days, and his psalms, and the service in the sanctuary at which they were sung, were truly results; Samuel's three chief means for this were the reformation of the people's morals, the upright administration of justice, and the regular organization of the prophetic order [d]. Like all true reformers, his object was to raise and elevate the people themselves; all the rest was sure to follow. Now of all his institutions, that which gave strength and life to everything else was the grand development he gave to the energy of the prophets by means of the schools which he founded for them. He trained in these schools men whose one business was earnestly to labour among the people for their spiritual good. As the priests and Levites laboured to preserve the Mosaic religion, its ceremonies and ritual, its types and sacrifices, its feasts and fasts and festivals, so the prophets laboured to preserve and impress upon the people's hearts all the great spiritual truths and ideas of the Mosaic teaching. After the return from Babylon, this great duty was performed by the synagogues, wherein the law, and psalms, and prophets were read every Sabbath day. Among us it is performed by the

---

[d] Of course I do not put these upon the same level. The first was the end sought also by the other two. I put them down in this order (illogical though it be), because Samuel brought about a national repentance first of all by his own exhortations (1 Sam. vii. 3-6), and then took means for making this revival of faith and morality firm and lasting by his other two measures. His annual circuits as judge would maintain a high standard of morality; the preaching and activity of the prophets would quicken the nation's faith.

services of the Lord's house, wherein the teaching of the Church and of the Bible is enforced by the living voice of the preacher. As I have said, I doubt not but that under the Mosaic institutions the priests and Levites were dispersed throughout Israel on purpose that they might discharge this duty: they did not discharge it, and Samuel now confided it to men trained by him for this one end.

In the text we are introduced to the first and earliest of the prophetic colleges, with its organization apparently complete and in full working order. We find prophets arranged in a regular company, duties about which they are engaged, and a duly appointed head presiding over them. Already in the tenth chapter we had read of a company of the prophets coming in solemn procession from some religious ceremony, preceded by instruments of music, whereas previously the name of prophet is most rare. And here we see them at their head-quarters, and subject to a settled discipline, with 'Samuel standing as appointed over them.' How appointed? and by whom? and whence arose these schools of the prophets, of which henceforward we read so much in the annals of the Jewish monarchy?

Now, first, the college of which we here read is at Ramah, a town which pertained to Samuel. His father Elkanah had dwelt there (1 Sam. i. 19, ii. 11), and at his death his possessions descended to Samuel, his first-born son. Thither at the end of each judicial circuit Samuel returned, 'for there was his house, and there he judged Israel, and there he built an altar unto Jehovah (Ib. vii. 17);' and there, finally, 'he died, and was buried (Ib. xxv. 1).' And, as I have before said, Naioth is not the name of any town or village, but means pastures, places apparently that were common property, and where the shepherds loved to congregate and pitch their tents. In these pastures, then, near Ramah, Samuel's dwelling-place, there were young men assembled, to be trained, as it appears, not in martial exercises, but in the rudiments of a higher education.

It is quite incidentally that the mention of them is made. Probably the Books of Samuel were compiled from records which he had himself commenced. Had Gad or Nathan written them, it seems incredible but that they would have told us more about the origin and discipline of these schools. For they had by that time grown into important institutions, and prophets who had learned in them arts so important as reading and writing, would have looked back with affection to their great founder, and told us more of his plans and ways. Not so Samuel. The prophetic colleges had grown up round him as it were by chance. He had not consciously intended to alter the whole course of things, and found a new era: but he had felt a want, a need, and tried to supply it. And his plans by prudent management had prospered. From small beginnings there had sprung up round him what virtually was a University[e]. Men had gradually gathered to his teaching, and learning advanced with rapid strides. Though Deborah records

---

[e] I will not enter into the vexed question whether Kirjath-sepher, Book-town, was a Canaanite University, but Ramah was plainly the first Hebrew University, and stands at the head of that long line of educational institutions which after the Saviour's time ended in the great schools of Tiberias, Sora, and Pumbeditha.

that there came to her from Zebulun 'those that handle the pen of the writer (Judges v. 14),' this is the last indication of the existence among the Israelites of that culture which they must have acquired in Egypt when living in close contact with a people so highly civilized. Nor can even this be depended upon, for the more probable translation is 'those that handle the staff or baton of the general.' In the sanctuary alone at Shiloh were the arts of reading and writing preserved. But now learning becomes common. The youthful David, son of the rich farmer of Bethlehem, standing there at Samuel's side when Saul's messengers came, was not only himself an educated man, but when he became king could gather round him accomplished scribes and competent historians. His son was to be the wonder of the age for literary skill. All this was Samuel's doing. I see not how David could have learned to read and write except in Samuel's schools. His skill in music may also have been acquired there. But be this as it may, from the days of Samuel till the repeated invasions of the Assyrians had wasted the land and destroyed its higher civilization, the Israelites [f] were a highly-educated and literary people.

His own education then in the sanctuary was bearing fruit. Samuel's predecessors had been warriors, men who fought for freedom sword in hand, but who had little idea of anything more. Samuel was no

---

[f] Like all energetic races they had an eager thirst for knowledge, and an aptness to learn and teach. 'The scholar and the teacher' are already mentioned in David's time (1 Chron. xxv. 8); and among the three precepts ascribed to Ezra in the Talmud is this, 'Teach: make numerous scholars.' See Nicolas, Des Doctr. Rel. des Juifs, p. 31.

warrior. Not but that at Ebenezer he put himself at the head of the Israelites, and won for them that great victory which gave them rest for many years. But he had higher purposes. To give Israel permanent and enduring superiority, he must raise the whole people mentally and morally, as well as religiously. If by his own teaching and example he could thus ennoble a few, they would be his instruments for ennobling the rest. He gathers round him therefore religious men, deepens their own convictions, awakens their zeal, fills them with earnestness, kindles in them the true prophetic spirit, and by them calls forth again into full force and activity those pure and elevating Mosaic beliefs which had at first nerved the people to quit Egypt, and enabled them in the next generation to conquer Canaan.

At first these young men probably dwelt in tents or booths on the open pasture land: for the ways of life were still simple, and houses [g] rare, and possessed only by those of higher rank. But as their numbers increased, and a regular constitution was given them, and a settled discipline, it is probable that their dwellings acquired more of a permanent character [h]. In the text they certainly appear as a regularly organized body: for we find 'Samuel standing as

[g] That the tent was the ordinary dwelling-place of the Israelites, except in the towns, is suggested by passages such as Is. liv. 2. So David is described as saying, 'I will not go into the tent of my house,' Ps. cxxxii. 3; and Isaiah, xvi. 5, calls David's house a tent. If such was the king's habitation, no wonder that all the people in Solomon's time still lived in tents, 1 Kings viii. 66, and long afterwards, 2 Kings xiii. 5, Jer. iv. 20, x. 20.

[h] At all events they would require something like a common hall, or place of meeting.

appointed over them.' Now these words may only refer to that religious service of song and chant in which they were engaged when Saul's messengers arrived. If so, they would show that they had arrived at that stage when the service of God was conducted according to a dignified and impressive ceremonial. But the words more probably signify that Samuel 'was chief over them.' Not appointed by any one: that is not the meaning of the Hebrew. As a prophet of the highest rank, he was by virtue of his office their chief. And thus the words suggest, what we should also gather from other things, that after the appointment of Saul to the kingdom, Samuel, for the remaining thirty years of his life, concentrated all his energies upon these schools. Hence the deep root they struck in Israel, and the vast effects they produced. And, following Samuel's example, other inspired prophets devoted themselves to the same high purpose, and the sons of the prophets looked to them naturally as their chiefs. Thus when at Jericho they saw that 'the spirit of Elijah rested upon Elisha,' they acknowledged him as their head by 'bowing themselves to the ground before him (2 Kings ii. 15);' and subsequently we find him recognized as their ruler by all the prophetic colleges among the ten tribes.

The training of these young men was partly in reading and writing, the two sole foundations of all intellectual culture, and the two greatest steps that men can take forward on the road from barbarism to civilization. But it was partly also, as we have seen, in music, with which was joined probably singing, such as subsequently formed the great charm of the temple services, as established there by David, Nathan, and Gad, all three, I doubt not, trained by Samuel himself. Now the introduction of psalms into the temple service was a great step towards an intellectual and spiritual worship. The sacrifices were full of typical meaning, but their chief attraction probably was the feast which followed. The Psalms were 'a reasonable—an intellectual—service,' and men's hearts rose up in them to God. The synagogues, after the return from Babylon, made this kind of service, with other similar additions of prayer and the reading of the scriptures, the ordinary form of Divine worship throughout the land. And we have inherited this service. The Christian Church was formed upon the model not of the temple but of the synagogue. Still we read the same law, and the same prophets as they read, and sing their psalms. To this day these Jewish Psalms are our best expression of praise and thanksgiving. When Samuel trained his young prophets in music, he introduced an innovation into Divine service which will continue and bear fruit as long as the Church shall last[i].

But this training was necessary also for the times. In a coarse and violent age like that described in the Book of Judges, music and poetry, which inevitably go together, exercise a powerful influence in civilizing men, and giving the softer arts, and the pleasures of a milder and more refined mode of life, value in their

---

[i] Yet here as everywhere else the root is in Moses. He first wrote a Psalm which Miriam and the women sang with timbrels and dances (Ex. xv. 20), and therefore the Psalms are very significantly ascribed to Moses in the Revelation, 'They sing the song of Moses, the servant of God, and the song of the Lamb (Rev. xv. 3).'

eyes. We now are subject to innumerable softening influences. It was not so then. Music, the song, the religious chant, the solemn dance at holy festivals, these were the chief, and well-nigh the sole civilizing elements of early times [k].

We must not, however, suppose that all the young men trained by Samuel at Ramah became prophets. Very probably at first he wanted men to aid him in the civil administration of the realm: and besides, though the sons of the prophets occupied a lower position than that held by men so highly inspired as Samuel and Gad and Nathan, and Elijah and Elisha, yet before a man was admitted even into the lower grades of the prophetic order, proof was necessary that Jehovah's spirit rested upon him; proof that he had the inner call to bear to men Jehovah's message. But men so called formed probably but a small proportion of those who frequented Samuel's schools. Certainly we find that David had returned to his ordinary duties at home when the war with the Philistines summoned him away from his obscurity. Yet we cannot be far wrong in concluding that he did not learn at Bethlehem either his extraordinary skill in writing or his mastery over the harp. We read

---

[k] In a fighting age the bard stands in the same relation to civilization as the newspaper of the present day. He was the organ of intelligence, the bearer of news, the representative of the ideas of his times. When men take to reading, the bard becomes a plaything. He may beguile the long hours of a winter evening, or increase the pleasures of a feast, but no more. In early times he was the educator also. His lays, as sung by himself, and repeated from mouth to mouth, formed the minds of his countrymen. The song, the ballad,— these were the intellectual food of the people. Of such ballads probably consisted the Book of Jashar, and the Book of the Wars of Jehovah, so often mentioned in the Bible.

of him too as dancing before the ark, and though not expressly mentioned, still we cannot doubt but that this formed part of the religious exercises of the sons of the prophets[1]. Still more conclusive is the elevation of his views as shown in his contest with the giant, his self-devotion, and early piety. From all this I doubt not that after Samuel had anointed David as Israel's future king, he had him with him as much as possible, and carefully trained him for his high destiny[m].

We find a proverb twice referred to connecting even Saul with the prophetic schools (1 Sam. x. 11, xix. 24). Two circumstances are mentioned, in both of which the ready wit of the people noticed that strange incongruity of character, which strikes us to this day in reading Saul's history. But we must not conclude from the proverb that Saul had ever had any such training. The history presents him to us as one who had no personal knowledge of Samuel (1 Sam. ix. 18) when God's providence brought him first to Ramah: and apparently he resided at Gibeah during the no very long period which intervened between his designation to the crown and the establishment of his authority by the defeat of Nahash. Saul was a man of great natural ability, with many noble qualities, who yet failed miserably in his probation. But his whole history is that of an untrained man, nor is there the slightest indication that he could read

---

[1] Compare Michal's reproach of David, 2 Sam. vi. 20, with what is said of Saul, 1 Sam. xix. 24.

[m] According to the ordinary chronology, Saul's second and final rejection was in B. C. 1079, and David's combat with Goliath in B. C. 1063. There is thus an interval of sixteen years, giving ample space for David's anointing and subsequent training for the kingly office.

or write, or that he possessed any of the accomplishments taught in the prophetic schools. The national wit, then, contrasted the tall, ungainly, uncultivated, but still stalwart hero with the educated and accomplished men whom Samuel was training for intellectual work. It did more. It contrasted the wilful, irreligious, wayward despot with the good and holy men whose conduct was regulated by settled religious principles.

Still the proverb shows that there was no impossibility in Saul having been thus trained. The incongruity seized upon by the people was that of his personal character. The probability is, that of those trained by Samuel, some, like Gad and Nathan, became Nabhis, prophets, and as a learned and devoted order of men filled an important place in the national economy; others returned to more ordinary duties, to the cultivation of their estates, or to a military life or office under the king; while, lastly, a large majority were probably Levites, and from the time that David brought the ark to the tent which he had pitched for it in Zion, they had the charge of the services there. For we are expressly told that the music in the house of Jehovah was according 'to the commandment of Jehovah by the prophets (2 Chron. xxix. 25).'

For Samuel was himself a Levite, and to the Levites he would naturally look for the men to aid him in his reforms. He recognized the high place they were intended to fill in the Jewish economy, and saw that they had not filled it: but while organizing his new institution on a freer footing, so far from excluding the Levites from it, he would still chiefly turn to them. The opposition between the priest and the prophet has often been noticed by writers of every kind: but of the comparatively few prophets whose lineage has been recorded, the majority are priests. And so when Samuel [n] added a more spiritual element to the services of the sanctuary, it was entrusted entirely to the Levites. Though the priests and Levites had not done all that Moses had expected, yet it is exceedingly probable that they had always maintained among themselves a higher standard both in morality and religion than the rest of the community. There was an opposition in the law itself between its spiritual truths and its burdensome ritual (Ezek. xx. 11, 25, Acts xv. 10), and yet the law contained and harmonized both elements. And so, if the prophet seized the law in its inner, and therefore its higher and more spiritual reality, while

[n] It is certain from 1 Chron. ix. 22 that Samuel commenced that reorganization of the Levites which David completed. From 1 Chron. xxv. we learn that all the great singers and musicians, Heman, Asaph, Jeduthun, &c., were Levites, and that Heman was a Kohathite, like Samuel himself (1 Chron. vi. 22, 28, 33). From the part taken by Gad and Nathan in the arrangement of the temple service (2 Chron. xxix. 25), it is exceedingly probable that it was modelled upon the same plan as that originated by Samuel in the schools of the prophets: and when in the text Saul's messengers found 'the company of the prophets prophesying, and Samuel standing as appointed over them,' there can be little doubt that they were engaged in a religious service, consisting of music and singing, like that subsequently instituted by David for the tabernacle, and performed by a chorus of 288 trained voices (1 Chron. xxv. 7). How impressive Samuel's service was we gather from the effect produced upon three successive sets of messengers sent by Saul, and subsequently upon Saul himself (1 Sam. xix. 20-24). From the last verse we learn that there were also solemn dances, in which Saul, clad only in a linen ephod, or tunic, such as David danced in before the ark (2 Sam. vi. 14, 20), took part so enthusiastically, that he finally fell down completely exhausted, and for many hours afterwards lay motionless.

the priest saw chiefly its lower and objective aspect, still the prophetic spirit was not denied to the priesthood; and often, as in Ezekiel, the two modes of thought were happily combined in the same man.

Such, then, was the new beginning of prophecy. The dismal state of things which preceded Samuel, and his own far-seeing and thorough remedies, made him need a more highly-educated class of men than Israel had ever before possessed. But the prophets were no mere literary class; I do not know that such a class has ever either merited or met with much respect; and certainly that was not what Samuel wanted. The very root of his reforms was his desire to see Israel more virtuous and more religious. His instruments, therefore, must above all things be men who themselves were holy. He needed a clergy. For them education was something: the grace of God was more. Now the prophets had ever been men who pleaded for God. Religion with them was the one thing essential. And though we cannot suppose that the Spirit of Jehovah rested in the way of direct inspiration on all the holy men trained by Samuel, still they earned and deserved the name of prophet by their intense conviction both of the truth and of the need of God's message to man. They were men who felt an irresistible call to work for God, and in whom God's Spirit wrought by a large outpouring of the ordinary gifts of grace. But there were also here and there among them men on whom extraordinary gifts were bestowed. Such men were Gad and Nathan in David's days.

What they were endowed with was no mere intellectual superiority; no mere human wisdom; but something directly supernatural. There were at David's court men of the highest worldly wisdom. Ahithophel was so wise that 'his counsel was as if a man had enquired at the oracle of God (2 Sam. xvi. 23):' but men knew that there was nothing divine about it, and David left his friend Hushai the Archite to frustrate Ahithophel's advice. There was nothing wrong in so doing: for Ahithophel's was mere worldly wisdom; his strong sense made him discern what were the best means for gaining his ends; but the question of right and wrong formed no element in his counsel. But the prophet ever spake of right and wrong, and duty. And when he went inspired with a message from above, like Nathan to David, it was the conscience that was addressed, not the intellect; and man's duty was, not to understand it, and judge of it, but to obey. It was a command given by the highest and final authority, from which there was no appeal.

But our business with the prophets at present is rather with their ordinary and every-day level. It is only by looking at them as they were in the large majority of cases that we shall be able to judge of the extraordinary elevation of those wonderful men, who stand out from time to time in gigantic vastness among the actors in the annals of Jewish history.

Now first, as regards the time, we have already seen that this remodelling of the Mosaic institutions by Samuel took place just at the period when the old method of consulting Jehovah by the oracle and Urim went out of use. This was but an unsatisfactory way at best, but it lasted just to the time when real prophecy, the real mediatorship between Jehovah and

His people, such as that with which Moses had been himself invested, was set free from its connection with the priesthood, and founded again upon a wider and freer basis by Samuel. From this time forward Jehovah was no more consulted according to the Mosaic enactments. His will could no longer be ascertained whenever the chief ruler wished. Henceforward the Urim probably answered no more. For Jehovah had now His own special servants, who declared His will not as and when men desired, but as He commanded. And this usually was as men least desired. The prophets were unwelcome visitors. Elijah meeting Ahab in Naboth's vineyard was a most disagreeable intruder; yet scarcely more so than Nathan with his 'Thou art the man' to David, or Gad with his three plagues, or Shemaiah bidding Rehoboam dismiss his army. Seldom is God's message received by man with joy.

And next we must repeat that, unlike the priesthood, the prophetic order was open to all, without respect of birth or even of education. Samuel's schools were as free to all of every tribe, as are our own universities open to every one now. But we must not connect prophecy too closely even with them. Neither were all prophets trained in his schools, nor were all trained in his schools prophets. But just as now a higher education is the usual preparation for the calling of a clergyman, so it was then with the prophets. Samuel no doubt intended his scholars to be prophets, and urged them to it. But not only was the highest gift of all absolutely untrammelled by any and every earthly ordinance, but even the lower gift would depend upon the personal fitness of the recipient. And these schools called forth men who were fit. But as the usual rule they were prophets by education only and calling. We find them in time gradually falling to a very low spiritual level; but this corruption was long after Samuel's days. Even in their worst day they were still called prophets. No practical inconvenience arises from the use of words in a higher and a lower sense. Neither the Nabhis whom Samuel set over his schools, nor the young Nabhis trained there, supposed themselves, or were supposed by others, to share the same gift as Samuel and Elijah possessed. It was only in bad and demoralized times, like the reigns of Jehoiakim and Zedekiah, that we find false prophets claiming direct inspiration (Jer. xxix. 9) for their lies, and denying it to the true prophet (Ib. 27).

After Samuel's days these schools greatly multiplied. His foundation had been at Ramah in Benjamin, but in the time of Elisha, when our accounts of them are most full, we find prophetic colleges existing at Bethel, at Jericho, and at Gilgal, places all of them, except Jericho, connected with Samuel's history[o]. But as they are mentioned only incidentally, it is very probable that similar institutions existed elsewhere. At all events prophets had become a very numerous class. For when, seven years after Elijah's great day of triumph at Carmel, Jehoshaphat wished Ahab to enquire at the word of Jehovah about

[o] This makes it highly probable that in the long period of thirty years and more between the anointing of Saul and the death of Samuel, the latter had established prophetic colleges in many other places besides Ramah.

the expedition to Ramoth-gilead, that king, in spite of Jezebel's cruel persecutions, was able to collect in one town, Samaria, where, as far as we know, there was no prophetic college, no fewer than four hundred men. The whole narrative shows that these men were by profession Jehovah-prophets, and they all prophesied in Jehovah's name. But there was something unsatisfactory about them: perhaps Jehoshaphat knew that God does not speak by people in crowds, and so he asked if there was not some one prophet of Jehovah besides; and the true prophet came unwelcome as usual. Now though we cannot but condemn the four hundred as flatterers, and that of such a king as Ahab, still even they probably were in advance of the mass of the people both in religion and morals. It is at all events but fair to remember, that but a few years before, when Jezebel was persecuting the Jehovah-prophets, large numbers of them willingly suffered death rather than abjure God's true worship.

No class of men ordinarily is very far in advance of the general state of feeling in the midst of which it lives; and thus until the days of Jeremiah we never find the Jehovah-prophets in Judah sinking so low as their brethren in Samaria. But however discreditable may be the behaviour of these men before Ahab, yet there are many particulars in which plainly great national progress had been made, which we cannot be far wrong in attributing to the prosperity of the prophetic schools under the able management of Elisha. Thus, long after the palmy days of David and Solomon, none apparently but the prophets were able to read and write till about this time. But now we are told of a writing addressed to Jehoram, king of Judah, in Elijah's name, which we must suppose that king could read (2 Chron. xxi. 12). Jezebel sends letters to the elders of Jezreel, and seals them with Ahab's seal, a proof that such communications had now become common (1 Kings xxi. 8). Jehu twice writes letters to the same elders (2 Kings x. 1, 6); even the king of Syria sends a letter with Naaman, and it is expressly said that the king of Israel read it (2 Kings v. 5, 7), though it is probable that it was written by some royal scribe. Henceforth letters and writing play an important part in all political matters. Now when we bear in mind Jezebel's persecution of the prophets, and then read how active and numerous they were under Elisha, and further see so very marked an advance in the liberal arts, we may safely draw the conclusion that the prophetic schools had long before struck deep root in the northern kingdom, and established a firm hold over the affections of the people. Plainly they were a great national institution.

The general government of the prophetic body, as well as of their colleges, would necessarily devolve upon whatever prophet was then inspired. And thus, as we have seen, no sooner did the sons of the prophets at Jericho perceive that Elijah's spirit rested upon Elisha, than by their deep obeisance they recognized him as their head. But besides this, he had also another claim, namely, that of having been Elijah's personal attendant. So probably Gehazi would have succeeded Elisha, had he not yielded, like Judas and Demas, to the seductions of covetousness [p].

[p] It is important to remember that Gehazi's fall was the fall of a man of high prophetic dignity. Just as being in the ark did not save

As head of these colleges we find Elisha leading a life of incessant activity. We read of him at Dothan, at Samaria, where he had a house, and usually dwelt (2 Kings v. 3, vi. 32), on Mount Carmel, at Shunem, and at Damascus; but chiefly we find him with the sons of the prophets. Thus he multiplies the oil of the widow of one of them, to enable her to pay her debts (Ib. iv. 1); at Gilgal he renders the poisoned pottage wholesome, and multiplies the first-fruits offered by the farmer from Baal-shalisha (Ib. iv. 41, 43); and here incidentally we learn that the college at Gilgal numbered a hundred men. Elsewhere we read of his accompanying them to choose timber for the enlargement of their dwelling (Ib. vi. 2), and restoring to one of them the axe-head lost in the waters of the Jordan. Again, he uses one of them as his

---

Ham, nor his apostleship Judas, so neither did the prophetic office save the prophet. A gift so high as inspiration was probably not attained to till after many internal struggles, and long wrestlings after grace. Yet Balaam fell, and Jeremiah has recorded his own long-continued resistance against God, ending finally in his submission; but the struggle might have ended otherwise. The prophets had their own probation quite as much as the apostles and all other saints, and when saved, they were not saved by the gifts they had received, but by grace: by faith and the work of the Holy Ghost on their hearts, just like other men. And if so many fell whose gifts were above nature, well may baptized Christians 'not be high-minded, but fear.' Gehazi, however, had never received the actual gift of inspiration, but probably hoped to attain to it upon Elisha's decease. This, however, was no necessary result of his position. Baruch, who held the same rank with regard to Jeremiah, never became a prophet, though he was a good and holy man. Some think that Jer. xlv. was written to comfort him under the disappointment. A common tradition in the East represents him as so vexed by the withholding of the gift, that after Jeremiah's death he apostatized, and under the name of Zerdusht, or Zoroaster, became the founder of the religion of Persia. The tradition is only so far interesting as illustrating the relation in which the great prophets stood to their immediate attendant.

messenger to Jehu (Ib. ix. 1), and everywhere plainly stands in the closest relation to them.

And, next, we must notice that all the express references to the schools of the prophets connect them with the northern kingdom. To the ten tribes belong those great prophetic heroes Elijah and Elisha; and God, Who is merciful to all, seems to have granted to those of the Israelites who loved Him a compensation in prophecy for the loss of the temple-service at Jerusalem, and for the withdrawal of the priests and Levites. If the great means of grace provided by the Mosaic ritual were no longer theirs, at all events they had the less regular institutions of Samuel to aid them in living unto God. Still it is hard to believe that no similar institutions existed in Judæa. The notices respecting the schools of the prophets in the northern kingdom are so casual, so entirely connected with the personal history of Elisha, that we can found no argument upon the silence of Holy Scripture respecting other places. And when we come to the books of the prophets, we find every one possessed of so intimate an acquaintance with the writings of the rest, that we feel sure they had some regular organization to render this possible. Thus Isaiah quotes, verbally and exactly, without even omitting the conjunction, a passage from the writings of a prophet of his own time, Micah. He could not have so quoted it but from a written book. Obadiah quotes in the same way from Jeremiah. Amos takes up the very words of Joel as his beginning, and concludes with other words from Joel which all but immediately follow his first quotation [q]. Nor is this

---

[q] Compare Joel iii. 16 with Amos i. 2, and Joel iii. 18 with Amos ix. 13.

all. The prophets use the same metaphors, dwell in the same circle of thoughts, employ the same phrases, have certain expressions always occurring in the same meaning: all this shows that they had some centre, some head-quarters, where they met, and where the young were educated, and the inspired writings of the great prophets made available for general use and study. It is exceedingly probable that they had some such college in Jerusalem, of which Isaiah in his days was head; and if so, the intimate knowledge which Jeremiah possessed of the writings of his predecessors is no longer so extraordinary. He was but a lad when called to be a prophet (Jer. i. 6), and one so eminently conscientious would doubtless prepare himself for his office by deep study of the Scriptures. Even if he did not enter the prophetic college, still, living at Anathoth, three miles from Jerusalem, he would constantly go thither to read the writings there laid up. At all events he knew them almost by heart. Nor is Jeremiah the only instance of this. Short as is the prophecy of Obadiah, a large proportion of it is in the very words of Jeremiah [r]; and though the rest write more freely, yet all of them show a large and exact knowledge of the works of the prophets who had gone before.

Now this was scarcely possible unless the prophets had some head-quarters, where the inspired writings of their great chiefs were preserved and read and studied. Though, as I shall hereafter show, the exhortations of the prophets were far more widely known, and attracted far more public attention than

[r] Besides constant allusions, the first seven verses of Obadiah are borrowed, with slight alterations, from various places in Jeremiah.

the negative critics suppose, yet this verbal and minute acquaintance, not merely with their general teaching but with the very words of the written text just as we read it at present, could have been acquired only by the eye, by the actual perusal, and the committing to memory of their works. But we have something like direct evidence upon this point. In the days of king Uzziah, a hundred years after Elisha's death, Amos, in answer to Amaziah the high priest of Bethel, says, ' I was no prophet, neither was I a prophet's son (Amos vii. 14).' Now the words 'a prophet's son' mean one trained or educated in the prophetic schools. But though Amos' mission was to Israel, yet he belonged to Judah, and his dwelling-place was Tekoah, twelve miles south of Jerusalem, on the borders of the great desert. We can scarcely doubt but that Amos in his answer referred to the state of things existing at that time in Judæa. If there were none trained to be prophets in Judæa, as Amaziah very well knew that Amos belonged to Judah, and in fact as all he wanted was to induce him to leave Bethel, and go home, it would have been very unnecessary for Amos to tell him that he did not belong to an order of men that did not exist. Thus his words serve to show us how little really we know of the social state and internal history of these kingdoms, and warn us against the too hasty conclusions of those commentators who have argued, that because the schools of the prophets are not mentioned after the days of Elisha, they therefore did not exist : and that they never existed in Judæa, because we have no express mention of them there.

It is, however, exceedingly probable that they

neither were so numerous nor so important in Judæa as in the sister kingdom; for many of their functions in this latter country were performed in Judæa by the priests and Levites. But the large number of prophets mentioned as writers of histories, and whose works are referred to in the Books of Chronicles, the high state of learning at Jerusalem, especially in Hezekiah's days, and still more the unity of symbolism employed by the prophets, forbid our imagining that they had no special training. The chroniclers and historians of Judah were probably educated in the same way as Nathan and Gad had been. In short, Samuel founded the schools of the prophets to give men a better intellectual culture and to fit them for God's ministry. The whole country is soon raised by them to a high level in literary matters, and though at first they flourished chiefly in Samaria, yet finally it was Jerusalem that became the centre of this learning, and of that class for whom these schools were instituted. It is not therefore very reasonable to suppose either that this culture existed in Judæa without the educational means which had called it into existence, or that so large a number of men would have followed this profession, unless there was still that special training which made men prophets in the lower sense of the word.

For mental culture is one thing, and the gift of inspiration another. It was one thing to be directly God's spokesman, and another to be a prophet like those who existed in crowds at Jerusalem, and who joined with the priests and people in shouting for Jeremiah's death because he prophesied as miserable a fate for the temple as had befallen Shiloh (Jer.

xxvi. 8). Jeremiah, who more than any one else has disclosed to us the internal state of Jerusalem just before its fall, always speaks of the prophets there as a large, powerful, and organized class[s]: but he does not speak favourably[t] of them. They were prophets as far as education and class-feeling could make them such, somewhat better possibly than the four hundred Jehovah-prophets at Samaria, who had nothing but good words for Ahab: certainly better than the mass of the people, because they were as a rule opposed to idolatry, with all its base accompaniments. They were moral, to a certain extent even religious men, as far as externals went, and joined, I have no doubt, eagerly in Hezekiah's and Josiah's reforms[u].

[s] See Jer. ii. 8, 26, iv. 9, v. 31, xiii. 13, xxvi. 7, xxxii. 32; they formed even a powerful class among those carried captive with Jeconiah to Babylon, Ib. xxix. 1, 2, but wrought more for evil than for good, Ib. 8, 9, 21, 31, 32.

[t] The prophets in Jeremiah's days must have been fearfully corrupt, see vi. 13, viii. 10, xiv. 13–16, xxiii. 9, 11, 14–32, xxvii. 9–18, Lam. ii. 14, iv. 13. Occasionally, however, he uses words which show that God had still His own true servants among them, Jer. ii. 30, xxv. 4, xxvi. 5, Lam. ii. 9, 20. The whole picture in Jeremiah shows how hopeless is the state of that nation whose very clergy have become demoralized, Matt. vi. 23.

[u] I have no doubt that the confidence expressed and felt by these prophets that Jerusalem would never become subject to Nebuchadnezzar (Jer. xxvii. 9), and that the captives would soon return (Ib. 16), was entirely founded upon the fact of Josiah's thorough reforms, and of the continuance of the temple-service in all its magnificence during his days and the days of his successors. It was, they deemed, a detestable act in Jeremiah to threaten Jerusalem with the fate of Shiloh so long as the sacrifice was daily offered, and the Levitical priesthood active in its ministrations (Jer. xxvi. 8). But Jeremiah took exactly the same view as all the true prophets. They did not care much for services (Is. i. 11–15, Jer. vii. 4), but set an enormous value upon repentance (Is. i. 16–18, Jer. vii. 5–7, xxvi. 3). Far more pleasant was the doctrine of the false prophets, that men can be saved by what others do for them.

Just the one thing they wanted was the heart touched by the live coal from the altar : the grace of God was not in them, and therefore they fell each one in his own way by his own besetting sin, and that in most cases was the love of the world, the love of power and praise and money.

And in them and with them the nation fell too. It was the solemn duty, the weighty responsibility of the priests and prophets to be, as the clergy ought to be now, the salt of the earth. Upon them, morally speaking, depended the purity of the people's faith, the depth of their religion, the sobriety of their practice. Individuals could be saved without them, but their influence told largely and directly upon the mass. If they then, with the advantage of special religious training, with higher associations, and louder professions, and solemn call to Jehovah's service, failed, what could you expect of the rest? Jeremiah tells us what was the natural and inevitable result: 'A wonderful and horrible thing is committed in the land; The prophets prophesy falsely, and the priests bear rule by their means; and my people love to have it so: and what will ye do in the end thereof? (Jer. v. 30, 31).'

In Jeremiah's days, then, we see the prophets fallen, but with true prophets still existing among them, and the inspired word rising to as high an elevation as in any previous age[v]. It was the un-

---

and that services are acceptable to God independently of the personal faith of the worshipper.

[v] To this period belong Jeremiah, Obadiah, Zephaniah, Habakkuk, and the writers of several psalms, besides the prophetess Huldah. Josiah was also aided in his reforms by pious priests, like the high-

inspired prophets that had fallen, and it is a mark of their fall that they claimed to speak in Jehovah's name (Jer. xxiii. 21), and also that they combined with the priests in seeking worldly ends. But we must not therefore underrate either their piety, or their services in earlier and purer ages, any more than we must those of the clergy of the Christian Church because of the low level to which they have occasionally fallen. At first they were men who had the inner call to the ministry: to this was added a religious training, and a higher culture than that ordinarily enjoyed by their countrymen. They could not therefore but be an influential class. But however useful they might be, and blessed to do much good, yet it was in the way of God's ordinary gifts of grace, and it does not appear that the highest gift of direct inspiration was often bestowed upon them. Nor again was it confined to them. If Gad and Nathan were thus trained, and if the Psalms were mostly composed by men so trained, still Elisha was called from the plough, and Amos from gardening. Yet they too were both educated men. Elisha was competent to take the supervision of the prophetic schools, and in the appropriateness and terseness of his metaphors, and in the judicious arrangement of his subject, Amos[w] even excels the other prophets.

priest Hilkiah, and equally pious laymen, such as Gedaliah, Maaseiah. Neriah, and others.

[w] Though some words in Amos are spelt peculiarly, and though his metaphors are taken from rural life. yet he was a well-taught man, who wrote simply and easily, and with true artistic feeling. How highly educated then must the Jews have been. when thus a gardener, earning but a scanty livelihood, and who had had no special training, could think and write so correctly! Reading was no easy matter then, nor

We must, however, still consider what was the ordinary mode of life of the mass of the prophets when their training was over. We find, then, first of all that they married. We gather this not merely from the special command given to Jeremiah not to marry, for reasons peculiar to his days (Jer. xvi. 2, 3), nor from Ezekiel's being married (Ezek. xxiv. 18), but are taught it directly in Elisha's miracle of multiplying the widow's oil (2 Kings iv. 1–7). She is described there as 'a certain woman of the wives of the sons of the prophets.' These young men therefore married. And next, the husband had incurred debts: from this it follows that their maintenance was not ensured them from any common fund, but from their own personal labours. At his death the creditor comes to take the two sons as bondmen[x] to work out the debt. The widow goes to Elisha, and he has no common fund out of which to relieve her, but asks, 'What hast thou in the house?' She has nothing but one pot of oil. They had separate houses therefore, and their own furniture, though poverty had in this case stripped the widow of everything. Was this oil grown by themselves, some of their own produce? It would not, however, follow from this that they possessed or farmed land, as two

---

were the means for learning so simple and readily attainable as with us since the invention of the art of printing. And Amos is but one proof among many of the advanced state of culture attained to in the southern kingdom before the Assyrians and Chaldaeans wasted the land, and which reached its highest elevation in Hezekiah's days.

[x] The words may even mean to take them absolutely as slaves. Either alternative was a violation of the Levitical law (Lev. xxv. 44-46), which however required that a debtor should himself be liable to work out in person his debt (Ib. 39).

or three olive trees might in a good season produce a large quantity of oil. Elisha finally bids her borrow vessels, and, having closed the door, to fill them from her one remaining jar, and then sell the oil thus multiplied, and pay her debts, and with her children live upon the rest.

After this it is but natural to read of Samuel's house at Ramah, of Nathan's in Jerusalem, of Ahijah's at Shiloh, of Elisha's at Samaria, of Ezekiel's at Telabib. As regards Elijah, it has been argued that his ascetic character and wandering habits were incompatible with a settled dwelling and a wife. But this is to confound modern with oriental manners. One would have thought St. Peter's life incompatible with marriage: not so our Lord. St. Paul even tells us that not only Peter but the rest of the apostles[y] and our Lord's brethren were accompanied by their believing wives on their circuits; and so we find St. Peter's wife with him at Babylon (1 Pet. v. 13). I do not know whether any one has ever supposed that St. Peter's[z] wife may have been in the number of those Galilaean women who ministered to our Lord,

[y] The phrase is so very strong as to imply that marriage was the all but universal rule with the apostles, οἱ λοιποὶ ἀπόστολοι, καὶ οἱ ἀδελφοὶ τοῦ Κυρίου (1 Cor. ix. 5). In the A. V. occurs one of those mistranslations which occasionally mar our beautiful version, 'Have we not power to lead about *a sister, a wife?*' the Greek means *a believing wife*, a wife who is a sister, that is, a Christian. The wives of the apostles, then, were all Christian women. The rendering in the margin is a violation of one of the commonest Greek idioms, but has some patristic authority, e. g. Clem. Alex. Strom. iii. p. 210.

[z] St. Peter certainly had the high privilege of doing more for our Lord, in earthly matters, than any of the rest of the apostles. His house was our Lord's dwelling at Capernaum, and his boat that in which our Lord so often crossed the sea of Galilee.

but certainly we find several married women among them, such as Joanna, and Mary the mother of James and Joses, and Zebedee's wife. If the mothers of apostles followed our Lord, so also may their wives. As regards Elijah and Elisha, the latter was more perpetually in motion than Elijah himself, yet he had a settled dwelling. It was so imperative a duty upon the Jew to marry, that it is a very hazardous thing to conclude that either of these prophets had departed from the ways and habits of their countrymen.

But though the sons of the prophets had thus their own separate houses, yet we find something of a collegiate life existing among them, probably during their training. Thus we read of a great pot in which they seethe pottage for the sons of the prophets (2 Kings iv. 38). Into this pot a man shreds a whole mantle[a] full of wild gourds. Evidently a common meal was in preparation for a large number of people. So when the farmer from Baal-shalisha brings firstfruits, a common meal was being prepared for a hundred men (Ib. 43). But the meal taken together is the great centre of a collegiate[b] life. Equally important is the common lodging. And of this, too, we find something. On one of his numerous circuits the sons of the prophets say to Elisha, 'The place where we *dwell with thee* is too strait for us (2 Kings vi. 1).' With Elisha at their head they go

---

[a] The word in the original is not a 'lap full,' as in our version. It is the בֶּגֶד the loose upper garment,—the *blanket*, as Mr. Grove calls it,—which was filled with these gourds; and implies a load as large as a man could carry. The Vulgate translates it very properly *pallium*.

[b] Hence, in Oxford, our usual term for the junior members of the University is Commoners.

to the Jordan, and there cut down every man his beam, to construct therewith some addition to their dwelling. But they had no community of goods; for we find them going, some with their own axes, and some with borrowed tools. Now from their going to Jordan, the place was probably Jericho. Certainly it was not Samaria, where Elisha had his own dwelling. To carry timber from Jordan to Samaria would have been beyond the power of so feeble a community. We gather, therefore, that the building which was thus to be enlarged by their common efforts was not Elisha's private property, but was one used for educational[c] purposes. The manner in which they describe it, as a place where they dwelt with Elisha, shows that he did not content himself with merely visiting these institutions, but took a real share in their management.

The offering brought by the man from Baalshalisha was intended for 'the man of God' himself: but it is probable that the students were in part maintained by private charity. Such, in later times, was constantly the case in the East; and so in Europe, during the middle ages, young men entirely without means did not hesitate to go into distant countries, wherever any University became famous for its teaching, sure of finding a maintenance, though often a very miserable one. And to give this help was long recognized in our Church as part of the

---

[c] The need of some such common lodging was early felt in our own University. The three hundred and ten marks bequeathed by William of Durham were expended on educational buildings; and John de Balliol's endowment was of a similar kind. From these benefactions our two most ancient Colleges reckon the date of their foundations.

ordinary duty of the beneficed clergy. They were required by the Injunctions both of King Edward VI and of Queen Elizabeth to maintain one student at the Universities for every hundred pounds of annual income. We have, however, no absolute proof that the sons of the prophets were thus supported by voluntary offerings; but, as such offerings were certainly made to the prophets generally, some part of the revenues of the colleges were possibly derived from this source.

But when their education was complete, the prophets, as forming an educated and literary class among those who could neither read nor write, would be too useful and necessary for the general good, not to be well paid. Many of course had private property like Elisha, who was apparently a rich man, with a good landed estate at Abel-meholah; but the narrative of the son of the prophet, who went out into the field to gather herbs, and came back with his mantle full of wild gourds, does not justify the conclusion which some have drawn from it, that the schools of the prophets were endowed with landed property. People do not grow the cucumis colocynthis on cultivated ground; and the word field[d] in our version is used almost exclu-

---

[d] Thus the plants and herbs of the field (Gen. ii. 5) are wild plants; so in this very place the 'wild vine' is in the Hebrew 'a vine of the field.' Even in Ex. xxii. 6, Gesenius explains 'the field' of wild herbs, olera agrestia, in opposition to those cultivated. So 'the beasts of the field' are the wild beasts (1 Sam. xvii. 44, Cant. ii. 7). So Esau is a 'man of the field,' a man living by hunting, and not by agriculture (Gen. xxv. 27). As for the wild gourd, it is excellently explained by Tristram, Natural History of the Bible, p. 452. He says that near Gilgal and all round the Dead Sea the citrullus or cucumis colocynthis grows most abundantly on

sively of the open country, the common land, where all might pasture their cattle, and which belonged exclusively to no one. Wandering over this the young man found a bed of wild colocynth, a plant which will grow in the driest weather, and gathering his mantle full he brought home as a great prize what had nearly proved fatal to the whole community.

While, then, there were probably offerings in aid of the juniors, the seniors whose education was finished would have to depend upon their own labour. Such as were priests and Levites would have their share of the revenues of their order. Amos had his fruit and cattle, and we find Jeremiah buying his uncle's land at Anathoth. The generality—like St. Paul, who supported himself in his missionary travels by his own hands—had doubtless some occupation or trade by which they earned their living. But besides this they had the offerings of the people who came to consult them. As men of greater literary attainments they would be useful in many ways to those among whom they dwelt. They would be the physicians, the lawyers, the advisers, the letter-writers of their neighbours, and their aid would be invoked not merely in difficulties like that which brought Saul to Samuel, but in numerous legal matters. Thus at the death of the head of a family

the barren sands, covering much ground with its tendrils, which reach a prodigious length, and bear great quantities of fruit. Elisha had just arrived at Gilgal, and the son of the prophet who gathered the fruit had probably come with him, and not being used to the plants in the neighbourhood, on going out to search for food had mistaken it for the wild melon, cucumis prophetarum, which it very much resembles, and which is perfectly harmless. Some one of the natives of Gilgal happily discovered the mistake, and Elisha transformed 'the drastic medicine' into wholesome nourishment.

some sort of assistance would generally be necessary for the arrangement of the property and its distribution according to the terms of the Mosaic law (Deut. xxi. 17). In the New Testament we find the scribes, who had the management of all such legal matters, a numerous and important class.

But besides law, medicine probably was an art specially cultivated by the prophets, and one that brought them no mean emolument. Thus we find Jeroboam's wife disguising herself in order that she may go to consult Ahijah at Shiloh about the sickness of her son. Being thus in disguise she would not wish to expose herself to detection by taking much more than the usual offering, and this in her case consisted of ten loaves, some delicate confectionary called *pricked cakes,* and a jar of honey (1 Kings xiv. 3). Jeroboam even offered a present to the man of God who came from Judah (1 Kings xiii. 7). We cannot doubt, then, that offerings[e] were made to the ordinary uninspired prophets, and many probably by their skill made large emoluments, and earned them as fully as they are earned now by those who practise law and medicine. But it is equally certain that these presents had a bad effect in the end upon the characters of many of them. For two

[e] These offerings may however be looked upon in a different light. In the East no one ever approaches a great man without a gift, and this is looked upon not as payment for services but as an act of homage. The quarter-shekel to be given to Samuel by Saul was, no doubt, a mark of respect. And similarly the offerings made to the prophets may be regarded not as fees, or payments for their services, but as homage done them. If so they must have held a very high place in the national estimation, and been looked upon as raised above the ordinary level of the people, when thus they could be approached only by gifts.

things were mixed up which are really incompatible, namely, the delivery of God's message, and the practice of arts which however honourable are still practised for the sake of gain. And thus men who were prophets merely by education were led to claim powers which they did not possess (1 Kings xxii. 11, Jer. xiv. 14, xxiii. 21, xxviii. 15, xxix. 31, Ezek. xiii. 2). Against these men the inspired prophets utter the severest denunciations, because they made Jehovah's people to err. Even as early as the days of Micah this degradation of the prophetic office had begun; for he accuses the princes of judging for bribes, the priests of teaching for hire, and the prophets of divining,—a thing strictly forbidden[1],—and that for money (Mic. iii. 11). Micah accuses them also of using terrorism, and compelling people to fee them by threats of false accusation; 'He that putteth not into their mouths, they even prepare war against him (Ib. 5).' To one so intensely truthful and just as Micah, such conduct must have seemed most abominable. His contemporary Isaiah, however, speaks of the prophets rather as failing in their duty (Is. xxx. 10, lvi. 10, 11), than as being consciously false. But the evil had begun, and it waxed in intensity, till, as we have seen, in Jeremiah's days the prophets were utterly corrupt, and Jerusalem a

---

[1] Deut. xviii. 10, 1 Sam. xv. 23, 2 Kings xvii. 17. The Hebrew in these passages, and many of similar import, is just the same as in Mic. iii. 11, Ezek. xiii. 23, &c., and implies, without doubt, a gross imposture. As I have before shown, the word for *prophesy* in Ezek. xiii. 17, as applied to the women, means a sham, a false pretence of prophecy; but when used just afterwards of Ezekiel, 'prophesy thou against them,' the word used is one that means true prophecy. We lose in our version the force of this opposition.

foul den, whose king and princes and priests and prophets were fit only to be 'removed into all the kingdoms of the earth, to be a reproach and a proverb, a taunt and a curse, in all places whither Jehovah shall have driven them (Jer. xxiv. 9).'

Even these uninspired men, therefore, were powerful alike for good and for evil; but they were not the men who wrote the Bible. The true prophets never spake smooth things, but had ever a message of reproof and warning. And to strengthen this message, it was ever brought by the holy, the self-denying, the suffering; by men to whom their high gift brought only trouble, and wrong, and contumely. And the world rejected both them and their message. Their history is a history of good done by them, and wrong done to them. The New Testament sums it up in these words, ' They had trial of mockings and scourgings, yea, moreover of bonds and imprisonment: they were stoned, were sawn asunder, were tempted, were slain with the sword: they wandered about in sheepskins and goatskins; being destitute, afflicted, tormented.' And who that reads the records of their ministry can justly challenge the Apostle's verdict, that 'they were men of whom the world was not worthy?' (Heb. xi. 36–38).'

LECTURE IV.

PART II.

THE ORDINARY LIFE AND DUTIES OF THE PROPHETS.

They were stoned, they were sawn asunder, were tempted, were slain with the sword: they wandered about in sheepskins and goatskins; being destitute, afflicted, tormented.—HEB. xi. 37.

To those acquainted with the Septuagint these words carry the mind at once back to the prophets of the preparatory dispensation, wearing their distinctive dress, ever actively in progress from one place to another, bearing every kind of contumely for Jehovah's sake, and often finally sealing with their lives the truth of their message. And in the main these words refer to the uninspired prophets — the men who formed the mass of the order—as fully as they do to those who had received the extraordinary gift of inspiration. Or rather they refer chiefly to them: for the writer was speaking of faith, of what everybody can attain to: and while we naturally perhaps think most of gifts of power, gifts such as that of working miracles and foretelling things to come, our Lord and St. Paul[a] both expressly teach us that God looks at these things very differently, and that in His eyes the gifts of grace are the more precious. For the gifts of power save no man. Men may have had the gift of prophecy and of working miracles, who nevertheless at the last day will be disowned by the Judge, 'I never knew you: depart from Me, ye that work iniquity.' The gifts of grace do save. The things that abide in life, and endure throughout eternity, are 'faith, hope, love; and the greatest of these—that which we are commanded to follow after—is love (1 Cor. xiii. 13, xiv. 1).' Great and extraordinary powers were bestowed under the Jewish dispensation for special purposes: but they were given sparingly, and at distant intervals. Usually the men who attained to them were such as had made extraordinary progress in the higher gifts of faith, love, purity, holiness. But the Divine purposes were sometimes even better accomplished by the bestowal of gifts of power on men less worthy. The glowing predictions of the man brought from the mountains of the East to curse God's people, but who was compelled to bless, more deeply impressed upon their hearts a firm faith in Jehovah than any other words could have done. But if Balaam fell, as Judas and Demas fell afterwards, it was because these gifts of power interfere with no man's probation. A man is neither saved nor lost by the number of talents which he possesses, whether they be moral, intellectual, or supernatural. They do but increase his powers of doing good or harm, and thereby make

---

[a] Matt. vii. 22, 23, 1 Cor. xii. 31, xiii. 2.

his responsibility heavier. There is but one way of salvation, and that is by faith in Christ, sealed by the work of the Holy Spirit on the heart. Prophecy and miracles do not save (1 Cor. xiii. 2), nor anything but the new and spiritual birth (John iii. 5).

Now it is probable that a large proportion of the ordinary prophets, at all events at first and in Judah, had God's better gift of grace, though, as we have seen, they gradually declined in spirituality, till in Jeremiah's days they were utterly fallen. Nor need we doubt this because we do not always find them very advanced in their views either in morals or religion. No class of men is ever very far removed from the level of its own age, and we must not therefore indiscriminately condemn the prophets in the northern kingdom, because many of them unquestionably reached but a low standard. Nor, on the other hand, can we form a high estimate of their moral state. That old prophet at Bethel who caused the ruin of the man of God from Judah was certainly a Jehovah-prophet. He speaks in Jehovah's name (1 Kings xiii. 18); was probably greatly struck by his fellow-prophet's doings, and thought possibly that in bringing him back he was himself working for a good end. 'But he lied unto him' (Ib.), and, by his false profession of a message from Jehovah, brought upon him fearful punishment. But in persuading the man of Judah to go back with him, he probably intended not so much to gratify his curiosity, or even to increase his own personal importance, as to strengthen the right cause at Bethel. It was a place where the king was doing his utmost to set up a false worship. This worship he and the other

Jehovah-prophets were opposing as far as they dared. If then this prophet from Judah, who had wrought such miracles, could, after refusing the king's present and hospitality, be prevailed upon to come to his house, and eat and drink with him, what a triumph it would be! What a proof that he was Jehovah's chosen mouthpiece! And how he would talk all the rest of his life of his noble brother from Judah, who had so helped him in his great struggle against idolatry! True, that such an acknowledgment would bring him power, honour, emolument. But this he would keep in the background. The excuse he would put off upon himself would be the great good he was doing for the right cause so unrighteously oppressed at Bethel. He was a man, then, who strained his conscience for the sake of his cause. And this is a temptation which assails many men in all ages. They so think their cause the one right cause, and so identify themselves with it, that they lose all definite perceptions of right and wrong. Like Uzzah, they think that God's ark cannot stand unless they hold it up. But God rejects them and their unhallowed aid. This old prophet was compelled himself to pass sentence upon the man of God from Judah for returning with him, and thereby to prove that God had not accepted his own previous labours. And most probably it was this condemnation of Jeroboam's calves, followed by the rejection of the Jehovah-prophets at Bethel, and the severe punishment of the true prophet for even eating with them, that made all the true worshippers of Jehovah quit the northern kingdom. The priests and Levites we know all left the ten tribes[b],

---

[b] 2 Chron. xi. 13, 14, 16 : and cf. xv. 9.

and so probably did many good men, from the conviction that Jeroboam's worship was one utterly rejected by the true God. The old prophet did not quit Bethel: but he showed his belief in the man of God's message by ordering his sons at his death to bury him in the prophet's grave.

Yet this old prophet had been brought up under the better influences of Solomon's reign, and within hearing of the teaching of true prophets like Ahijah. What wonder, then, if at Samaria seventy years afterwards they were ready to flatter a powerful king like Ahab! Yet even here we miss not the one true prophet. It is the glory of Jewish history that it always has the one true man. Even if its great hero David falls into sin, there is the man found ready to go with his life in his hand and carry to him God's reproof. Nathan reproving David is something infinitely nobler than Clitus rebuking Alexander: as much nobler as is the repentant David than Alexander murdering his reprover, and dying of surfeit and intemperance.

But it is not the greatness or nobleness of the few that is the true proof of the acceptance with God of any order of men. God gives His people, from time to time, men of extraordinary powers, whose mission it is to rouse up the great mass of the community to a higher life and truer faith in Him. And thus He gave the northern kingdom those two great heroes of prophecy, Elijah and Elisha. Priests and Levites had abandoned Israel (2 Chron. xi. 13, 14): the mass of the prophets had fallen to a very low ebb. But Israel is not yet rejected. It may yet repent and take its share in God's great work of saving mankind. Its sons may yet be the heralds of salvation to the heathen, and the word of Jehovah go forth, not from Jerusalem only, but from Samaria also. There rises then, first of all, that wonderful prophet Elijah; and he summons, by God's especial directions, Elisha to carry on his work. Their individual greatness proves nothing in favour of the northern kingdom, nor of the prophets there. Rather the contrary. Israel was sinking so fast that no ordinary help could save it. Nor did these two men save it. They gave Israel its last call to repentance, and that a mighty call, but it availed not.

Naturally they first addressed themselves to the prophets, and for a time had great influence over them for good. For, as I have said, they formed a sort of irregular clergy, and though such a body always holds a close relation to the state of morality and religion and thought prevalent in its day, yet its members are always among the first to be influenced by, or even to originate, religious movements. If they are cold when others are cold, lax in morals in a careless age, negligent at a time of indifference, they are also the most earnest when men's minds are aroused and quickened with energy. It is very seldom that religious movements have begun with the laity. The priest Wyclif, the monk Luther, the pastor Calvin, the Anglican clergyman Wesley, may serve as examples of a general rule. Even unbelieving and neologian movements often find some of their promoters among the clergy: for where religion is the one subject of thought, there must ever be those who range themselves in opposition to the dearest convictions of the rest. So it was of old. The intellectual life of the Jewish nation centred in its priests and prophets. And not only were many of the greatest prophets themselves priests or Levites, but even men like Elijah and Elisha would look to those trained in the prophetic schools as the only men who could give final success and permanence to their labours.

I have already shown that the order was numerous and powerful; and that there were special schools for its training, certainly in Israel, and most probably in Judah. I have shown that in these institutions there was something of a collegiate life, but no traces of any common fund or endowment, except in their buildings. How long a time was spent in these schools does not appear, nor whether many were educated in them besides those intended for the prophetic calling. In Judaea it is probable that a large number of the Levites were thus trained. For the temple-service was a direct result of the music and singing in the prophetic schools, and some such service was probably offered to Jehovah even in Israel, perhaps on the high places[c]. But however this may be, doubtless a large proportion of the 'sons of the prophets' devoted themselves to the more distinctly religious life. And of these many probably made no gain of their profession, but gave themselves up entirely and unreservedly to preaching and teaching. But evidently other arts were also taught in the prophetic schools, such as medicine[d]. Not only do we

[c] Hezekiah was the first to remove the high places even in Judah (2 Kings xviii. 4, cf. xv. 4), and probably they were the sole resource of the true worshippers in Israel.

[d] Originally medicine must have been studied also by the priests. Witness the considerable knowledge they were expected to have of the symptoms of leprosy.

find Ahijah consulted by Jeroboam's wife about her son Abijah, but we read also of Benhadad sending Hazael to Elisha, and saying, 'Take a present in thine hand, and go, meet the man of God, and enquire of Jehovah by him, saying, Shall I recover of this disease? (2 Kings viii. 8).' In the history of the cleansing of Naaman, every one, from the little Jewish maid to the king of Syria, regards it as perfectly natural that recourse should be had in sickness to a prophet; and the rich presents which Naaman brought would have sufficed to have raised Elisha to the height of affluence had he deigned to accept them. It is exceedingly probable that considerable medical knowledge was accumulated in the prophetic colleges; and Isaiah, who was probably their Rector in Judaea, displayed no mean skill as a physician in his treatment of Hezekiah's disease. Many commentators suppose that Hezekiah's malady was the same as that which so suddenly smote down the army of Sennacherib. In a country wasted by war pestilence is sure to appear, and the plague[e] which

---

[e] The pestilence is called the angel, that is, the messenger of Jehovah, just as that sent to punish David's sin is so called in 2 Sam. xxiv. 16, 17. Both visitations were more than providential. They had been foretold, and were both the direct interference of God with the laws of nature, yet acting in and by the laws of nature for moral purposes. Just. then, as it was God's messenger who smote David's realm with pestilence, so most probably pestilence was the natural means used by the angel in smiting the camp of Sennacherib. A remarkable illustration of this method of God's dealings may be found in the plagues of Egypt. With the exception of the smiting of the firstborn, they are all natural occurrences, though many of them heightened to a supernatural degree. Hail and lightning, though very rare, do occur in Egypt. The rest are all based on phenomena by no means unusual there. I may add that Ewald, Hist. Is. i. 218, enumerates the natural calamities to which Palestine is subject. Only one of these, locusts, occurs among the ten

broke forth so violently in the camp of the Assyrians probably remained for some time in the country, though in a milder form. Ulcers have been a symptom of the plague in all ages, from the plague of Athens down to the plague of London. But be this as it may, Hezekiah's recovery from a malady, which would otherwise have been fatal, is expressly attributed to the medical skill of Isaiah. No doubt there was God's especial blessing, but it was a blessing resting, as is usual with God's operations, upon the right use of means. Naturally we have in the Bible but a very brief summary of Hezekiah's sickness, and of the means used by Isaiah for its cure. The Bible is not a medical work, and is concerned only with the moral and religious significance of the event. Still it does tell us an important symptom of the malady, and suggests to us that Isaiah wrought a cure by his method of treating it.

I will add upon this point but two remarks; the first that the healing art has always been regarded as something sacred. It was so in Greece and in Egypt; throughout the East the Hakem, the wise man or sage, is usually too the physician of the community. So among us it is a calling which not a few in holy orders follow professionally, and many more unprofessionally. A man is scarcely fit to be a missionary who is not well versed in it. The second and far more important remark is, that when in the manifestation of our Lord prophecy reached its highest

---

plagues of Egypt. This is very remarkable, and a proof that the Book of Exodus is a narrative of real facts. Had it been written in Palestine in Samuel's days, as Colenso supposes, the plagues would have been such as were known in Palestine.

elevation, so also did the power of healing. The two-fold occupation of the Saviour, as He wandered from place to place perpetually throughout the land, was healing and teaching. And when He sent out the seventy disciples two and two, His command was, 'Heal the sick (Matt. x. 8).' Even the false gods claimed a knowledge of the symptoms of disease: and thus the messengers of Ahaziah were on their way to enquire of Baal-zebub, god of Ekron, whether the king would recover from his accident, when Elijah met them, reproached them for not making their enquiry of the prophets of the true God, and foretold Ahaziah's speedy death.

But, as the one educated class, there would be numerous occasions on which their aid would be indispensable to the people. And though here and there cases might occur of poverty, yet no one can read the prophetic books without being convinced that the prophets formed a very powerful order, great in influence, large in numbers, with ample sources of revenue, working generally for good, but sharing in Judah's decay, and by the time of Jeremiah hopelessly corrupt, time-serving, covetous, and false. Not perhaps so much in doctrine. Professionally they were opposed to idol-worship: and yet Jeremiah charges them with it. Adultery, spiritual adultery was, as everybody knows, the phrase applied by the prophets to idolatry; and of this Jeremiah accuses them: 'I have seen in the prophets of Jerusalem a horrible thing: they commit adultery (i.e. idolatry), and walk in lies: they strengthen also the hands of evildoers, that none doth return from his wickedness (Jer. xxiii. 14).' Only a few perhaps fell thus utterly;

yet of the mass he says, 'Mine heart within me is broken because of the prophets.' 'Both prophet and priest are profane.' 'I have not sent these prophets, yet they ran: I have not spoken to them, yet they prophesied (Ib. 9, 11, 21).' No wonder that Jerusalem was as Sodom, and the inhabitants thereof as Gomorrah (Ib. 14), when that order of men, who as God's clergy were especially bound to preach holiness, and whose privilege it was to be required to enforce the spiritual part of the law, and not its mere ritual, were themselves hopelessly corrupt. A believing clergy cannot by itself save a nation. That will depend upon whether the nation accepts their teaching or rejects it. But an unbelieving clergy is simply ruin. It is morally impossible for religion to survive the apostasy of that order of men who are especially devoted to its maintenance. Things must already be far gone when the very salt has lost its savour. Yet even then God sent a Jeremiah. His justice waited till the last call had been made and rejected. So it is ever. No nation utterly falls till it has again and again refused to hearken to God's voice.

But the prophets had thus formed a separate and numerous order long before the power and wealth which prophetic gifts brought with them had led to its corruption. And as its duties were different from those of ordinary life, so probably it would be distinguished by a peculiar dress. Such we find to have been actually the case. When Ahaziah's messengers return to the king with so stern a rebuke, they describe the person who had stopped them on their way to Ekron thus: 'He was a hairy man, and girt with a leathern girdle about his loins (2 Kings i. 8).' Such are the words of our version; but plainly it is absurd to describe a man by his long hair or beard, and girdle. The words really mean that he wore a garment [f] made of hair, long and loose fitting, and to this is fitly added the description of the belt with which it was girt about his waist. Now this garment, generally made of camel's hair, and the leathern girdle, formed the distinctive dress of the prophet. When then his messengers told him that the man who had so sternly rebuked them was thus clad, Ahaziah knew that it was some prophet, and rightly guessed that it was no other than Elijah the Tishbite.

The marginal references make this plain. The first is to Zech. xiii. 4: 'In that day the prophets shall be ashamed every one of his vision; neither shall they wear a rough garment to deceive.' Now if you turn to the Hebrew, you will find that the passage is very loosely translated. Zechariah does not say a *rough garment*, but uses the proper word for that garment of hair which was the prophet's peculiar dress. The word is *Addereth*, a term four times applied to Elijah's garment in the Book of Kings, and there translated *mantle*. That mantle plays, as you know, a very important part in Elijah's history. It is to him what his rod was to Moses. It was the possession of this garment which assured Elisha that his prayer for a

---

[f] The Hebrew is literally 'a man master of hair.' This may no doubt mean that he wore his own hair long, but it may equally well mean that he was clad in a mantle of hair-cloth. Just as in Latin *dominus abollae* means a philosopher, and in the middle ages *dominus cuculli* a monk, so the Hebrew phrase means *dominus vestis pilosae*, in other words a prophet.

double[g] portion of his master's spirit had been accepted
(2 Kings ii. 9, 14); and with it he smote the waters
of Jordan, and they parted hither and thither. By
wearing it he claimed to be a prophet, and the sons of
the prophets acknowledged him as such—as Elijah's
successor, and their own head and chief. And then,
next, we can see the meaning of the second reference
to Matt. iii. 4. John the Baptist's dress is there
described as consisting of a cloak or robe of camel's
hair, and a leathern girdle about his loins. This dress
was not of his own choosing, still less was it the dress
of a self-inflicted asceticism. It was the regular prophetic costume, and was a claim on John's part to the
prophetic rank and dignity. St. Matthew's words are,
in short, the right translation of the description of
Elijah's dress as reported to Ahaziah.

Now, instead of this hair robe, the Septuagint uses
the term *sheepskin*, μηλωτή. It describes Elijah's
mantle in this way. In the cave at Horeb it says
that he wrapped his face in his sheepskin, ἐν τῇ μηλωτῇ
αὐτοῦ. So it thrice uses the term in the account of his
translation, and in other places. It does not of course
follow from this that the prophet's robe was really
made of sheepskins, but only that the translators
of the Septuagint identified the Addereth, the hair

[g] Many persons misunderstand this passage, and imagine that Elisha asked for twice as large a gift of God's Spirit as had rested on Elijah. Really, he asks for the portion of the first-born son. Among the Jews, when the father died, the property was divided into a number of shares exceeding by one the number of the children. If he had two sons, it was divided into three shares; if three sons, into four shares; and so on. The first-born then took two shares, the rest one a-piece. Thus he had always twice as much as any one of the rest (Deut. xxi. 17). Elisha, then, prayed that he might—not excel his master, but—be in the position of the eldest and favoured son.

mantle [h], of the Hebrew, with the meloté, the sheepskin of their own days, a rough cloak worn probably by some class of men in Egypt. In the passage therefore chosen for our text, instead of that vague general notion which too often passes current for a knowledge of Holy Scripture, we find an exact description of the prophets on their frequent journeys clad in their distinctive dress. The person stoned was not Naboth, as the parallel reference might lead you to infer, but Zechariah, the son of Jehoiada, stoned in the very court of the Lord's house (2 Chron. xxiv. 21), and possibly Jeremiah stoned at Tahpanhes. The prophet sawn asunder has been generally supposed to be Isaiah. To be tempted or tried was the common lot of all; of Elijah when he fled from Jezebel's threats to seek new strength at the mount of God; of Micaiah when cast into prison by Ahab; of Elisha when the king threatened him with death because of the famine at Samaria; of Jeremiah obliged to flee for his life from Jehoiakim, and reduced to silence during the last seven years of that despot's life, and again cast into the pit by Zedekiah. It was Urijah, the son of Shemaiah, who was slain by the sword (Jer. xxvi. 23), though this was the common fate of prophets. Jeremiah compares Jerusalem to a murderess, whose very garments were dabbled in their blood: 'Also in thy skirts is found the blood of the

[h] Strictly speaking, the word means a robe, a loose upper garment enveloping the whole body. Made of rough materials, and black in colour, it marked the prophet; but it was often made of the most costly textures, and thus what Achan stole is described as Addereth-Shin'ar, a Shinar or Babylonian robe (Josh. vii. 21); and so the king of Nineveh wears an Addereth (Jonah iii. 6). Even the prophet's Addereth was not necessarily of camel's hair; it might be made of sheepskins.

souls of the poor innocents (Jer. ii. 34):' for during the whole reign of Manasseh the prophetic voice was silent, owing to the violence of that unhappy monarch, who slew them 'till he had filled Jerusalem with innocent blood from one end to another (2 Kings xxi. 16).' So, too, of their wanderings, when the apostle speaks in the next verse of 'deserts and mountains, and dens and caves of the earth,' Elijah in the cave at Horeb in the desert of Sinai and Elisha dwelling on Mount Carmel (Ib. ii. 25, iv. 25) are the two most notable examples. But in the text, 'they wandered about' is a wrong translation. The word περιῆλθον refers to no purposeless wandering, no restless mendicancy, but sets before us the picture of a calm and regular but never-ceasing activity. So Samuel, περιῆλθε, went about on circuit to judge the people. Like the apostles afterwards, the prophets were ever on foot, going from place to place, bearing with them words from God. We find this especially the case with that prophet whose history is given us at greater length—Elisha. While Samaria and Mount Carmel seem to have been his chief abodes, we read of the rich woman at Shunem proposing to her husband to make for him a little chamber that he might lodge there whenever he chose; for, said she, 'I perceive that this is a holy man of God, which passeth by us continually (Ib. iv. 9).' In these circuits we find him visiting the schools of the prophets at Gilgal (iv. 38), at Jericho (vi. 1), at Bethel (ii. 23); again, we find him at Dothan (vi. 13), not far off when Jehoshaphat and Jehoram, in their march against Edom, were in danger of perishing for want of water (iii. 11), going even as far as Damascus (viii. 7), but always with a purpose. Such, too, was the journey which Amos took throughout the ten tribes, though limited to a set time, and for the one object of giving Israel a final call to repentance while, during the victorious reign of Jeroboam II, it still enjoyed internal prosperity. The prophetic life was no life of self-willed asceticism : it was the far higher and worthier life of practical usefulness.

In these circuits the prophets ever wore their distinctive dress. By it the Shunammite knew that Elisha was a man of God. Amos would wear it while on his mission, but would probably lay it aside at Tekoah when his mission was over. From the words of Zechariah, quoted before, we learn that all those who were prophets by profession regularly wore it, as certainly would Isaiah, Jeremiah, and Ezekiel, called by express vision to their office for their whole lives. So also did John the Baptist. Of Isaiah we have an express prophecy relating to his dress. For three years he is to loose the sackcloth from off his loins, and walk naked and barefoot (Is. xx. 2). The word *naked*, both here and in several other passages of Scripture, means clad only in the close-fitting under-garment, or rather it means simply that the loose upper robe had been thrown off (1 Sam. xix. 24), or parted with through poverty (Job xxii. 6, xxiv. 7, 10). And this loose robe is here called *Sak*, translated *sackcloth*, but the word does not necessarily refer to the material. Usually it was made of hair, and, thus clad, the two witnesses are represented in the Revelation of St. John as prophesying for the thousand two hundred and threescore days (Rev. xi. 3). Plainly it was a coarse rough garment, which in times of sorrow and self-abasement was worn by any one, and often without the tunic underneath. Thus Job says, 'I have sewed sackcloth upon my skin (Job xvi. 15);' and at the famine at Samaria we read that when the king, passing by upon the wall, heard of the women eating their own children, 'he rent his clothes, and the people looked, and, behold, he had sackcloth within upon his flesh (2 Kings vi. 30).' In these two places the sense requires us to understand that the under-garment was made of that coarse material usually employed only for the outer robe. But when Ahab was reproved by Elijah for the murder and robbery of Naboth, 'he put sackcloth upon his flesh, and lay in sackcloth (1 Kings xxi. 27);' and when Joel proclaims a general fast, he bids the people 'lie in sackcloth (Joel i. 13),' in both which cases we may best understand it of their wrapping themselves in this mantle of hair. Thus, then, we find that the prophet's ordinary dress was that worn by the people as a mark of sorrow. The sheepskin, $\mu\eta\lambda\omega\tau\eta$, was, on the contrary, the dress of the poorer people. Now as the prophet's message was ever a warning of woe impending because of sins unrepented of, his proper dress would be the garb of mourning. Still very fittingly he might also wear the dress of poverty; for doubtless those who had the real inward call to the prophetic office would give up all worldly interests in order to do God's work. It is very probable that the more intensely ascetic life adopted by Jeremiah was intended as a protest against the worldly spirit of the prophets in his days.

But great as was the necessity of a more than ordinary rigid life on his part (Jer. xv. 17, xvi.

2, 5, 8), yet were the prophets generally ascetic and self-denying men. Even Isaiah, high in authority and influence at the court of Hezekiah, walks naked and barefoot for three years (Is. xx. 3); and Ezekiel weeps in bitterness, and sits among his people astonished for seven days (Ezek. iii. 14, 15). The Baptist in the wilderness, poorly clad and fed, but whose summons to repentance reached even the city and the soldiery, is their type; and yet there is such freedom about them, that no prophet is bound by the practices of another. They were earnest men, whose care and thought was of duty and holiness; yet, under different circumstances, and with different parts of God's message to deliver, they were limited to no one type. Our Lord is the very highest type not merely of the prophetical but also of the spiritual life, and He had nothing distinctive in dress or manner or habit. He came eating and drinking, and was as thoroughly occupied in doing the duties of a prophet when feasting in the house of Matthew the publican, or with the rich Pharisee, or at the marriage in Cana of Galilee, as John gathering his solitary meal of locusts and wild honey in the wilderness. It is the prerogative of the Gospel to sanctify to God the ordinary duties and relations of human life. To abandon these duties and relations is to fall below the level of Christianity. The Christian is not to abandon the world, but to win it for God, and in its ordinary routine he must lead the life of prayer, of self-denial, of devotion to God, and active work for man. Especially is this the duty of the clergy, who in so many respects hold a position analogous to that of the prophets under the preparatory dispensation.

To leave the world would be to abandon their profession ; to lead a worldly life is to be false to their profession, to be a stumbling-block in the way of others, and bring ruin on their own souls. Yet both their outward life and the manner in which they seek to maintain the spiritual life within them, will depend very much upon external circumstances. Scattered throughout the land there will be places where a more rigid life may be necessary, and much have to be foregone in itself right, because a more forcible example is necessary to raise men sunk in foul and degraded habits. Yet naturally Christ is the highest pattern of our life, and our desire should be, under every outward diversity, to aim at that thorough holiness of which our Lord was alike the teacher and the example.

And this brings me to the prophet's work. Now this was wider than the work of the clergy in the present day: for we find them not confining themselves to religion and morality, but also taking part in politics. I suppose that it would be the duty of the clergy now to take part in politics, if the government attacked either religion or morality. Whenever current political ideas are based upon immoral or irreligious principles, it is the duty of the clergy, as teachers, to enforce Christian principles in opposition to them: but this is more frequently and better done by means of the press than in our ordinary parochial ministrations. But religion was the basis of the Jewish commonwealth. It existed for a religious purpose, and even after the appointment of kings, Jehovah was still the supreme ruler and the prophets His representatives. Certain political maxims, therefore, formed part of that cycle of truth, which every religious man was bound to maintain, as far as in him lay, in its integrity. That cycle of truth consisted of ideas relating partly to the Divine nature, partly to human life and duty, partly to the right theory of government. Now it was especially the duty of the prophets to maintain those ideas, and their chief means for so doing was oratory. They were the great public speakers, I may even say the great public men of ancient time, who, when they saw king or people violating any truth, or entering upon any course of action opposed to those fundamental ideas upon which the Jewish theocracy was based, stood forth manfully, and resisted this wrong policy with powerful and spirited appeals to men's consciences. Sin and impiety they boldly rebuked even in princes: warned all men of the inevitable consequences of violating the law of God, whether natural or revealed: and often gave fresh energy to their addresses, or stimulated the curiosity of the people, and woke up new attention to their words, by symbolical actions. Sometimes, as when Jeremiah took his stand in the temple on some solemn day of gathering there, it was the national conscience that was addressed (Jer. vii. 2, xxvi. 2): sometimes, as in the roll of that same prophet which Baruch copied at his mouth. it was the conscience of the ruler, or of some powerful individual or class. The grandest day of Jewish prophecy was undoubtedly that on Mount Carmel, when Elijah stood forth alone, braved singly the anger of the king, and the more determined and fanatical malice of the queen, confronted the serried ranks of the priests and prophets of Baal and Astarte, and forced the hesitating and reluctant nation to give in its adherence to the truth, and cry, 'Jehovah, He is the God, Jehovah, He is the God (1 Kings xviii. 39).' Such crises are rare: but upon all the great occasions in the nation's history, the prophets ever stood forth as the boldest, the most disinterested, and the most powerful actors. Through them Israel attained to the greatest of all blessings, religious truth. If there be such a thing on earth—and what would earth be without it?—they won it for their nation. And then One came of Whom the prophets had ever spoken: and He gave truth, religious truth, to the whole world (John xviii. 37).

Necessarily, then, under the theocracy the prophets, as the representatives of Jehovah, took great part in all political matters, and we find them even bestowing the crown. It was Samuel who chose Saul, and when he failed in his probation it was again Samuel who anointed David in his room. At his death it was Nathan who was foremost in advising that not Adonijah, the first-born, but Solomon should be placed upon the throne (1 Kings i. 11, 1 Chron. xxii. 8, 9). In the history of the subsequent kings the narrative is too brief to enable us to judge how far the influence of the prophets may have been exerted in selecting one son before another for the succession: but in the reign of Asa we find Oded the son of Azariah the prime mover in the extirpation of idolatry in Judah, and able even to prevail upon the king to depose Maachah the queen-mother from her office, which was one next in rank to that of the king himself. In Israel it was Ahijah the Shilonite who chose Jeroboam to be king: and though henceforward the annals of that kingdom scarcely present us with more than a succession of murders and military usurpations, yet the one dynasty which did retain the crown for four generations, and which under Jeroboam II gave Israel its last epoch of success and glory, was called to the throne by Elijah and Elisha. The whole narrative shows that the command of these two men was looked upon not merely as ensuring the success of Jehu's enterprise, but also as conferring a valid title to the crown. Humanly speaking, the long continuance of the dynasty, and the ready obedience of the people, were the result of the general conviction that Jehu was the duly appointed king.

Even in the military affairs of the nation the prophets exercised not merely a great, but often a preponderating influence. It was the continuation of that appeal to Jehovah, as the king of the nation, by the Urim and Thummim, which we find in general use from the death of Joshua (Judges i. 1) to the early years of David (2 Sam. v. 23). In David's wars of conquest the prophetic voice was silent; but when a foreign enemy attacked Israel, or the two kingdoms warred with one another, the prophets constantly interfered in a very peremptory way. Thus when Rehoboam had collected 180,000 warriors to compel the ten tribes to return to their allegiance, at the command of Shemaiah (1 Kings xii. 21-24) the attempt was given up, sorely, no doubt, to the discontent of Rehoboam, a violent and godless man, with an Ammonitish mother: but he had no choice. To persevere was useless; for the people recognised in the prophet's voice the decisive command of Jehovah. The same Shemaiah subsequently averted from Rehoboam the worst consequences of the Egyptian invasion (2 Chron. xii. 7), possibly by having counselled submission, whereby the expedition of Shishak passed away as a mere temporary evil. Soon afterwards we find Hanani reproaching Asa for having purchased the services of the king of Syria, instead of himself preventing Baasha from fortifying Ramah (2 Chron. xvi. 7), and, as a punishment for his want of faith, Hanani declares that henceforward he shall be troubled by perpetual wars, a denunciation to which Asa replied by casting him into prison. This did not however deter Jehu, Hanani's son, from denouncing utter destruction against Baasha (1 Kings xvi. 1), nor from reproving his own sovereign Jehoshaphat for his ill-starred alliance with the house of Ahab (2 Chron. xix. 2). We have seen this same Jehoshaphat unwilling to go to battle without enquiring at the word of the Lord, ill-content with the loud assurance of the four hundred Jehovah-prophets of Samaria, and asking for the one true man. Subsequently, when attacked by Moab and Ammon, Jahaziel instructs Jehoshaphat in the conduct of the war, and promises him victory (2 Chron. xx. 14): while his partnership with king Ahaziah in ship-building, and his attempt to revive the old commerce of Solomon with India, are condemned by Eliezer, and the wrecking of the ships foretold (Ib. 37). When, too, Amaziah had hired 100.000

fighting men from Israel, and paid them a hundred talents, sorely against his will he had to forego their help, lose the large sum of money already expended, and incur the bitter anger of the mercenaries at the bidding of a man of God (Ib. xxv. 7). So, too, Hezekiah consults Isaiah in the war with Sennacherib, and sends to him the insulting letter he had received from that king, by the hands of the noblest princes of the realm.

All this is very remarkable. It shows us the prophets possessed of an authority before which the very kings had to bow, even in cases where to yield was most painful to them. Still the kings of Judah professed allegiance to Jehovah; but we find plain indications that the Jehovah-prophets exercised a similar influence also in the northern kingdom. Thus the war between Ahab and Ben-hadad, king of Syria, is carried on in accordance with the directions of a prophet, who speaks in Jehovah's name (1 Kings xx. 13). In Jehoram's reign Elisha gives the king repeated information of the ambuscades laid for him by the Syrians (2 Kings vi. 9, 10), and when Samaria was so pressed by siege that its surrender seemed inevitable, Jehoram determined to behead Elisha, as though the issues of war lay in his power (Ib. 31). Finally, Elisha makes Jehu king in the place of Jehoram, and on his death-bed sends for Joash, the grandson of Jehu, and gives him encouragement, and the promise of thrice-repeated victory in the long struggle between Israel and Damascus (Ib. xiii. 19). When we bear in mind this constant activity and interference of the prophets in matters of peace and war, it no longer surprises us, but seems perfectly natural, that Elisha should be found in the host of Jehoram and Jehoshaphat in their expedition against Moab. For, one purpose for which the spirit of prophecy was given was the preservation of Israel's political existence. Israel existed that God by it might give mankind the one true and sole way of salvation. It could not therefore be destroyed. The mighty realms of which we read so much, Nineveh and Babylon, Egypt and Macedonia, have passed away with their people. You could not find, search where you would, any remains of them. The Arabs, and tribes of Mongolic race like the Turks, have wasted and destroyed those realms once so powerful. Israel could not be destroyed, for in it all mankind was to be blessed : and, even now, the Jew still remains, the best proof and evidence of the unchangeableness of God's counsels.

Still, important as was the preservation of Israel's national existence, it was yet only a means for an end. Far more important was the work of the prophets for this end. Israel existed that the world might be taught the nature and attributes of the one true God : and the great duty of the prophets was to maintain the worship of the one true God in its purity. And this is the explanation of the fact that it was in the northern kingdom that prophecy first assumed such grand proportions. It is not true that it arose there. On the contrary, for a long period after the disruption of Solomon's empire, all the prophets whose names occur belong to the southern kingdom. Shemaiah, the man of God who went from Judah to Bethel, Iddo, Azariah, Hanani and his son Jehu, Jahaziel, Eliezer, all belonged to Judah. Ahijah alone still dwelt at Shiloh in Mount Ephraim. During the long period from the beginning of Jeroboam's reign down to the time of Ahab, we find the prophets full of life and energy in Judah, forbidding or rousing the nation to war, ever actively mixed up in all political matters, and possessed of enormous influence : while in the kingdom of Israel we find only that old Jehovah-prophet at Bethel, who played so dubious a part in relation to the man of God who came from Judah. Had we not been told so, we should never have guessed that God had numerous prophets in Israel during this time, and that they were earnest enough in the cause of religion to bring upon them the cruel anger of Jezebel.

Now during this period the kings were all nominal worshippers of Jehovah. Jeroboam's calves were not the images of a false god, but were a false way of worshipping the true God. Even Ahab never directly broke off from his allegiance to Jehovah, but, like his predecessors, took part in that corrupt and schismatical form of worship established at Bethel and at Dan. Upon his marriage, however, things changed; for his Sidonian wife did her very utmost to destroy the worship of Jehovah, and substitute that of Baal in its place; and Ahab made no opposition to her wishes. He even built, at her suggestion, a temple to Baal in Samaria, and reared in it an altar, and made an image of Astarte[1] (1 Kings xvi. 32, 33).

---

[1] The word rendered in our version *grove* is in the Hebrew *Ashērah*, which is merely another form of the word Astarte, or Ashtaroth. Her image in ancient times was a roughly-carved beam of wood fixed in the earth; while the statues of Baal were made of stone. As the Asherah could thus be cut down and burnt (see Judges vi. 25), our translators concluded it must be a grove of trees. As for the meaning of the word, Asherah is probably a name for the planet Venus, and signifies *good*

Now this was an entirely new state of things. It was the public establishment of a licentious nature-worship, and joined with it the determination to uproot the worship of Jehovah. Upon how grand a scale Jezebel set up her idolatries we learn from the fact that there were four hundred and fifty prophets[k] of Baal, and four hundred prophets of Astarte, who ate at the queen's own table. And not satisfied with this she put to death the true prophets, as we learn incidentally from Obadiah's speech, who urges his interference in their behalf as a reason for Elijah excusing him from a mission which he regarded as equivalent to his own death-warrant. Even after that great day at Mount Carmel, Jezebel flinched not. Resolute against God, all undaunted[l] by what

luck; the root being connected with the well-known word Jashar, and implying prosperity and success. But that beautiful planet soon became the symbol of lust, and Baal, the sun, the husband, and Astarte, the star of love, were degraded into mere representatives of the reproductive powers of nature, and worshipped by acts of the most unbridled profligacy.

[k] Evidently Jezebel did not consider that she had done enough for her national deities till she had surrounded them with a vast retinue of persons who imitated the Jehovah-prophets. Doubtless they, too, claimed to be inspired by Baal and Astarte, and to speak in their names. But we thus have an unintentional proof of the importance of the true prophets, as elsewhere the attendants upon the heathen deities were not prophets but priests.

[l] None perhaps but a woman would have set herself thus desperately to uproot the national religion of a country whither she had gone as a wife, in order to establish in its place that in which she had been brought up. It was a woman's entire devotion and unwavering faith, degenerated into fanaticism. Like her daughter Athaliah, she had a fearless energy, which shrank back from no deed, however atrocious: but Athaliah's was a selfish wickedness, while Jezebel, like Philip of Spain, may have thought she was labouring for God. And how fearlessly she fell! Arrayed in queenly attire, as careful of her beauty as if she was preparing, not for death, but for some high ceremonial, she boldly

evidently made the deepest impression upon Ahab, she defied Elijah at the very moment of his victory, and bound herself by an oath to destroy him. Such a struggle as this between truth and falsehood had never existed in Israel before, and God was pleased, in order that the people might not fall for lack of knowledge, to raise prophecy to a far grander height than it had ever reached in previous times.

The open worship of Baal and Astarte had no doubt roused all the deeper religious feeling of the nation; and persecution had purified the motives and quickened the faith of the worshippers of Jehovah, while it had also separated the lukewarm from their company. But who would have supposed when reading of that old Jehovah-prophet at Bethel, with not a word to say against Jeroboam's calves, though ready to tell any number of falsehoods to obtain the countenance of the true prophet; who would have supposed that he was the representative of a class who preferred death to the entire abandonment of Jehovah? Yet so it was! The only voices raised against the calves had all come from Judah. Thence came the man of God who denounced Jeroboam to his face: thence came Jehu the son of Hanani to condemn Baasha. But when they are required to abandon Jehovah's worship altogether, and force is used, and the sword wakes up, men's better principles resist, and death seems preferable to so shameful a desertion of their creed. And in this nobler state of mind there springs up from

---

confronts one whom she deems an usurper, and provokes him with a bitter taunt. And then her pride, her determined purpose, her unflinching courage, her queenly dignity: the end of it all was a crowd of curs yelping over carrion!

among themselves one of the most heroic men that ever bore witness for God's truth; and for a time he stays the nation in its downward course, and gives it a fresh opportunity of repentance.

And this is ever the way of God's doings with mankind. He is longsuffering and merciful, and deals with His people, not, as some seem to suppose, with the technicality and harshness of the letter of the law, but with a largeness and fulness of mercy such as befits His perfect nature. In David's time we find the prophets Gad and Nathan engaged in the comparatively unimportant duty[m] of arranging the singing and ritual of the temple-service (2 Chron. xxix. 25): but when the usual means of grace were taken away, when Jeroboam's impious worship had driven from his realm all the believing priests and Levites; when the solemn feasts and festivals, the sacrifices and offerings of the Mosaic law were lost, and ordinary men ministered instead of the true priests at altars devised to serve the purposes of worldly scheming; God gave then to His true worshippers some compensation in the increased vigour and power of the prophetic order. God withdraws not His grace till men have long struggled against it. Long and often do men grieve the Holy Ghost before His light is finally quenched in the heart, and not unfrequently grace at length gains the victory. Ill were our lot

---

[m] This duty was not, however, really unimportant: for we owe to that temple-service the Book of Psalms. And while uninspired men might have been sufficient for arranging the service in itself, yet we cannot say that prophetic aid was unnecessarily lavished upon that which was to give the Church, throughout all time, her best manual of praise and devotion.

if it were not so. Ever throughout the Bible God is revealed as one 'Who waiteth to be gracious (Is. xxx. 18):' and who deals with us not according to the harsh letter of some statute, but so as may best serve for our own moral and spiritual good. And thus as religion declined in Israel, as the nation rejected or lost one after another all its means of grace, and the more pious members of the nation withdrew from a country where Jehovah could not be served in truth, He was pleased to give a last loud call to repentance and faith, by the grand development of the prophetic schools, and the extraordinary energy of individual prophets.

Who can estimate the influence of men like Elijah and Elisha? But few in the whole Bible rise to so high an eminence as they! On the mount of transfiguration it is one of them, Elijah, who appears as the representative of the prophetic order, uniting Moses to Christ! And never did men more truly work as prophets. They kept religion alive in the hearts of the people, encouraged the fainthearted, and were the centres of resistance against all the attempts of Jezebel to make Baal and Astarte usurp the place of Jehovah in Israel's worship. Gross sins in king and people they openly rebuked: disclosed to view the Divine vengeance following with speedy step upon each act of national apostasy, and foretold the final ruin which would inevitably follow upon persistence in idolatry. And yet it is noteworthy that neither the schools of the prophets, nor the influence and unparalleled energy of Elijah and Elisha availed to save Israel. Had Jehu been more free from worldly ambition, less ready to shed blood, and more singleminded in his faith, he would have abolished Jeroboam's calf-worship, and restored the Mosaic law. In this case the labours of the prophets, united to the influence of the state, might have been blessed with happier results. As it was, there was no national repentance. After all, it is the use or neglect of the ordinary means of grace upon which our weal or woe depends. And so even the prophets were no compensation for the loss of priest and Levite, the degradation of the priestly office by thrusting into it unworthy men, the separation from Jerusalem, and the enforced absence from the great festivals celebrated there. I doubt if any extraordinary gifts, however great, can compensate for the loss or neglect of God's ordinary gifts; or, rather, I have no doubt that they cannot. For our Master has plainly taught us so: 'If men hear not Moses and the prophets, neither will they be persuaded though one rose from the dead (Luke xvi. 31).' The greatest possible miracle would not be so efficacious in bringing a man to God as the simple reading of the Bible. The resurrection of Christ did not move those Jews who had heard Christ preach, and heard in vain.

And so Israel, cut off from Jehovah's true worship, and resolutely abiding by her calves, fell rapidly into moral and religious ruin: and, as is ever the case, national corruption was but the prelude to national decay. Judah still flourished and gloried in a Hezekiah and a Josiah long after Israel had ceased to exist. Not a single monarch in the long line of Israel's kings was a good or a pious man, though many were able statesmen and brave warriors. And such as were the kings, such also was the people.

Ever it sank lower and lower, and those who were moved to better things, and who might by their presence have resisted the growing degeneracy, preferred rather to withdraw to Judah, where they could enjoy those religious privileges which were denied them at home. They went where they could worship God as He had commanded men to worship Him: and where they recovered their full share in the blessings of the covenant, and the actual enjoyment of its privileges. Thus it was one of the tribe of Aser who held the infant Saviour in her arms at His presentation in the temple (Luke ii. 36). But though one here and one there of the ten tribes was thus restored to the Church (Acts xxvi. 7), the mass fell gradually more and more away. We know of no Israelites now. They are all 'Ιουδαῖοι, Jews, descendants of Judah. Of the ten tribes we know nothing. Where they are, or whether they still are, and what purpose God may yet have for them, or whether they have been finally rejected, all this is matter of debate and uncertainty. As regards those passages of Scripture which seem to refer to them, every man has his own doctrine, and his own interpretation of their meaning.

And yet one remark more, and one only. Judah, too, became corrupt, and in the place of the good, or comparatively good kings that had sat on David's throne, an Ahaz, a Manasseh, and a Jehoiakim, set the people the example of substituting the gross licentiousness of idolatry for the pure worship of Jehovah. And then God gave prophecy as grand a development in Judah as previously it had enjoyed in Israel. It was not of the same type. Isaiah has little in common with Elijah: Jeremiah in personal character is the very reverse. Round Jeremiah there was gathered one of the noblest circles[n] of men that ever lived. There is nothing comparable to it in the whole history of the northern kingdom. And prophecy in them saved Judah. The captivity of Israel was for aye. It had no return. The exile of Judah was for seventy years, and it had a return (Jer. xxiv. 5–7). Judah returned to work out that purpose for which God had called the Jewish Church into existence, and watched over it from the days when Abraham first left his birthplace. That purpose was the giving the one true religion to the whole world. Weary, footsore, in tears, the saddened exiles toiled on their homeward journey: there was in their poor array nothing of wealth or pomp, of glory or earthly splendour, and yet they bore with them all that we hold best and dearest. Of them sprang a carpenter's son, and some fishermen: and they were the Saviour of the world, and His apostles. On so slight a thread seemed to hang the destinies of mankind, but really that thread was a chain of adamant. For God had declared by His prophets, that 'out of Zion should go forth the law, and the word of the Lord from Jerusalem (Micah iv. 2, Is. ii. 3).'

[n] Jeremiah's labours were seconded by all the foremost priests and laymen of his time. It is enough to mention the high priest Hilkiah, the nobles Shaphan, and his son Ahikam, Neriah, and his son Baruch, the prophets Zephaniah and Habakkuk, and the prophetess Huldah.

LECTURE V.

THE COMMENCEMENT OF WRITTEN PROPHECY.

*Built upon the foundation of the apostles
and prophets.*—EPH. ii. 20.

WE have now traced at some length the upgrowth of Jewish prophecy, but thus far we have been occupied with it only in its earlier stages. Yet even in these early stages, when apparently it was engaged mainly in the lower work of maintaining the kingdom of Israel in its integrity, and of making ready the earthly scene of Christ's labours, it was ever true also to its higher duty of preparing for Christ Himself, and for the doctrines which have not only raised Christian nations to a level so far surpassing what even was best and noblest in heathen philosophy, but in which we believe that we have 'the words of eternal life.'

If we would understand what was its office and work directly as regards our Saviour, it seemed necessary that we should thus study it throughout the whole period of its existence. For prophecy forms a grand whole, of which we shall lose the right interpretation if we regard it merely as the fitful display of extraordinary powers granted to men here and there of high intellectual gifts. Such men there were; men who stood far above the general mass of the prophets, and whom God called by a supernatural impulse to be the teachers in His name of truths which man could not by any exercise of his own powers have learned for himself. Of these men St. Paul speaks when in the text he says that we have been 'built upon the foundation of apostles and prophets.' For while all truth centres in Christ as the one corner-stone, yet it was the especial duty of the prophets before His coming, and of the apostles after He had come, to give us the doctrinal explanation of His person and office, and of the manner in which we have salvation through Him.

But besides these men who spake under the direct impulse of the Holy Ghost, there were prophets 'in companies,' on whom God's Spirit rested in the way of His ordinary gifts, and who wrought for God as men may work for Him now. And if we would understand our Bibles, we must study what is said of these men too, and examine all the agencies and influencies employed by God in His dealings with His people throughout the whole period of its existence, and not those only which were supernatural. Abraham was called by God, and Israel formed into a nation for the noblest of all possible purposes—the bestowal upon mankind of the one true religion, and of the one Saviour, in Whose Name alone we can be saved. Hence the interest that attaches itself to every portion of the Old Testament. We read it not as the history merely of a very remarkable and singular people, but as the opening scene and gradual progress of that which very closely concerns ourselves. We are looking in the Old Testament at our own foundations; and it is well that we should be again and again reminded that our religion did not spring out of nothing. We are not people of yesterday, or the day before. Our Lord was the chief corner-stone—λίθος ἀκρογωνιαῖος—of a building that had long been in course of erection. If in these days of scientific enquiry there are difficulties about the first chapter of Genesis, yet, on the other hand, it is worth remembering that ours is the sole religion that goes back to the day of creation itself: and that we claim that throughout the long series of records which describe God's dealings with mankind, beginning with that account of creation, one, and one plan only has been steadily carried out, and that that plan was completed and made perfect in Christ. No type of the law, no teaching of the prophets, has failed of its fulfilment.

It is the spirit of prophecy which thus binds the Old Testament together, and gradually leads it onward to the final and perfect teaching of our Lord and His apostles. Two stages of this we have already considered, the era namely of Moses and that of Samuel. Now the distinguishing characteristic of prophecy, as it existed in Moses, is that it gives the whole outline of Gospel truth. There is, indeed, one remarkable exception. Moses did not clearly teach the Israelites the doctrine of a future judgment and of an eternal state of rewards and punishments. He did set it forth typically. There is in Paradise a tree of life, and fallen man must be driven from Paradise, lest 'he put forth his hand, and take of the tree of life, and eat and live for ever (Gen. iii. 22).' As the Bible begins so does it end with that tree of life: but its meaning in the last chapter of the Book of Revelation is no longer veiled, but, as 'the pure river of the water of life' is the grace of the Holy Ghost, so that tree of life is 'the living bread which came down from heaven, of which if any man eat he shall live for ever (John vi. 51).' The doctrine, then, of eternal life is contained in the teaching of Moses. He expressly states the possibility of man living for ever. (For implicit teaching see Matt. xxii. 32). Why, then, was it not taught more clearly?

We obtain the answer to this question by the study of the mental and moral state of the Israelites when they left Egypt. The more closely we examine their state, the more unfit we find them for any just ways of thinking about God. Still this did not prevent Moses from setting many high spiritual truths before them; but as regards the immortality of the soul we must remember that the Egyptians held that doctrine, but in such a way as tended more to the debasement than to the ennobling of human nature[a]. It might be better, therefore, for the people to have the doctrine withheld from them for a time, than for it to be associated in their minds with gross conceptions of what happens after death. And in fact we are expressly taught by Ezekiel that this is the principle of God's revelations in the Pentateuch, namely, that while in many respects it set perfect truth before the Israelites, in other respects it taught them what was good only

---

[a] On the views of the Egyptians, see Wilkinson, Manners and Customs of the Egyptians, vol. ii. 2nd series, 1841, p. 381 sqq. Ewald, Hist. Isr. ii. 134, very well remarks, 'The religion of Jehovah, while dealing a blow to all the mythology that had hitherto prevailed, especially abhorred the generally gross heathen conceptions of events after death, because its thoughts respecting God and man's relation to Him had so totally changed.'

for the time, the utmost that they could attain to, but which was in itself imperfect, and not good, compared with what the prophets subsequently were permitted to reveal. For first he says, 'When I caused them to go forth out of the land of Egypt, and brought them into the wilderness; I gave them my statutes, and shewed them my judgments, which if a man do, he shall even live in them (Ezek. xx. 10, 11):' and then he adds, 'But when they despised my statutes, and polluted my sabbaths, and their eyes were after their fathers' idols, then I gave them also statutes that were not good, and judgments whereby they should not live (Ib. 24, 25).' I need scarcely remind you how generally the fathers exaggerate Ezekiel's meaning; and how constantly they use the word Deuteronomy, 'the second law,' in the way of reproach, as a burden imposed upon the Israelites for their sins [b]. But we

---

[b] I do not know that I can refer to any place where this patristic teaching is more unreservedly carried out than the 26th chapter of the Didascalia Apostolorum, ed. Lagarde. This work, though spurious, and guilty of putting into the mouths of the apostles somewhat unscriptural doctrines, is very good evidence of the views current in the fifth century. The chapter referred to is addressed to the Jews, and tells them that the law which David asserted to be perfect (Ps. xix. 7), and which our Lord said that He came not to destroy but to fulfil (Matt. v. 17), is the ten commandments only. After giving for this a puerile reason, namely, that the symbol for ten is the Hebrew letter yod, which yod or jot our Lord said was not to pass away (Ib. 18), and which, too, is the first letter of His own name, it draws the more important distinction between the decalogue, as the law given before Israel's apostasy (Ex. xxxii. 1-6), and those 'distinctions of meats, and offerings of incense and sacrifices and burnt offerings,' which were subsequently imposed upon them for their sin, and which it calls the Deuteronomy, or second law. Till then, the author argues, sacrifices had never been expressly commanded, though offered spontaneously by Abel, Cain, and Noah: but for Christians to offer them, or submit to the yoke of any part of the Levitical law, would be a violation of their baptism, &c An earlier

must not therefore forget his warning. The law had a twofold character. On the one hand it marked out the whole length and breadth of the divine counsels. It foretold that man should be raised from his fallen state by the wounding for him of one Who was to be the woman's seed. It showed by its sacrifices that sin could be atoned for only by the death of a spotless victim, and God approached only by that victim's blood. It set God forth as a personal God, keeping covenant with His people, and showing mercy, but that will by no means acquit the guilty. It taught all this, and much more. But this teaching had to be accommodated to the moral and mental state of the Jews. If the world was fit for Christ's coming only after long ages of preparation, the very fact of the necessity of this preparation shows that there must be a development, a progress in revelation itself, and consequently that there must be much in the earlier stages that was temporary, partial, incomplete.

and more trustworthy evidence is the Persian bishop Farhad, whose homilies are dated respectively A.D. 337, 344, and 345, and who was present at the Council of Seleucia in the latter year. In his Homily on the Distinction of Meats, discussing the passage quoted from Ezek. xx. 11, he asks, 'What are these commandments and judgments, which if a man do he shall live in them? They are the ten commandments, which God wrote with His own hand, and gave them to Moses, that he might teach them to the people. But when they had made them a calf and apostatized from Him, then He gave them commandments and judgments that were not good; such as those of offerings and purifications and defilements and sacrifices for sin,' all which he contrasts with the terms of the Gospel in Matt. xi. 28-30. Dr. Wright has lately edited the original text of these Homilies from a MS. dated as early as A.D. 474, and the passage will be found in page 318 of his edition, and also in page 334 of that of Antonellus, who edited an Armenian version of several of them at Rome in the year 1756, but wrongly ascribed them to St James of Nisibis.

Remembering this, it is the more extraordinary that Moses should nevertheless have marked out so thoroughly the whole domain of revelation; and have stood in a more close relation to God than any subsequent prophet. No one besides has so completely filled the prophet's office, and been the mediator between God and man. Other prophets there were many: but a prophet like unto Moses God gave but one, even Him, Who came as the Son over that house of which Moses, great as he was, had been the steward only.

During the long period that followed, the work of Moses languished. Great men rose—men instinct with the Spirit of God—but they did not labour directly for religion, and even in temporal matters Israel seemed in danger of being permanently conquered by the Philistines. It could not, indeed, be so. For salvation was to be of the Jews (John iv. 22, Is. ii. 3). The purpose for which God had summoned Abraham to leave his country must be carried out to its full end. And so, just when the country was ripe for him, God sent Samuel, and from his days there is no break in the activity of the prophetic order. Violent men like Manasseh might silence the prophets for a time by the sword; Jehoiakim might compel Jeremiah to quit Jerusalem; but the work went on. The world, under their teaching, was daily growing more ripe for Christ's advent: men were advancing in morality, in intellect, and in the power of understanding spiritual truths. And simultaneously the plan of redemption was being more and more plainly declared. The time of the Saviour's coming, His birthplace, His nature, His office, all were becoming more definite, more exactly foreshown. Isaiah has so clearly unfolded the nature of Christ's sufferings for us, that not even the apostles after His crucifixion could give a more complete doctrinal statement of the manner in which they avail for our redemption.

Before the prophets could attain to this elevation it was necessary that they should be set free from lower duties. Although the idea of the theocracy required that the prophet, as God's mouthpiece, should also direct the government of the state, yet, as long as human nature is such as it is, this really placed the prophet in circumstances more likely to put difficulties in his way than to keep him singleminded. Moses, Deborah, Samuel, had combined the two offices in spotless integrity. But there were great dangers in the union; and thus Samuel unwillingly, yet by God's express monition, separated the two for ever (1 Sam. viii. 22). Under Saul and David Israel soon obtained not freedom only, but empire. That, as usual, was but a dubious blessing. But though the prophets remained so much mixed up with political and worldly matters, that it became a snare to many of them, yet, set free at least from having any direct share in the government of the nation, they could henceforth devote themselves more entirely to God's immediate service, and to the higher duty of teaching the people.

We see this in Samuel's own case. Released from the toils of government, he could give his time and thoughts to the management of the prophetic schools. By their means he obtained for Israel, first of all, a higher culture, and, secondly, a large and active class of men who laboured directly for religion. In both these respects we find ourselves at the close of Samuel's days in a state of things removed by a vast gulph from the days of the Judges. Idolatry has disappeared. The people are everywhere making great advances in learning, and a high tone of morality and religion generally prevails. The one blot upon the time is David's lust of war, bringing men like Joab to the front, and debasing David's own character. But the prophets were too true patriots to approve of this. They disapproved of it, and laboured that his throne might be filled at his death by a man of peace. Even he, too, disappointed them. Religion pined under the costly trappings of an imperial court. Vice followed close upon the heels of luxury. The people were ground down by forced labour, exacted from them to rear works of royal magnificence, and a lasting schism tore into two petty nations what had once been a powerful state. If ever God wrote His verdict plainly upon ambition and aggressive war, he wrote it upon the wars of David. They brought the stain of two foul crimes on David himself; ruined his own domestic peace and happiness; ruined, by the possession of too great power, that one of his sons who started so wisely and so well; and ruined the kingdom, which broke asunder of its own weight. Absalom saw clearly enough that the flaw in David's government was his neglect of the administration of justice at home (2 Sam. xv. 2-6). If he had followed Samuel's example (1 Sam. vii. 15, 16), or provided, as Jehoshaphat did afterwards, for the upright administration of the law in every city (2 Chron. xix. 5-7), instead of devoting himself to war, he would have knit the tribes of Israel into one united and compact monarchy.

But it is probable that this schism in the kingdom was for Israel's real good. The work of the prophets at all events was made more easy thereby. I can scarcely see how an institution so free, so independent, so brave in resisting sin even in the mightiest, could have existed in the face of a powerful and despotic court. We find Asa casting prophets into prison, Manasseh and Jehoiakim putting them to death. Means such as these would soon have reduced the prophets to the condition of those at Samaria, who must perforce say to Ahab 'go and prosper,' or be content with prison fare and the cruelties of a dungeon.

But, in these petty kingdoms they had, as a general rule, full scope for their powers, and we have seen to what grand proportions prophecy attained in the persons of Elijah and Elisha. Even they, however, were men of action only; we have not yet come to the days of written prophecy. It was by oratory, by personal addresses, that the prophets moved the people, but we are now approaching the time when they began to write their prophecies, or at least some memorials of them. The prophecies of Amos and Jeremiah are records of long and unwearied labours, the former an orderly and well-arranged account of one important mission, the other the rough and unarranged jottings, as it were, of a life of incessant activity and constant suffering, closed by a violent death, nor does the prophet seem ever to have had any period of tranquillity during which he had leisure enough for reducing to order the narrative of his noble zeal. Micah's prophecy, so vigorous and terse, so abrupt and broken, seems but as the heads of discourses often urged upon the people. On the other hand, the last twenty-seven chapters of Isaiah, the prophecies of Habakkuk, Joel,

Nahum, and others, are probably written compositions, never orally spoken in public, but from the first committed to writing. These written compositions were less powerful at the time, and the influence of the prophets far smaller than it had been in Elijah's days. But to us the change is all-important. We are admitted by it within the circle of inspired teaching [c]. We can appeal to that teaching, can compare our Lord's life and death and doctrines with what the prophets had long before said of Him. The New Testament comes not down to us single-handed. We can point also to the Old, and say, Read both these books; both these collections of books; compare them with one another: and you will see that in Christ all is accomplished that prophets had foretold; and you will see also that, from the first, men had been bidden to look forward to, and expect, and pray for all that is found in Christ. This is a thing to be noted and remembered, this unity of teaching and doctrine, beginning with the earliest records of God's dealings with mankind, and ending in that book

---

[c] Christians are sometimes twitted with being 'the people of a book,' and our respect for the Bible is called bibliolatry and other bad names. So the Mohammedans are called 'the people of a book,' and having thus a fixed standard for their religion, they have a consistency among themselves, and a backbone for their creed, which has hitherto made them very unmanageable opponents of even Christian missionaries. But we are not 'people of a book,' but of thirty or forty books, all for convenience' sake bound together in one volume, but none the less distinct books. While this widens the field of attack, it also makes the defence more decisively successful. It is to be expected that clever and brilliant fallacies will be brought forward from time to time, and urged as unanswerable attacks upon some part or other of the long line which believers have to defend. But what else than truth can make so long a line really defensible!

which sets before us the only sufficient Saviour, the only religion worthy of God and man, the only revelation that invites and can endure the closest scrutiny. Such a fact is no chance-work. Either Christianity is true, or you must believe that mere human agency has for many thousand years steadily persevered in preparing for, in producing, and in maintaining the noblest and purest delusion. A creed utterly unlike what men could have invented, which raises and ennobles man, gives him the mastery over himself, works only for purity, chastity, and holiness, and which is nevertheless false. A creed supported by a vast and solid mass of evidence, none the less solid and vast because little holes have been picked in it, but which no evidence may be allowed to prove. Those may believe so who like. But those who think the question too important to be prejudged, and are content to weigh the evidence calmly, know that the balance of that evidence is largely in favour of Christianity, even though there are difficulties enough to try our faith. As prudent men, too, they will wait to see whither the apostles of doubt intend to lead them. We know the value of our faith: we may reasonably ask what is to be the substitute, before we part with what we have.

The early prophets, then, laboured for the maintenance of the true religion in Israel; the later prophets laboured to raise Judaism from being a mere local worship to its true dignity as the catholic religion, the one true religion for the whole world. The first was an absolutely necessary part of God's scheme of mercy for man. Our Lord must have some place where He could be born, and give proofs of His

Messiahship, and die. There must be there men able to witness, to understand and to record His doings, and to teach them to others. Men must be prepared also for their teaching. A certain cycle of doctrine, relating especially to the nature and attributes of God, and to man's relation to Him, must be impressed first upon the minds of the Jews, and then, through them, upon the more thoughtful of the heathen, among whom the Jews were dispersed, apparently for this very purpose. Nor was this preparation confined to Judaea. The conquests of Alexander, the empire of Rome, the translation of the Septuagint, and the gropings of philosophy after truth, were all ordained by the Divine Providence, and so regulated as best to lend their aid also to this part of the preparation for Christ. A vast external work was necessary, as well as a body of pure and spiritual teaching. In Israel, and outside of Israel, everything combined to make that the very fulness of time when Christ came. When we see the vast scale on which, far and wide, all earthly things had been fitted and made ready for the manifestation of God's mercies to mankind in Christ, we need not wonder at the high rank held by Elijah among the prophets, even though he committed no prophecy to writing, and his work chiefly belonged to this, the outer and material, preparation for the Saviour's ministry.

But already the inner work had begun, of giving to men the abiding record of the faith, and its firm memorial as long as the world shall last. Even the early prophets did not confine their activity to oral teaching, the effect of which, however powerful, is nevertheless transient. Already there had been added to the law of Moses works of history and psalms. Both begin with Moses. Repeatedly he is commanded to lay up written memorials of certain great events within the ark: and psalmody commenced with that hymn of triumph sung by Miriam and the women on the shore of the Red Sea, with timbrel and dance. But these again had a new beginning in Samuel. The singing in the temple is expressly said to have been the work of the prophets (2 Chron. xxix. 25), and it was in the prophetic schools that Samuel revived the art of music, and made it part of the regular course of instruction given there; while history we find was the special study and business of the prophets. The annals of each king's reign were kept by prophets, and numerous biographies written by them are referred to in the Books of Chronicles. The Jews call all the historical books of the Old Testament the 'books of the early prophets.'

But though histories and psalms were composed thus early, the prophets did not as yet record their own addresses to the people. And this continued to be the rule for rather more than three hundred years, from the time of Samuel till the uprise of the Assyrian monarchy. During this period Israel and Judah were left to work out their own destinies, with no worse evil than their constant rivalry with one another, and no more powerful foreign foe than the Syrian kingdom of Damascus. The most prominent figures in this era are Elijah and Elisha; the most remarkable fact the grand development of prophecy in the northern kingdom. Written prophecy began with the Assyrian period, so called because the relations of Israel and Judah to Nineveh form the leading features of the times. It lasted about a hundred years, commencing about 800 B. C., in the reigns of Jeroboam II, king of Israel, and Amaziah, king of Judah. The prophets of this era were Jonah, Joel, Hosea, Micah, Isaiah, Nahum. The third or Chaldaean period witnessed the life-long struggle of Jeremiah, the fall of Jerusalem, the seventy years' captivity, and the final outburst of prophecy among the returning exiles. And then for four hundred years there was silence, till the Precursor came, announcing the advent of the prophet like unto, but greater than, Moses, in Whom God gave mankind the fullest light that would avail for their good. We have no new revelation to expect. The Old Testament ever looked forward to, and spake of, latter times: the New Testament bids us earnestly contend for a faith that has been once for all delivered to the saints.

It was in these two last eras that, with a message still for Israel, 'the spirit that was in the prophets testified beforehand the sufferings of Christ, and the glory that should follow (1 Peter i. 11).' The earlier prophets had laboured to keep Israel true to its mission. They tried to maintain the worship of Jehovah in its integrity; instructed the people in the great doctrines of God's unity, His omnipresence, His spiritual nature; resisted their longings after idolatry, and strove to make them worthy of their high vocation of being Christ's brethren after the flesh, and His future ministers for teaching mankind the true faith. To bring about these ends, the prophets had hitherto taken great share in things political; but now, without altogether abandoning this lower field (Is. vii. Jer. xxxii. 3–5, &c.), they yet constantly rise above it, and look onward to a new covenant, made not with one small nation, but unto which 'all nations shall flow (Is. ii. 2).' In a people so exclusive as the Jews, whom Moses had so separated from all the neighbouring kingdoms, whose patriotism was so fierce and so narrow, who looked with such open aversion upon all foreign races, and who refused to admit even proselytes into full equality with themselves until the fourth generation, it is the more remarkable that their prophets speak of the deliverance of Gentile as well as Jew, of the bestowal of a common Saviour, and of the founding of a universal Church. Up to this time they had been content with trying to save Israel from idolatry; they now attack idolatry itself, and summon the whole world to witness God's controversy with idols. The Jews are no longer to be the one people possessed of truth, but must be made fit to be the apostles and teachers of a suffering Messiah, who died 'not for one nation only, but that also He might gather together in one the children of God that were scattered abroad (John xi. 52).' For this end the prophets now expand, simplify, show the living spirit which animated the teaching of the law, free it from all that was local, temporary, national, and labour to make Judaism the religion of all lands, and people, and languages. The first, and imperfect, and preparatory Church, is fast growing into a Church perfect, final, universal. The flickering taper of Judaism is changing into a dawn preceding the rising of the Sun of Righteousness.

You see this in their own writings. Passing by the first chapter of Isaiah, written, as the contents plainly show, when the prophet was gathering his earlier prophecies together, to form an introduction or preface to the whole volume; passing this by, we find in the second chapter Isaiah's programme—his leading idea. And it is given in a very remarkable way. He quotes three verses from a contemporary prophet, Micah, not omitting even the conjunction *and*[d] at the beginning, as if he had nothing to add to or subtract from Micah's message, but only to explain and enforce it. Or perhaps it was to remind the people that there was something that came before that *and*. For what was Micah's message? A very painful one; so painful that the people would have gladly seen Micah put to death, if Hezekiah would have permitted it (Jer. xxvi. 18, 19). In good Hezekiah's days, when there was so much to justify the expectation of an era of great national happiness, Micah warned them that 'Zion should be ploughed as a field, and Jerusalem become heaps of ruins (Micah iii. 12).' Why? Because it had to make room for something else, something better. 'In the latter days,' a phrase which always with the prophets means the days of the Messiah, 'in the latter days the mountain of the house of Jehovah shall be established on the top of the mountains, and to it, the Christian Church, not Jews only, but all nations shall flock. Out of Zion the law shall go forth,—of old it had stayed within it, —and the word of the Lord from Jerusalem.' And this, not to found an empire of force, like that of David, but an empire of peace. 'Nation shall not

---

[d] In our translation the conjunction is translated *but* in Micah iv. 1; in the Hebrew it is *and* in both places. It is the form of the verb, however, which proves that Isaiah quotes from Micah, and not Micah from Isaiah.

lift up sword against nation, neither shall they learn war any more (Ib. iv. 1–3, Is. ii. 2–4).' If ever there was anything contrary to the whole tenor of Jewish thought, it was Christ's command to go out into all the world, and make disciples of the whole creation. That command, even now, has not been fully obeyed. Missionary enterprise soon died out, and its revival is a matter of recent date. Man's supineness and disobedience have too long delayed this promised reign of peace. No such reign, too, will come till Christianity has been more fully received at home, and has established a more complete authority over the bad passions of fallen human nature. But Micah and Isaiah spoke of a duty incumbent upon every one who has been brought near Christ, when they described this expansive power which has ever been a note of real Christianity; and in this empire of peace they showed what would be the result, if the principles taught by Christ had obtained full mastery, first over our individual selves, and then, through us, over all mankind.

Now how came Isaiah to quote these words as his programme? You cannot say that he took them in a less threatening sense than we do, for Jeremiah has told us how greatly Hezekiah and the people— Isaiah's contemporaries—took them to heart (Jer. xxvi. 19). You cannot say that Isaiah had no particular purpose in quoting them, for he refers to them six or seven times elsewhere (Is. xi. 9, xxv. 6, 7, 10, lvi. 7, lvii. 13, lxv. 11, 25, lxvi. 20). You cannot say that he thought only of an extension of Judaism; for the prophecy expressly declared that the 'mountain of the house,' the area on which the temple was situated, was to be 'as the high places of the field,' as the hill-tops, which rise barren, and lone, and desolate in the uncultivated wilderness. You cannot say that Isaiah shared in the popular alarm that the Assyrians would capture Jerusalem. He expressly assured Hezekiah of the contrary. You may take refuge with some of the new critics in saying that the words had no meaning, or that we cannot tell what that meaning was. But if the words have a meaning, it can be no other than this; that instead of that mountain of Zion on which stood the temple, and of the dispensation of which that temple was the centre and symbol, God would have another, a holy mountain, a dispensation of which holiness would be the distinguishing characteristic: that in it all nations would have equal rights with the Jews: and that this dispensation would be first published from Jerusalem, but that afterwards that city would have nothing more to do with it. Titus may destroy Jerusalem, Arabs and Turks waste it: but in doing so they are wasting the site merely of a dispensation that has fulfilled its purpose. 'The Law has gone forth from Zion:' it is not there now. 'The word of the Lord has gone forth from Jerusalem:' it has no special head-quarters, no local centre now. 'In every nation he that feareth God, and worketh righteousness, is accepted with Him (Acts x. 35).'

It is quite possible that Isaiah did not himself distinctly contemplate or understand all that was contained in his words. It is the nature of prophecy not to be capable of being fully understood until it is accomplished. But 'borne along by the Holy Ghost,' Isaiah took as his programme a text that showed that

Judaism was to pass away, and that the business of prophecy henceforward must be to prepare for that better and enduring dispensation, of which the grand features are nowhere else so clearly set forth as in Isaiah's own predictions. In this second stage, then, the prophets laboured not for the means only but for the end [e]: not for Israel, as God's instrument in giving man the true religion, but for that religion itself, for Christ and His Church. And therefore they wrote their prophecies, because they had not merely a temporary but an eternal use and value. 'They were written for our learning—the instruction of all Christians: that we through patience and comfort of the Scriptures might have the hope.'

And we,—possessing these writings, and daily reading therein of the hope and consolation of the true Israel, who are Abraham's seed by being sharers in that faith which God accepted in Abraham while he was yet uncircumcised,—we, having these lively oracles of God ever before our eyes, are in danger not of over-estimating their value, but of under-estimating the importance of the work of those prophets who left behind them no written memorials of their teaching. The place which Elijah holds in the New Testament may serve to warn us that we are wrong in our view of them; and yet, when we compare him with an Isaiah, or a Jeremiah, we may wonder why he should have been chosen, as the representative of the whole prophetic order, to stand on the Mount of Transfiguration between Moses and Christ, as the link which

---

[e] Of course the Christian Church and its ordinances are really means only: means for bringing men to God. But as regards the Jewish Church, they were the ends for which that Church existed.

unites the law to the gospel. Moses of course was there. He had showed what God is. Go where you will; search where you will among all the cosmogonies and philosophies of ancient and modern times, but you will never find anything so true, so simple, and so sublime, as the opening words of Genesis. God the Creator, the sole active, intelligent, life-giving, spirit: matter dull, heavy, void, shapeless, created by God. And besides this, he showed what God is with relation to man: what man was, how he fell, what he needs, how those needs must be supplied, how sin can be atoned for, and man raised up again, and the breach between heaven and earth repaired, and all once again be as at first 'very good.' Moses must be there, for in him God gave man the full outline of the marvellous plan of redemption. But why Elijah? Because, you will perhaps say, of his high personal merits, of those qualities which made it meet that he should be exalted to heaven in the chariot of fire. But Elijah was there as the representative of the whole prophetic order, and not by reason of his personal merits. You will say then, perhaps, that Elijah was the great preacher of repentance, and that repentance is the true preparation for faith, the Baptist cry that must precede the preaching of the Gospel. But this is scarcely enough. You have on the Mount of Transfiguration Moses, Elias, Christ: the law, the prophets, the Gospel. You can scarcely say that repentance is the equivalent of the second term.

May not the reason then be that Elijah and his contemporaries were the real founders of the prophetic teaching? and that written prophecy was the result, the product of their work? That product is all-important to us: by being committed to writing, prophecy took a firm, lasting, and permanent shape. Yet the men who first taught those truths, which Micah and Isaiah penned, may justly hold a higher place in the view of Him Who judgeth not according to the semblance, but according to reality. For with one exception the prophets all belong to, and give expression to the same grand circle of ideas. They speak plainly, clearly, decisively, and harmoniously. Each retaining his own individual character, his own style and mode of thinking, they yet utter no confused and uncertain cries, but all teach the same truths. Now God, even in His highest gifts, yet works by means. And, as I have shown, prophecy was a great institution, numbering its ordinary members by hundreds and thousands, with its inspired teachers few, yet so grand and elevated in their characters and powers, that they stamped the impress of their thoughts deeply upon the minds of their disciples, and of all the religious and earnest men of the nation. I have shown you that this lasted for three hundred years before Joel and Jonah penned the first written prophecy. Shall we be wrong in concluding that so great an institution had a soul as well as a body? a purpose for which it existed as well as an organized existence? If there were so many and such flourishing prophetic colleges, are we to suppose that nothing was taught in them except the simplest rudiments? They were religious corporations, and therefore must have had some doctrines, something that they believed. We may be sure, then, that what the later prophets taught, and have left us in written records, the early prophets taught also: yet probably God gave these truths, these spiritual ideas about man and God and a Saviour, gradually. They were slowly won by the piety and faith of these early prophets: many of them probably by the close study of the law of Moses, yet not without the Spirit's direct aid. Humanly speaking, we should say that the circle of truth penned by the later prophets was the result of the teaching of the prophetic schools during these three centuries. Thus Elijah stands on the Mount of Transfiguration as the representative of the prophets, because the truths committed to writing by later prophets were those which he and his contemporaries had won for men, and which they had taught their disciples.

We are not left, however, to conjecture and reasoning upon this point. As I mentioned, the prophetic schools were closely connected with the temple-service. Prophets arranged that service: the psalms sung there were the work of men educated in the prophetic schools, and composed, many of them, long before the era of written prophecy: the Levites who sang them had there also their training. Now psalms and hymns f, I grant, are not the proper means for

---

f Psalms and hymns constantly have their origin in doctrines, and thus they indirectly bear witness to them. But their use to inculcate doctrines began with heretics. Bardesan first used them to make Manichæan ideas popular in the East, and Ephrem Syrus then wrote his poems 'Against the Enquirers' to frustrate his purpose. So Peter the Fuller convulsed the Greek Church by inserting into the hymn ' O holy God, holy Almighty, holy Eternal, have mercy upon us!' the words ' That wast crucified for us,' but was anathematized by the council of Constantinople for his pains. So in St. Chrysostom's time the battle between Arianism and Orthodoxy was fought with hymns. But it was an evil necessity which led to controversial hymns, and all such, especially when intended to enforce the pet notions of some sect, are

teaching doctrine. A doctrinal hymn is a hymn that has mistaken its vocation, and congregations are sorely to be pitied who have to sing them. Psalms and hymns ought to be the voice of praise and thanksgiving, mounting up spontaneously from glad hearts to glorify God for His goodness. And this is the character of the Psalms of the Bible. They are the expression not of controversy, but of devotion, and spring not from the intellect, but from the heart. Still in pouring forth of its fulness the heart will give unpremeditated utterance to those thoughts which most deeply agitate it, and little as the early psalms have in them of distinctive doctrine, yet they do show us something of the belief of the saints who lived in times anterior to the first book of written prophecy. What, then, do we find in them? Exactly the same great circle of ideas as that given us in prophecy, forming at all events the back-ground, and giving the occasion often for the burst of praise which follows. You have the prophetic view of the intrinsic worthlessness of sacrifices, and that God's true offering is thanksgiving (Ps. l. 8–15, xl. 6–8): the prophetic view of repentance, that it is the contrite heart, and a renewed life (Ib. li. 17, 10). Sin is forgiven by our iniquity not being imputed unto us (Ib. xxxii. 1, 2). The Jewish priesthood is to give place to one higher and better, after the order of Melchizedek g (Ib. cx. 4).

painfully out of place in public worship. Naturally, however, Christian hymns will have more of doctrine in them than the early psalms, because more doctrine has been revealed; but a hymn of praise, springing from a heart filled with thankfulness at God's dealings with us in grace is one thing, and a hymn intended to indoctrinate us, and drag some new notion in, is altogether another.

g On the authorship of this psalm see Ewald, Poet. Bücher des A. B. ii. 56, and Rev. C. Taylor's 'Gospel in the Law,' p. 18.

There is a mysterious tale, too, of suffering, an oft-repeated promise of especial love for the poor and needy, and anticipations of a universal empire over which a Son of David shall rule, of Whom it is said, 'His name shall endure for ever: His name shall be continued as long as the sun: and men shall be blessed in Him: all nations shall call Him blessed (Ib. lxxii. 17).' But it is not doctrines only which connect the psalms with the prophets. They are full of pure, noble, spiritual thoughts, such as the prophets everywhere give utterance to. Now many of these psalms are written records of those early times when as yet the prophets preached only, and did not preserve any memorials of their sermons: when it was only by the living memory that the truths taught by Samuel and Nathan and Elijah and Elisha were preserved in the prophetic colleges. And it was right that thus the earliest written memorials of prophetic teaching should be these glorious psalms of praise to God. The first-fruits were ever God's share, and when they had been offered, the rest was thereby sanctified to man's use and enjoyment.

But, farther, one prophet, as I said, stands apart from this cycle of ideas; that is Daniel. In him prophecy has a new development: it breaks away from the bonds of Jewish thought, and sets before us the grand onward march of the world's history, and the Christian Church as the centre and end of all history. Prophecy would not have been complete had not this new direction been given to it. For 'the world is Jehovah's, and the fulness thereof.' If in Judaism there was a special preparation for a certain end, that end belonged to the world outside of Judaism, and prophecy must put the two in their right connection. When the Jew read in Daniel that the world was greater in God's eyes than Judæa, and that his own especial work was nearly over, and that therefore the city and sanctuary would in a few weeks be destroyed, and the sacrifice and oblation cease, and that God would set up a kingdom that would never be destroyed, and that this kingdom would not be Judæa, he was puzzled and offended, and though he could not help inserting Daniel in the canon of Scripture, yet he would not admit him among the prophets, but placed the Book of Daniel between Esther and Ezra, in its chronological order, as a sort of historical writing. Now God works by means. It was necessary that prophecy should have this development, and whom did He choose as His instrument for giving it? One carried as a child to Babylon, probably a prince of the blood royal of Judæa, but brought up to serve as a eunuch at the king of Babylon's court. He is not educated at any prophetic college, but in the wisdom of the Chaldæans. No doubt he would often meet and converse with many of those believing men who had been brought captive to Babylon with Jeconiah, and would read with them the law of Moses, and the recent prophecies of Jeremiah ; for they, we know, were the great study and comfort of the exiles; but he would not be able, as Jeremiah had been, to pore over and meditate day by day upon the great mass of prophetic literature stored up in the college at Jerusalem. And when he arrived at man's estate, he became a mighty ruler, busied with the government of a vast empire, and necessary alike to the Chaldæan monarchs, and to the Medes, their conquerors. Intensely deep as was Daniel's religion, and tender as were his love and reverence for Jerusalem, yet his thoughts are not as the thoughts of the prophets who preceded him, nor of Ezra and the returning exiles. God placed him in such circumstances as made it easy for him to look at Christ's kingdom not with Jewish but with Gentile eyes. He is the link between Jewish prophecy and the Christian Church.

And thus, then, I have endeavoured to show that St. Peter was not wrong in assigning so high a place among the prophets to Samuel (Acts iii. 24), and that Elijah was the right representative of the prophets, as the bond of union between the law and the Gospel. Prophecy did not grow out of nothing, nor does God, so infinitely wise and good, bring about effects without causes, or govern this world by chance-medley. His providence moved Samuel to found his schools; it freed him from the cares of government, by appointing Saul to be king; and it prolonged his life for more than thirty years after that event, that his schools might take deep root and be strengthened for lasting and powerful influence. In these schools there grew up under the teaching of inspired men a definite body of doctrine, having its foundation in the law, but in close connection with the more spiritual part of its teaching; that part which Ezekiel described as statutes by which the soul might live. Its effects were first felt in God's own service. To the burdensome ritual of animal sacrifice was added a spiritual sacrifice of praise and thanksgiving. That service has lasted from its first commencement in Samuel's schools to our own day.

Psalms written by that youth who found refuge at Naioth from the violence of Saul and his messengers are sung by us now. May they not have been first sung by Samuel and his choir? One of that choir probably was Heman, the son of Joel, Samuel's firstborn (1 Chron. vi. 33, 1 Sam. viii. 2), and he there acquired that mastery of music which made him one of the three singers selected by David and the captains of the host to arrange and preside over the temple-service (1 Chron. xxv). Blessed with a numerous family, who all seem to have inherited his musical ability, Samuel trained them all 'for song in the house of Jehovah with cymbals, psalteries, and harps (Ib. ver. 6),' and it is remarkable that no less than fourteen out of the twenty-four courses of singers were Samuel's own descendants, and that as long as the first temple stood they were the chief performers of that psalmody which he had instituted. Their 'songs of Jehovah,' then, give us the earliest glimpses of the teaching of the prophets, but when in due time it was so far perfect as to be fit for permanent use, God moved the prophets to commit the revelations made them to writing. And thus we know what were the truths for which Samuel and Elijah and Elisha and so many others laboured. For the new knowledge vouchsafed ever confirmed the old, and belonged to the same cycle of thoughts, only it made them more clear, and pointed them more definitely to Christ. Finally, if we read our Bibles intelligently, and observe how, from the days of Moses downward, one great purpose has been steadily carried out, and then examine the religion of Christ, and see what it has done for mankind, and for the soul of each believer, at all events we must acknowledge that the claims of Christianity are not to be carelessly and lightly thrust aside. One might venture, perhaps, to say, that a true religion is the best and most precious gift that God could bestow upon the noblest of His earthly creatures—man: if so, it would justify the great and extraordinary preparation made for it; and this vast preparation proves again the greatness and value of the gift.

But written prophecy also requires a close and exact examination; and to this I shall proceed in my next Lecture.

LECTURE VI.

THE FOUNDATION OF TRUTH LAID BY THE
PROPHETS JONAH, JOEL, AND HOSEA.

Saying none other things than those which the prophets and Moses did say should come: that Christ should suffer, and that He should be the first that should rise from the dead, and should shew light unto the people, and to the Gentiles.—ACTS xxvi. 22, 23.

ST. PAUL, in these words, affirms that the one subject of his preaching was the fulfilment of prophecy in Christ. Now it may seem natural that our Lord Himself should constantly refer to the Old Testament as the proper proof of His ministry; that He should say, 'Search the Scriptures: for they are they which testify of Me.' And, again, 'Had ye believed Moses, ye would have believed Me: for he wrote of Me (John v. 39, 46).' And that first to the two disciples going to Emmaus, and then to all the apostles, 'beginning at Moses, He should have expounded to them in all the Scriptures the things concerning Himself (Luke xxiv. 27, 46).' This seems quite natural. Our Lord was speaking to Jews, and they confessedly had been brought up in the belief that a national deliverer was to come, and that in their Scriptures there were certain marks and signs by which they were to recognize Him when He did come. But it was St. Paul who gave a wider scope to Christianity, and carried the message of salvation far and near to those who otherwise would never have heard it. We find in the Acts of the Apostles very slight traces of any readiness on the part of the apostles to obey our Lord's command to make disciples of the whole creation. Even the Christians scattered abroad upon the persecution that arose about Stephen preached to Jews only. With slight exceptions, such as the mission to Samaria, and Peter's journey to Lydda and Joppa, we always find the apostles on all occasions at Jerusalem, or in the immediate neighbourhood. It is a matter of pious belief that they did become missionaries, but they apparently learned their duty from St. Paul. His noble example brought home to them the solemn responsibility laid upon them by their Lord.

It was St. Paul, then, who was God's chosen minister for the fulfilment of that which Christ Himself had proved to the apostles to be the teaching of the Old Testament, namely, 'that repentance and remission of sins should be preached in His name among all nations (Luke xxiv. 47).' And what is so remarkable is, that St. Paul takes to these nations the same proof as that to which Christ had appealed at Jerusalem. He, too, appeals to the Jewish Scriptures. He can give the Gentiles no stronger evidence of the truth of Christianity than the fact that in a long series of books, written gradually in the course of many centuries, and of which the most modern was composed four hundred years before the Saviour's birth, there was the most distinct preparation for the religion which He came to found, and a vast array of passages which found in His person and ministry a most exact fulfilment.

One proof which especially would come home to their minds, is the undeniable fact that prophecy had from the first distinctly contemplated the substitution of a catholic for a local religion. 'Moses and the prophets taught that Christ should proclaim light to the people and to the Gentiles.' St. Paul, no doubt, spoke Greek before men like Festus and Agrippa; but in the vernacular tongue of Jerusalem it was but a single letter that separated the Jews from the Gentiles. They always spoke of themselves in the singular number as 'the people.' They were the one people, the chosen, the beloved, to whom all God's mercies belonged, who had an exclusive right to His favour. All mankind besides were 'the peoples' in the plural number, who lived outside the circle of God's care, beyond the pale of His providence, with no right to His mercies. Now, as we have seen, the call of the Gentiles was one of the most important points of that circle of doctrine taught by the prophets. And yet it had not made the slightest impression upon the popular mind at Jerusalem. When Stephen preached that Jesus of Nazareth would destroy Jerusalem, an event which Daniel had foretold (Dan. ix. 26), and which Titus, during the lifetime of that very generation, accomplished, they stoned him. Christ again and again had taught what St. Stephen preached (Matt. xxi. 41, Luke xix. 44, xxi. 6), and as He hung upon the cross His murderers taunted Him with His prediction that the temple—the symbol and centre of Judaism—should be destroyed (Matt. xxvii. 40); and yet, in the Church itself, we read but of one besides Stephen who comprehended the full meaning of the Saviour's words, and saw that Judaism and Christianity could not exist together. That one man was St. Paul. He had consented to Stephen's death. He made glorious compensation by taking upon himself Stephen's work, and building up not a Jewish sect, but a catholic Church, gathered from all nations, and whose doors were open to all of every country and rank and degree.

And how was he treated? They resented with the bitterest hatred his attempt to do what their own prophets had foretold. In every city the Jews were his resolute enemies; his friends were those devout Gentiles, who knew the Old Testament, and read it in the Septuagint translation, and who, not being blinded by Jewish prejudices, could both understand the sublimity of its teaching, and also see that it had promises for them. As for the people of Jerusalem, when the Roman garrison had rescued Paul from their attempt to beat him to death, and had obtained for him a hearing, they listened to his defence till he used the hated word *peoples* in the plural, and then their patience broke down, and they cried, 'Away with such a fellow from the earth, for it is not fit that he should live (Acts xxii. 22).'

Now, as I have shown, Micah and Isaiah had prophesied just exactly the same truths as those which Stephen and Paul preached. Those two prophets happily escaped violence. They lived in good times, and Hezekiah used their prophecies rightly. A prophecy is never merely a prediction. The heathen oracles simply foretold an event. So to do is an act of divination or soothsaying,—a thing always condemned in the Bible in the strongest terms. A prophecy always has a moral purpose, and Hezekiah used Micah's prophecy for its proper purpose when he repented, and urged the people to repentance, and besought the Lord to avert the evil. But their repentance was short-lived; and other prophets arose with the same 'burden,' the same sentence upon Jerusalem, and they were met with as fierce an outcry as Stephen and Paul. Urijah repeated Micah's prophecy, and king, princes, and people were all indignant, and the prophet fled from their rage, but fled in vain; for Jehoiakim sent men to Egypt, who 'fetched Urijah forth thence, and he slew him at Jerusalem with the sword, and cast his dead body into the graves of the common people (Jer. xxvi. 23).' Undeterred by this cruelty, Jeremiah proclaimed the same truth, and great again was the popular rage at Jerusalem. 'Thou shalt surely die,' they said; and with difficulty was he rescued from their violence (Ib. 8). The Jews read all this, and in Paul's days no prophet was so highly esteemed as Jeremiah [a]. But as for the truths he had taught, they were as unpalatable as ever. Jeremiah declared absolutely that Jerusalem should become as Shiloh, and a curse to—that is, a thing cursed by— all the nations of the earth. St. Paul did no more

---

[a] In Matt. xxvii. 9, Jeremiah's name is used as equivalent to the whole circle of the prophets. But it is chiefly in Jewish legends that we find how great a place he held in the popular imagination. Thus in 2 Macc. ii. 5 he is described as hiding the tabernacle and ark and altar of incense in a cave; and in ch. xv. 13-16 he appears as 'a man with grey hairs, and exceeding glorious, and of a wonderful and excellent majesty,' who prays much for the people and for the holy city, and summons Judas Maccabeus to its aid, and girds him with a sword of gold. Hence the expectation of his reappearing, John i. 25.

than preach to the Gentiles. Even that he did only when the Jews rejected his message. Everywhere he spake to the Jews first. And yet they were so enraged even at this, that they cried, 'Such a one is not fit to live.'

The destruction, then, of Jerusalem, the rejection of the Jews, the call of the Gentiles, were plainly taught by the prophets Micah, Isaiah, Urijah, Jeremiah. But what do we find at the commencement of written prophecy? for it has been said that prophecy takes its colour from contemporary events. 'The Psalms of David,' we are told, 'and the writings of Solomon, gave utterance to the feelings of a time when the hopes of Israel came to at best but a typical fulfilment. The prophecies that followed were to comfort Jehovah's people for the loss of this splendour.' And these by no means comforting prophecies of the removal of the Jews, took their colouring, it is said, from the gloom cast by those vast and restless monarchies of Nineveh and Babylon over the neighbouring states. Now I am quite prepared to grant that very often a lower reference is possible. Many a psalm which speaks of Christ's universal empire begins with a possible allusion to David's wide-spread dominion, or to the calm peace of Solomon's reign. But rapidly it breaks away from this narrow beginning, and uses words which not merely surpass the bounds of Oriental imagery, but would be fearfully impious if applied to any being less than God. So the troubled relations of Jerusalem with the Assyrian monarchy may have made the prophets, on the one hand, forebode Jerusalem's fall, while, on the other, they could not but feel that a nation chosen so specially must have, in spite of present difficulties, a grand future before it. Grant all this—though it is only right to say that Jewish expositors do not grant it; they know nothing about this theory of a second sense of prophecy—but grant it, and what follows? Nothing: nothing, at least, that in the slightest degree invalidates the argument from prophecy. It rather strengthens it. The voices of the prophets are in exact relation to their times; in other words, the history of the Jewish people combines with the express teaching of their holiest men in establishing that wide circle of doctrine which finds in Christ and in Christianity its exact fulfilment. But then, besides, there is a vast mass of teaching in the prophetic books which you cannot thus account for. Even that which does grow out of some fact or circumstance in Jewish history quickly leaves behind it all reference to that present event, and hastens on to 'the latter times.' But much has no such reference, and would have been absolutely without meaning to the prophet's contemporaries, had not they as well as he been trained and habituated to look forward to the times of the Messiah as those in which all the national hopes should be fulfilled.

The Jews, as I said, do not hold this theory of a primary and secondary sense of prophecy. Their Targums and all their early expositors refer a large number of passages peremptorily to king Messiah and to Him only. The rest, in an equally absolute manner, they refer to the prophet's own times. But the Christian view rather is that you cannot thus separate the Bible into two parts, one belonging to Christ, and one having no reference to Him. We affirm that there are many passages which belong to Christ only, which have no reference to contemporaneous history, have nothing to do with anything Jewish, and were not suggested by anything local or temporary, but were opposed to and contradicted all Jewish prejudices and modes of thought. The most evident example of this directly Christian teaching of the prophets is the complete portraiture which they give of a suffering Messiah, and any one acquainted with the Targums and with Jewish expositors is well aware what an utter puzzle this portraiture was and is to them, and how it contradicted and still contradicts all their deepest feelings and their patriotic hopes. They were equally puzzled, too, with that other teaching, that while the Jewish Church was to live on for ever, it was nevertheless to be a Church of the Gentiles. But while we affirm that such ideas as these of a suffering Christ and a Catholic Church were entirely alien to the whole tenour of Jewish thought, we also affirm that much may finally have a real fulfilment in Christ, which has also an equally real reference to something Jewish. It may have begun with man, but it ends with God: it may have begun with some event or person belonging to the preparatory church; but it moves onward, and rises to a fuller and nobler—yes, and a truer meaning. Psalms occasioned by some temporary occurrence, prayers bursting from hearts overcharged with emotions arising from present mercies, narratives and persons in strictest harmony with their times, yet leave constantly those times far behind, and suggest thoughts of Christ, and shed light upon His office and work for us. If this occurred once only, or twice, or ten times, you might say it was chance work. If it were mere spiritualizing, a forced and far-fetched interpretation, it would not have any argumentative force, however capable it might be of adaptation to pious uses. But the interpretation is natural, obvious, plain. It is so general a rule in all the prophetic books, that you do not get rid of its force by hunting up with petty minuteness some present occurrence to which the declarations of the prophets may in some few cases, here and there, possibly refer.

For, after all, it is not on separate passages that we depend for our proof, so much as on the manner in which the whole Bible prepares for and teaches Christ. The whole atmosphere of the Old Testament is instinct with prophecy; Judaism from first to last is a progress towards the Gospel. You have, I grant, many very remarkable predictions which came exactly true: this is something—a great thing. Still, far more weighty is the fact that these express predictions are but the highest summits as it were of a whole region rising up everywhere to Christ. The facts and persons of the Old Testament typify Him: the Mosaic law and the ritual of the temple teach us the nature and efficacy of His work for us and in us; its psalms, and prayers, and songs of rejoicing speak not merely of present blessings, but of a coming Saviour: while the thoughts of the prophets ever dwell among those 'latter times,' when the work of Israel is done, and God's new covenant bestowed upon mankind. All the institutions of Judaism, the whole state of things which it sets before us, as well as the express teaching of its sacred books, look forward to and converge in Jesus of Nazareth. Eighteen centuries have passed since Jesus of Nazareth came, and Christians still, as they read the Old Testament, find there the same truths as in the New. We read it without note or comment, and without an effort it tells us of Christ's offices, and Christ's work. We need not ask, Of whom speaketh the prophet this? With calm, clear, powerful voice it sets before us the Man of Sorrows, Who died that we might live. You say this is fanaticism; but fanaticism never reasons. It never compares truths with one another, nor can it stand the test of enquiry and cool reflection. But it is to our reason that this argument, drawn from the unity of the two Testaments, appeals, and men, as they compare them, cannot but see that they do hold a definite relation to one another. Necessarily imperfect, veiled, reserved, the Old Testament yet leads up directly to the New, and forms a connected whole with it. It does fit exactly into its place, and that in a large grand way of which no minute criticism can lessen the force.

Still, as St. Peter reminds us, Christianity does not owe its light to Judaism, nor was either Judaism or Christianity the effect of the external state of things by which they were surrounded. I have shown that there was nothing in the state of Israel when it left Egypt to account for Moses, nothing in the time of the Judges to account for Samuel. It would be labour thrown away to show that there was nothing in the state of things under the kings of Judah and Israel to account for the pure, spiritual teaching of the prophets. As St. Peter says, 'the prophetical word was a lamp shining in a squalid place,' while Christianity is the day-light, and the morning star (2 Pet. i. 19).'

The one is a small light, the other a great and glorious light, but the place was but αὐχμηρὸς τόπος. But both lights infinitely excel the mental and moral condition of the people by whose instrumentality God gave them. The Jews had many great and noble qualities, but the Bible everywhere describes them as a stubborn and rebellious race. Their history is a disappointing one, with little in it of earthly grandeur and nobility. But there is just one point in which they do excel all nations. They had a true religion, and were God's means for bestowing it upon mankind. But this religion was no product of their own; no national growth. They were not a race naturally philosophic or pious, and their history is the history rather of a continuous resistance to God's purposes. As a rule, they did their very utmost to corrupt religion. There was not one of those spiritual truths taught by the prophets from Moses to Malachi, which they did not do their best to degrade, and from which they would not willingly have escaped. It was the few,—one here and one there,—the few, yet men never wanting in the Jewish Church, by whom God gave mankind His light. As for the mass, they were uncircumcised in heart and ears, and Stephen truly said of them, 'Ye do always resist the Holy Ghost: as your fathers did, so do ye (Acts vii. 51).' They were but a squalid place, yet God deigned to put His light there, and that light was God's express gift, for it was the light, not of natural, but of revealed truth, dim often, yet ever growing in brightness, and pointing onwards to Him Who is the Truth.

Even the few, the men by whose instrumentality God gave mankind the light, were seldom men possessed of great originality, or of what we should call creative minds. Moses in the Old Testament, St. John, St. Stephen, St. Paul in the New, had minds thus powerful, but most of the prophets and apostles were practical men who received truth slowly, and only gradually yielded their assent to new ideas. A vast gulph separates them from our Lord. In Him truth welled up as from an inner fountain, without struggle or effort. Of Him alone could we say, not that He had attained to truth, or spake truth, but that simply He was the Truth.

And truth in Christ St. Peter declares to be no lamp or torch, but sunlight. And like the light of the sun it belongs to all. It is no private property, but Gentiles and Jews alike share in it. It is too large and universal for it to be possible that there can be any exclusive right to its possession. Now if there be anything plainly taught in the prophets, it is, that Judaism was to give place to a catholic, a universal religion. And it taught this in direct opposition to every hope and aspiration of the Jew. The Jew dreamed of successful war, and of the Gentiles trampled ruthlessly under foot; his Messiah was to be a fierce and pitiless zealot, whose sword would be drunk with slaughter. The prophets spake of a suffering Messiah, of a religion of peace and love (Micah iv. 3, 4), of a church which Jews indeed were to found (Ib. 2), and of which they were to be the first teachers, but which would very soon turn against them, and regard them with the bitterest hostility (Jer. xxiv. 9). It is painful constantly to read in the Fathers their rooted and unreasoning antipathy to the Jews, and the aversion remains to this day.

Jeremiah's words have proved true. The Jew is a curse in the mouth of all the nations of the earth (Ib. xxvi. 6).

Now what I wish to point out to-day is, that this grand catholic teaching is no afterthought, but that written prophecy starts at its very beginning with as wide a programme as that of Micah and Isaiah, in the days of its fullest development. The two oldest written prophecies are those of Jonah and Joel. The object of the former of these books is to set before us the nature of prophecy itself, while Joel strikes the key-note of that spiritual teaching which has made the prophets the instructors, not of one age, but of all ages and all peoples. These two books form the proper introduction to the whole series of the prophetic records, but instead of arranging them in chronological order, we have adopted from the Jews a method apparently devised to make it impossible to read our bibles intelligently[b]. The Book of Jonah would never have been regarded as a mere tale, nor its importance missed, if it had held its proper place at the head of the roll. And so of Joel. Ewald[c] has well remarked

---

[b] Though there is comparatively little uncertainty as to the chronological order of the prophetic books, we nevertheless arrange them according to their length, and thus Hosea, the prophet struggling with apostatizing Israel, is put after Daniel, the link between the Jewish and Gentile Churches. The confusion of the New Testament is even worse. Not only are St. Paul's Epistles arranged according to the supposed political importance of the place to which they were addressed, but, contrary to the rule of antiquity and the authority of manuscripts, the Catholic Epistles, with their general teaching, are placed after the specific teaching of St. Paul!

[c] 'Jesaja wäre ohne Joel und andre grosse vorgänger unmöglich gewesen, er schliesst sich an sie, und führt ihr werk in lebendiger fortsetzung weiter.' Ewald, Propheten d. A. B. i. 273.

that Isaiah would have been, morally speaking, an impossibility, had not Joel and other spiritual prophets preceded him, and yet we put Isaiah first, while Joel, whose teaching prepares the way for that of Isaiah, is put into a corner, as if the importance of a prophet depended solely upon the number of chapters which he wrote. So, too, Isaiah's quotation from Micah would have been much more obvious and forcible, if Micah had held his proper place in the canon : while Jeremiah's narrative of the outcry raised against Micah in Jerusalem, and of the effect produced by his prediction upon Hezekiah's mind, and of the national mourning to avert Jehovah's anger, all this and more would have come home to us with double force and fuller meaning, if in the course of our daily readings that narrative had followed instead of preceding the prophecy which led to such remarkable events.

Now what is the nature of the teaching of this Book of Jonah ? The first thing that strikes us is that this, the earliest book of written prophecy, is a narrative of a mission to a Gentile city, which was the sworn foe and enemy of Israel. Jonah did labour for Israel, as we learn in the Book of Kings (2 Kings xiv. 25): but in his written prophecy Israel holds no place. And next it is an errand of mercy. Nineveh repents at his preaching, and is spared. Now the prophets generally have a message for the heathen nations round ; only two or three confine themselves to Israel and Judah. The heathen nations do not lie beyond the pale of God's providence; and thus Nahum's one subject is Nineveh, Habakkuk's is Chaldæa, Obadiah's is Edom. But this is no case merely of sending them a warning, or recording a condemnation of their sins. Jonah has to labour in person among these heathen, and his whole Jewish nature rises up against such a service. He will flee to the ends of the earth rather than so violate his prejudices. His name, Jonah, means a dove; but he cannot brook the thought of carrying the olive-branch to these hateful Assyrians. Nothing short of evident necessity can induce him to obey God's command. So it was with the apostles. Simon Bar-jonah will not go and receive the Roman centurion, Cornelius, into the Church until he has thrice had a command from heaven not to call, in his Jewish way, that common and unclean which the Holy Ghost had sanctified. Had Jonah been quite sure that Nineveh would be destroyed, then he would have nerved himself to obedience. What he could not endure was the feeling that there might be mercy for these ruthless Assyrians. 'This was what I said when I was yet in my country, and therefore I fled before Thee unto Tarshish: for I knew that Thou art a gracious God and merciful, slow to anger, and of great kindness, and repentest Thee of the evil (Jonah iv. 2).'

Jonah knew, then, the nature of prophecy better than most expositors do now, and his book is more remarkable for what it teaches us about prophecy, than even for the fact that he was sent to labour in a Gentile city. The great lesson of the Book of Jonah is, that prophecy is no blind fate, threatening men with an irrevocable destiny, but that it has a moral purpose, and is a warning given by an omniscient but merciful ruler to beings capable of repentance, and of reversing thereby the decrees of justice. In the heathen world you ever find the idea of evil impending upon men without the possibility of escape. This is the one ground-thought of the Greek drama, and the more innocent the sufferer the more tragic and interesting is the onward course of events, by which, through no fault of his own, he is doomed to destruction. This, too, is the one idea of all ancient oracles. Obscurely and in enigma they predict some calamity. The prediction must be so given as that it shall not serve as a warning, but, if possible, rather invite its victim to his fate. In the opening book of prophecy all these detestable views are carefully guarded against. It is no blind fate, but a kind, a merciful, a man-loving God, Who orders all earthly things for man's good, and Who directs the course of history, and guides the very laws of nature so as to make them serve for moral purposes. If there is one lesson clearly taught in the prophetic writings, it is God's longsuffering. It is even startling to find Jeremiah declaring in Jehovah's name to Zedekiah, but a short time before Jerusalem was captured, that if he would even then submit, God would spare him and the city (Jer. xxxviii. 17). Our patience has long been too utterly exhausted with that weak bad man for us to imagine that God's patience is not exhausted too. But His compassions fail not. There is mercy even after the eleventh hour has struck. It is man who obstinately persists in his evil courses. The danger of a death-bed repentance does not consist at all in God not being ready to spare, but in the moral certainty that such as a man has lived, such will he also die.

Now if the Book of Jonah had held its proper place at the beginning of the prophetic writings, men.

could never have confounded prophecy and fatalism. Nothing could be plainer and more express than Jonah's prediction, 'Yet forty days and Nineveh shall be overthrown.' But it was not an absolute decree, but conditional. Repentance could and did reverse it. Now I am not prepared to enter upon the question what God's decrees are, when looked at from above —from God's side. So regarded they are probably absolute, unchanging, inevitable. But the discussion would lead me into the mazes of the controversy how man's free will can coexist with God's omniscience and omnipotence. If you work downwards from definitions of these two divine attributes, it is easy to show that everything must have been predestined from the beginning, and be irrevocably fixed; and if you include the idea of God's absolute immutability, you will get an argument by no means easy to answer in proof that there is no such thing as the world at all, with such disturbing elements in it as sin, and repentance, and prayer, and reward, and punishment. But it is possible to begin at the other end: to begin with man, and this created world around us, and the facts of our own nature and experience: to begin, that is, with what we understand, and not with that which we cannot understand. And thus we find ourselves free, and the Bible speaks of us as free; for it says that we are made in God's own image, and endowed with dominion over nature (Gen. i. 26). But to be like God, and to rule, and yet not be free, is an absurdity. And so, then, I look at prophecy in the same way, from man's side, and as it is set before us in the Bible; and there I find it clearly declared to be conditional. God's dealings with us would not be moral dealings if they were irrevocably decreed, and if human repentance and human prayer availed nothing with Him. If this were so, instead of a personal God, a blind, harsh, cruel, relentless fate would rule man's destinies, and crush him with stony calmness and scientific precision. Thank God, this is not what the Bible sets before us. Jonah's prediction was moral, that is, it had man's good for its object, and was conditional upon the behaviour of the people of Nineveh; and Jonah was sent to declare it to them, not for so unworthy a purpose as that they might know an inevitable future, but that they might repent. If they repented, the whole purpose of the prophet's mission was gained. A prophecy can only be said to have failed when it has wrought no moral effect whatsoever.

For the God in whom we believe is a God of providence, a God who made man free to serve or disobey Him, and who can justly reward and punish because He still governs man by moral means. Fate, destiny, the changeless sequence of nature, the immutability of law, every idea that human actions are governed by an inflexible necessity, all this belongs to heathen, and not to Christian men. A Christian believes in repentance, and it is the very law of repentance that it reverses God's previous decrees. The Scriptural phrase, that 'it repented God,' may be very unphilosophical. Really and truly, as Scripture tells us, God cannot repent. But the phrase teaches us a great truth—a truth without which religion could not exist, namely, that human actions produce a change in the order of Providence, or seem to us to do so; for I am looking at things in the only intelligible way in which men can look at them, namely, as they appear to us and concern us. To frame a constitution for man as a moral agent from *à priori* notions of God's nature, deserves to be set side by side with that other folly, of deciding what creation ought to be from the same sort of views. As certainly as the creation of the world is incompatible with *à priori* notions of God's immutability; as certainly as the existence of sin and sorrow in the world is incompatible with *à priori* notions of God's wisdom and goodness; so certainly is man's moral freedom incompatible with similar notions of God's foreknowledge and omnipotence. That is, it is incompatible with man's *à priori* notions. Of course this is a very sad predicament for those who regard man as the ultimate and perfect measure of all things, and suppose that that which to man *seems to be*, also really *is*. To the Christian it is no difficulty at all. We start with the confession, that now we know only in part (1 Cor. xiii. 12). But it would be well for all to remember, that men cannot really argue from ignorance. Of course I do not mean but that plenty of people as a matter of fact do thus argue, but what I mean is that no legitimate conclusion follows from such arguments. Absolutely we know nothing of God's real nature, such as it is in itself. He has revealed to us what He is towards us, what His attributes are, and what His nature is, relatively to man, and so far as man can understand Him. But who can mount up to the contemplation of the one eternal I AM, such as He is in Himself? No being can rise to any idea higher than that of itself elevated to the utmost degree of such perfection as it is capable of, and purged from all imperfections. It is part of the promised bliss of heaven, that we shall know as we ourselves are known (1 Cor. xiii. 12). For 'when God shall have appeared, we shall be like Him, for we shall see Him as He is (1 John iii. 2).' But even this does not mean that man will ever fully comprehend God, or that our nature will be commensurable with His nature. What it means is, that whereas now we have no other notions of God than those derived from our own nature, hereafter we shall understand somewhat of God's real, heavenly nature, such as it is in itself. And thus we are content to leave many an enigma unsolved (1 Cor. xiii. 12). We know that here we are limited on every side, but we look forward to a better and abiding home, where, in the beatific vision, we shall be freed from the infirmities, physical, mental, and moral, which in this, our trial world, constantly remind us that it cannot be our rest.

Viewed, then, thus from below, we find ourselves living in a world of the conditional, a moral world, as we call it, because human actions in it are influenced by pleasure and pain, reward and punishment. And this is the great lesson of the Book of Jonah. It teaches us that prophecy, like all God's dealings, is for man's good, and not for his destruction. The threatenings of the prophets are no absolute decrees, no predictions of an inevitable necessity, but may be averted by repentance and prayer. As I said before, no prophecy could be more express. The time is fixed, 'Yet forty days.' The event specified, 'Nineveh shall be overthrown.' The people repent, and the city is spared. Jonah, naturally, is very angry. A man's one-self is of much more importance to him than six hundred thousand other people, and better they perish than Jonah's word fail of a literal accomplishment. But by his sorrow over the gourd God makes him condemn himself, and shows him the wickedness of his conduct.

And this most important lesson certainly did not grow out of anything either in the feelings or in the history of the Jews themselves. In opposition to that narrow and concentrated patriotism which so marked the whole nation, and of which we see plain proofs in Jonah's flight and refusal to carry to heathens a call to repentance, and his desire that repentant Nineveh might still perish; in opposition to all this he is made the instrument of teaching that prophecy is for man's good, and that its errand of mercy is not confined to the Jewish Church, but embraces within it all mankind. So St. Paul declared that this was the one object of any threatenings of evil in his own writings: 'Knowing the terror of the Lord we persuade men (2 Cor. v. 11).' But persuasion is impossible where there is no hope. No state is so dangerous as that of the man who gives himself up for lost. But there is no trace of this detestable fatalism in either the Old Testament or the New. It is a message of mercy from first to last, and warns man of his dangers only that he may be moved to escape from them. And how is he to escape from them? It is by prayer and repentance. It is prayer which 'brings up Jonah's life from corruption;' it is repentance which saves Nineveh. Not even in the Gospel itself is the efficacy of prayer and repentance more plainly set forth.

But in the Gospel you learn why prayer and repentance avail. The time had not come in Jonah's days for the full revelation of the manner in which God saves us. Yet, as our Lord Himself teaches us (Matt. xii. 40), there is in Jonah the sign of that death and resurrection whereby we can die to sin and rise again to a renewed life. It was a sign not understood at the time, nor intended to be understood. Even when our Lord referred to it, none probably could tell what His words exactly meant. It required other teaching to explain it. But when Christ had risen from the dead, then the full significance of the sign became plain. And thus, then, in the earliest written prophecy[d],—for we may, I think, accept the date given by Mr. Drake, namely B. C. 840, in the reign of Adrammelech II, as the most probable;—in this earliest prophetic record we are taught, first, what is the nature of all prophecy, namely, that it is conditional, for man's good, to move him to godly sorrow,

---

[d] Supposing, however, that the Book of Jonah were a mere tale, a fiction, as the neologists assert, you then, without losing any of the force of its teaching, have a problem to solve more difficult than ever. Of course the Book of Jonah must be put at a much later date, because on neologian principles it was the fall of Nineveh which suggested it; and yet the purity of its style, which nevertheless has something very personal and individual about it, will not let it fit in well even with the Chaldaic period. Supposing, however, that with Ewald (Proph. d. A. B. iii. 237) you assert that it belongs to the end of the sixth century before the Christian era, how do you account for the teaching of the book? Who was the wonderful man who entertained this view of prophecy so much in advance of even Christian commentators? Whence came his enlarged views towards the Gentiles? his conviction that God cared for them? I can find no era in Jewish history when such views would have had a hearing, or any book containing them have been admitted into the canon except upon the conviction that the writer was a prophet. It was the popular view of prophecy that its business was to curse the Gentiles and bless the Jews. They would have trampled the Book of Jonah under foot unless its external authority had been irresistible.

and no disclosure of destiny, but a warning of the necessary consequences of sin unless averted by repentance: secondly, we find a type of the central facts of Christianity, Christ's death and resurrection: and lastly, we have a foreshowing of the call of the Gentiles, and of their acceptance of the call. Surely such a prophecy was a fit preface and introduction to the whole prophetic canon; for it gives the outline and measure of that which succeeding prophets did but fill up and complete. It is Jewish, and yet it transcends all Jewish ideas and notions, contradicts their prejudices, and sets before them a nobler mission than any they ever contemplated, even that of being the messengers of love to mankind. There is a tenderness too in it, a purpose of healing the ills of all mankind, which even the apostles with difficulty realized. It needed the call of Paul, the Roman citizen, the Hellenist trained at the Greek university of Tarsus, the inhabitant of trading Antioch, before even the Christian Church could throw itself heartily into the work of bearing the Gospel of love to all the Ninevehs, the fierce, debased, heathen cities of a world lying in darkness and estranged from God.

And next in the list comes Joel; and his teaching, too, is spiritual, and not Jewish so much as catholic, with a lesson for all mankind. The occasion of his prophecy was a two-fold national calamity; the first a general drought, the second and more terrible the appearance year after year of vast armies of locusts, whose ravages are described with wonderful force, and also with the greatest truth and most exact agreement with nature. Many commentators have supposed that the description of the locusts is symbolical, but a passage in Amos iv. 9 shows that the land was really desolated by these insects, and it is far more probable that the misery caused by the wasting of their crops was what moved the prophet to urge the people to repentance, than that he introduced these details as mere poetical colouring for his exhortations. When we bear in mind that, in spite of the help given them from this country, one fourth part of the people of Ireland died from the failure for one year of a single article of food, we may to some extent form an estimate of the distress occasioned by successive years of famine. No wonder that 'joy had withered away from the sons of men (i. 12),' and that not only had they parted with their silver and gold to the Sidonians and Philistines to purchase corn, but had even sold their children to the Greeks (iii. 4–6), thinking slavery better for them than death, or lost, it may be, to all feelings of natural affection from the greatness of their despair. Finally, so utter was the famine, that the meat-offering and drink-offering, and probably all the sacrifices of the temple, had to be discontinued for want of means (i. 9).

In this extremity of grief Joel summons them to a solemn fast. All the people must gather together, the priests and the ministers of the altar, the elders and the inhabitants of the land: they must assemble at God's house with fasting, with weeping, and with mourning; but withal he warns them that it must be a rending of the heart and not of the garments (ii. 13); it must be a true, real, earnest, heartfelt repentance. If so they return to God, He will withdraw from them His chastisements. The early and latter rain shall come in abundance, and the fertility of the land in future seasons shall amply compensate them for their lost treasures. 'I will restore to you the years that the locust hath eaten (ii. 25).'

Thus far, then, we have the simple but grand lesson of God's Providence. As the Book of Jonah had taught that prophecy is given for a moral purpose, so the Book of Joel teaches that God's dealings with man in nature have also their moral lessons. The God of nature is also the God of grace. He may speak more plainly to us in His holy word than He does in the world around us, but the lessons taught are the same. And men try to escape from them however they are taught. Man prefers to be alone in the world—he will not brook the presence of any active intelligent power higher than himself; and thus he will see in nature only the endless procession of cause and effect moving on coldly, senselessly, purposely, in obedience to fixed laws, which laws have either no lawgiver, or one who must not watch over, or control, or influence them. Christians believe that the so-called laws of nature mean only the presence of God's almighty will, and that they are so even, perfect, apparently changeless because His will is calm, perfect, unchangeable. But they believe that from the beginning God so ordered these laws as that they should minister to man's probation, and to the individual good of all who love Him (Rom. viii. 28). And thus Joel's lesson is, that under all the dealings of God's providence there lies a moral purpose. That this is so may not be capable of proof by inductive reasoning, but it is taught us by the faculties of our soul, proved to us by the facts and experience of our daily life, acknowledged by us in every act of prayer, grasped firmly by our spiritual instincts. The belief in Providence is the belief in God's active presence in the world. Without this belief, what a mockery life would be! What a blank atheism would lie before us as the alternative! And as regards any other world, if God be present here only as a power inherent in laws which move darkly forward without any intelligent or moral purpose, how can we dare hope that we shall find Him an intelligent or moral governor in any other world, whether existing now elsewhere, or yet to come into being?

But from the lesson of Providence Joel draws other lessons. If the events of our lives, and whatever happens in the world around us; if chastisement and mercy, joy and sorrow, are all intended to move man to repentance, and wean him from sin, and win him to God, what follows upon this? Why should men repent? And is repentance perfect in itself, or a condition for something better? The answer is, that upon repentance follows God's gift of grace. 'I will pour out My Spirit upon all flesh; yea, even upon slaves and maidservants in those days will I pour out My Spirit (ii. 28, 29).' Repentance has its own happiness, and this Joel has described as the restoration of that which we had lost. But to those who have God gives more; and thus His people, freed from the curse of sin, move onward to higher privileges. Repentance opens, as it were, the door by which we may enter upon the spiritual life. And so, eight hundred years afterwards, John the Baptist preached again Joel's sermon, but in a new form. He preached first of all 'the baptism of repentance for the remission of sins (Mark i. 4);' that was a mere preparatory stage. His other words were, 'He that cometh after me is mightier than I: He shall baptize you with the Holy Ghost, and fire (Matt. iii. 11).'

Now this is a universal truth belonging to all times, and to every individual man. It matters not when, or who; there is but one entrance to the Christian life, and that is repentance. He who lives in sin unrepented of is no Christian. Yet Joel connects this truth with one special time, concerning which however he knew only that it was the time of the Messiah. He speaks indefinitely; 'It shall come to pass *afterward*.' And again, '*In those days* will I pour out My Spirit.' St. Peter tells us (1 Pet. i. 10) that the prophets laboured diligently to find out more exactly when these times should be; but, excepting to Daniel, only signs of them were given whereby not the prophets themselves, but men subsequently might be able to recognize them when they came. So our Lord Himself gave only signs of that dread coming of the Son of Man in the destruction of the Jewish Church and commonwealth, which that very generation was to witness. Its exact date He declared was no proper subject for revelation; for if times and seasons were made known to us, probation would be rendered impossible. And thus the prophets necessarily spake indefinitely, and their words must often have been an enigma to themselves and to their contemporaries. Yet even the men of those times were taught a valuable though general lesson. Jonah taught them the wideness of God's mercy, and the efficacy of prayer. Joel taught them the present blessedness of repentance, and that it is the indispensable condition for receiving still higher gifts.

And if these early writings had deeper, fuller teaching stored up for the use of future times, is not this exactly what we should expect of revelation? If the Bible is God's word, must it not speak to men throughout all ages? It is a thought difficult to realize, that God's word must be so constructed as to speak with living power to men at all times, of all nations, in all stages alike of civilization and barbarism, of learning and ignorance, of progress and of decay. Till our Lord came the word of God was growing, but in Him revelation became complete, and its record ends with a curse upon the man who shall add to or detract aught from the words of the Book of Life. But, complete as it is, must it not have lessons for the future as well as for the present and past? Would not the Bible soon grow stale and obsolete if there were no deep meanings wrapped up in it which only the course of time can unfold? Surely it is this fulness of meaning which makes each generation turn to it for the solution of the problems of its own days. It has been well said [e], that the Church never understood St. Paul's Epistles till the era of the Reformation; and even then it was one vital doctrine rather than the whole of St. Paul's teaching that attained to its true importance. We seem once again in danger of losing that insight into his marvellous teaching which then so stirred all the more intellectual minds in the Church. But those very minds failed to realize the value of St. James' teaching, which to us seems so absolutely necessary in order to complete the true portraiture of faith. The

---

[e] Hofmann, Weissagung u. Erfüllung, i. 46.

time, perhaps, is fast coming when the Revelation of St. John, excluded no longer from our services, may speak with trumpet tongue to us, and the messages of our Lord to the seven churches may be seen to be a clear, plain message to churches now. And may I not ask, Is not the Old Testament a sealed book to most of us now? 'The Jews misuse it: Christians know not how to use it [f].' The study of Hebrew has been so neglected that while to one here and there it is not destitute of meaning, to the mass it teaches but little. But when the time comes described by St. Paul in Rom. xi., the Old Testament may once again speak with living force, and be the means of welding Jew and Gentile into a Church whose vast proportions and firm hold of evangelical truth may far surpass everything that exists now.

For mark how even an apostle could fall short of the full significance of the words of God. St. Peter, at Pentecost, quoted Joel's prophecy (Acts ii. 16-21). It was the day on which the prophecy was fulfilled. And Joel evidently was much studied by the apostles, for they quote him continually. But though Peter repeated the words, 'I will pour out My Spirit upon all flesh,' it needed an express revelation and direct command before he could be persuaded that all flesh meant more than Jewish flesh. When the Holy Ghost was poured out upon Cornelius, Peter and they of the circumcision were astonished beyond measure, and though he submitted to what he felt to be God's will, yet his affections remained concentrated upon his own people. Not that

[f] Hofmann, as above.

there was any doubt that 'all flesh' meant all mankind. Peter would never have argued that the phrase either had or could have any other meaning. But that meaning had never presented itself definitely before his mind. So, often all our lives through, we have words in our mouths, and read and hear them, and yet their true, full meaning never strikes us. The truth is familiar to us, it is daily confessed and repeated by rote, but has never reached our hearts; then perhaps at length something wakens us up, and henceforward the truth is a living reality, influencing and moulding our lives; or, it may be, we die, and have never understood it. So, at the day of Pentecost, half Joel's words suddenly came home to Peter's mind. With joy he witnessed servants and handmaids inspired with God's Holy Spirit; but all his life long he gave but an unwilling assent to the other half, that Gentiles should henceforward share the gift of the Spirit as freely as Jews.

But if Joel had stopped even here, could we have said that he and Jonah between them sketched out the full outline of Christian truth? God's presence in the world, supernaturally in Revelation, naturally in Providence, the sign of a Saviour's death and resurrection, the efficacy of repentance and prayer, the outpouring of the Holy Ghost, this is much, but is it all? They were no sorry teachers who taught this; but what of man? Supposing that he chooses to stand outside of this, and lets things take their course, and leads merely a natural life, virtuous, because virtue makes life happy, but content with virtue and its present reward,—what then? Why should he not? Why should not nature be enough? and man's highest aim be to live according to nature? To this question Joel gives the answer. He it is who first spake of a general judgment. Now this is a truth which gives vitality to every part of religion. Without it man's duties and hopes would begin and end with this world. But the life according to nature is not enough if we have to give an account hereafter of our actions. Nature gives us neither knowledge enough of the principles upon which our conduct will be judged, nor help enough to enable us to conform our actions to the Judge's will. If there be a judgment, then there is another life following upon our few years here. Nature is but a poor guide even for this mortal life. For the life to come her guidance is absolutely naught.

Now it was Joel who first placed personal religion upon a settled basis by teaching men the doctrine of a general judgment. The Church, whether the Jewish of old or the Christian now, is the outer organization in which God's dispensation of grace is embodied, and it is grace alone that will suffice for the judgment day. At the very root of all, before we can believe in anything supernatural, in divine gifts of any kind, or even in a God, we must believe in the immortality of the soul, and in its responsibility to its Maker. To believe in God, without believing in any relation between God and man, is to believe in something so remote and abstract that at most it is a speculation and not a belief. Now I am quite ready to grant that it was very slowly that the doctrine of a general judgment attained to its due proportions. Its full proportions indeed it never did attain to till Christ came. He it was who brought to the light the eternal life of heaven, and the immortality of the soul (2 Tim. i. 10). Until these were understood men could have had but a faint notion of the meaning of words such as these, 'Multitudes, multitudes in the valley of decision: for the day of the Lord is near in the valley of decision (Joel iii. 14);' or of what was meant by those metaphors under which he described the whole world as ripening for judgment. But there, in Joel, the truth stood revealed, and in due time its full importance was seen (Dan. xii. 2, 3). And no sooner had the Incarnate Word come than an apostle could describe it as an elementary part of religion, that men must believe not only in the existence of a God, but that God rewards and punishes human actions (Heb. xi. 6). Surely this is an extraordinary phenomenon. In the words of Dr. Pusey [g], 'To this unknown prophet Joel, of whose history, condition, rank, parentage, birthplace, nothing is known, nothing beyond his name, save the name of an unknown father; of whom moreover God has allowed nothing to remain save these few chapters; to him God reserved the prerogative to be the first to declare the outpouring of the Holy Ghost upon all flesh, the perpetual abiding of the Church, the final struggle of good and evil, the last rebellion against God, and the day of judgment. "The day of the Lord, the great and terrible day," the belief in which now forms part of the faith of all Jews and Christians, was a title first revealed to this unknown prophet.' And again, 'To Joel it was first foreshown that the Gentiles too should be filled with the Spirit of God.

[g] Introduction to the Book of Joel.

To him was first declared that great paradox or mystery of faith, which after his time prophet after prophet insisted upon, that while deliverance should be in Mount Sion, and the stream of God's grace should issue to the barren world from the temple of the Lord, those in her who should be delivered should be a remnant only.'

Now these doctrines which Joel taught form an inseparable whole. The doctrine of a future judgment would crush man with insupportable terrors, were not repentance possible. But what would repentance avail, if we sorrowed for sin only to return to it again? It is God's gift of the Holy Spirit which makes repentance the starting-point of a renewed life; which makes it possible for a man 'born from above of water and the Holy Ghost' to live henceforward unto holiness. And this again deepens our responsibility towards our Judge. If no grace were offered us, if a renewed life were impossible, if the natural life were all that we could attain to, in hatred and bitterness we should defy the terrors of a day which offered us nothing but despair. As it is, we have only to use our privileges aright, and that day will be to us a day of mercy and blessedness.

I will only add to-day that Hosea completes by his one most touching lesson the great truths taught by Jonah and Joel. His prophecy is one long wail of sorrow over the impenitent; we may even truly say that it is God's lamentation; for God constantly speaks in it in His own person. If any perish it is not because God's love fails. Israel was not rejected from the covenant until after long warnings;

nor until God had exhausted every possible means for its recovery. And when it hardened itself against all God's love, even then its rejection was thus tenderly bemoaned. Can man's final ruin be less a grief in heaven than was Israel's earthly abandonment? We may be sure it cannot. Of the manner of God's dealings with the heathen, with those whom the preaching of the Gospel has never reached, with those born and brought up under such circumstances that a life of sin seems inevitable; how God will deal with such cases we have no means of knowing. Here, as elsewhere, it is a note of revelation that it tells us nothing to gratify a foolish curiosity. It tells us only how we may be saved or lost ourselves. Even where our Lord declares that God's judgment will be just, and our stripes be according to our knowledge, He was speaking of the servants only (Luke xii. 47, 48). But God's yearning love even for the impenitent, as proved by the words of Hosea, plainly teaches us that as God must necessarily be just in all His dealings, so will He also be merciful and good. But if we, the servants, members of God's house, and sharers of His covenant, if we reject all God's love, then equally does Hosea warn us that our final doom is certain. Israel was rejected. God's goodness did not, could not, save the impenitent. And so with us: God's longsuffering, His repeated calls to repentance, the ever renewed struggle of His Holy Spirit with us; all this leaves us without excuse. We are living in the clear light: if we love darkness, what plea can avail us at the last day?

It was the office, then, of these, the three earliest

prophets, to declare general truths. They do give utterance to prophecies of Christ, but they are faint, and couched in symbolical terms; not express, full, exact, particular, like those of the later prophets. But the great outlines of truth, the doctrines which were to be the special distinction of Christianity, and the nature of the Christian Church, these it was their business to teach, and they do teach them fully and exactly; as fully and exactly as their successors teach the great truths which relate to Christ's office and person. The method of prophecy is a strictly scientific one. It begins with general doctrines and catholic truths, and gradually it moves onward to particular and specific truths. The later prophets do not so much develope as fill up the outlines of the Gospel which the early prophets sketched in full, large, and grand proportions. Together they combine in setting before us the perfect lineaments of the truth.

LECTURE VII.

SPECIFIC PROPHECIES OF CHRIST IN HOSEA, AMOS, ISAIAH, AND MICAH.

To Him give all the prophets witness, that through His Name whosoever believeth in Him shall receive remission of sins.—ACTS x. 43.

I MENTIONED in my last lecture that the earliest written prophecies were occupied with the great doctrines of Christianity, while it is the office of the later prophets to set Him before us in Whom these doctrines became the vital principles of the Church. And this is a method that commends itself to our reason. For many ages under the Jewish dispensation men felt no need of anything more than Moses had given them. Their state mentally and morally was such as to make them content with the possession of the land of promise, and with the general knowledge that Jehovah—their covenant God—was a God of love and mercy, in Whom there was pardon for sin upon repentance. But when at length they found, as all men find, that no earthly good can fill man's heart, and that there is ever a craving for something more perfect: when the sin-struck conscience found sacrifice and offering insufficient, and sought for some more efficacious remedy (Ps. li. 17): when the instinctive longings of our nature for a nearer approach to God made the

Israelites impatient of those types and shadows of better things, and that mere outer court of truth into which the law of Moses had admitted them, it was fitting that they should first be taught those eternal and catholic truths, which are the very ground-work of religion, and which a man must believe before he can come to God (Heb. xi. 6). Upon this in due time would follow the particulars and details of the plan of salvation. But these details would have been meaningless had not man first been taught general truths which explained to him his needs, made him understand the meaning of his own emotions, and revealed to him the relation in which he stands to God, and what are God's purposes towards him. Thus taught, he would study with growing interest every detail of the means whereby his restoration was to be accomplished, and the breach, caused by sin, between God and man made whole [a].

[a] No doubt in this there is a great mystery. To many it is a thing not easy to understand why a preparation should have been necessary. They argue that man might have been so created, as that all should have been exactly equal, with the same advantages, the same difficulties, and the same probation to undergo. As a matter of fact this is not the case. Men differ not only in their outward circumstances, but in their inner selves: and that not only in things intellectual, but in things moral. Not only is the lot of a heathen entirely different from that of a Christian, but the probation of the inhabitants of a Christian country differs immensely according to the place where they live, the character of their parents, the nature of their education, of their calling in life, and so on. But all that this means is simply that the law of life is progress. Without progress this would be but a poor world, and it is the hope of progress which nerves to their work statesmen and moralists, and all who hope in any way to benefit mankind. Progress, then, is God's law, not only in the Old Testament, but in the New, for the Church (Matt. xiii. 31-33), and for each individual Christian (Ib. 12). In old time it was the office of the prophets to

If the writings of the prophets seem wanting to us in method, it is simply because we arrange them according to their length, or what we are pleased to consider their comparative importance, and not according to their chronological sequence. If we study them in the order in which God gave them, we shall find that they began with large and general ideas, and that the early prophets having thus laid a sure foundation, others built thereupon the exact and finished edifice of truth. If I have succeeded at all in my object, I shall have shown in these Lectures that the prophets formed a large and organized community, thoroughly conversant with one another's writings, trained up in the study of them, anxiously searching out their meaning, comparing statement with statement, and, as St. Peter says, slowly tracking out—ἐρευνῶντες—both the time and the nature of that salvation of which the Spirit of Christ that was in them did testify beforehand (1 Pet. i. 10, 11). I doubt not that many a later prophecy was the result of patient and prayerful study of what had been already revealed; and hence the constant reference and allusion made by each succeeding prophet to the writings of those who had preceded him.

And thus, though the Jews as a nation would not hear of such a thing, it was the unanimous teaching of the prophets that Judaism was to give place to something better and more perfect. If Jonah teaches

---

labour for human progress, it is now especially the office of the Church. Within her the highest possible probation is offered mankind. It is her duty to labour that this probation may become possible for millions now living in the darkness of heathenism, and more perfect and more easy for those within her fold.

this truth in a general way, it is Isaiah who describes the nature of that universal Church which was to take its place, and Jeremiah (xxxi. 31-34) and Ezekiel (xxxvi. 26, 27) who show that its sanctions are to be spiritual, that religion in it is not to consist of ceremony and ritual, but of God's law written in men's hearts, of sin forgiven, and of iniquity remembered no more. But neither they nor Isaiah more clearly taught the spiritual nature of religion than Joel did. Isaiah's office was to add to Joel's teaching more distinct ideas of Christ's work for man.

For, as we have seen, Joel taught the presence of God in Providence, the restorative power of repentance, the gift of the Holy Ghost to repentant men, and, as a necessary consequence, the certainty of a general judgment. Now we are expressly taught in the New Testament that two of these doctrines are absolutely essential even to the very lowest form of religion. Any one that cometh to God must believe that there is a God, and that God rewards and punishes. But certainly by the existence of a God is not meant here the existence of a power merely to keep the dull machinery of material laws in motion, and who must not venture to exercise any act of volition. Such a Deity neither could nor would reward or punish: for material laws perpetually confound the innocent with the guilty, and involve both in one common fate. It must mean a God Who practically concerns Himself with man, Who has subjected him to a state of probation for some moral purpose, Who by His providence leads him on to repentance, Who will accept that repentance, will after repentance give him all necessary aid for living a holy life, and Who therefore can and will reward and punish justly, because man has a real choice between God's service and disobedience to Him. And thus, then, the teaching of the New Testament, in this most important and fundamental passage (Heb. xi. 6), exactly agrees with that of Joel. If there were no restorative power in repentance, if no aid were granted man in leading the life of faith, there would be no possibility of God rewarding any, and punishment would not be just where the condemnation of all alike was inevitable.

Still it was very slowly that the prophets unfolded what seems to us a necessary result of such teaching; namely, that there must be a world to come, and that the soul can not perish at death, but lives onward, to bear the consequences there of what it has been here. Fully revealed this doctrine never was till Christ came. For He it was Who, in St. Paul's words (2 Tim. i. 10), made death a nullity by the clear light cast in the Gospel upon the doctrines of eternal life and of the incorruptibility of the risen body. It was the privilege of Daniel, who in so many respects stands apart from the rest of the prophets, to declare this elementary truth in words as clear as any in the Gospel itself. 'Multitudes that sleep in the dust of the earth shall awake, these to everlasting life, and those to shame and everlasting contempt. And they that be wise shall shine as the brightness of the firmament; and they that turn many to righteousness as the stars for ever and ever (Dan. xii. 2, 3).' The meaning of words such as these none could mistake, but many, I doubt not, pondered long and anxiously over the language used by Joel, and wondered what it might mean. Now it is not enough to say, that there—in Joel's words—was the truth waiting only for the fulness of time to attain to its full proportions: taught clearly, if not clearly understood: and in due season to become an elementary part of the Christian religion, and a fundamental tenet without which we cannot see how religion could exist at all. This is true, but not enough. The prophets spake to their own times as well as to us : and what they said was intended to be carefully studied and examined by their contemporaries. It was so studied, and its meaning was ever more and more fully understood. Men's hearts mused upon their teachings, and looked eagerly forward to the time when, instead of this lantern light, the Sun of Righteousness should Himself arise to illuminate the dark region of this world (2 Pet. i. 19). But neither one nor the other was any light of nature, or product of human wisdom ; for, as St. Peter tells us, ' Prophecy was never brought by the will of man, but men carried along by the Holy Ghost spake of God (Ib. 21 according to the Vatican codex).'

Time will not permit me to show the continuity of the teaching of the prophets step by step. I can only illustrate it by touching very briefly upon some of the more salient points. I shall notice then as regards Hosea and Amos, the prophets next in order, only this fact, that they are the first who connect the promise of the Messiah with the lineage of David, and that in a very remarkable way. You have in the Psalms an anticipation of the eternal duration of David's throne (Ps. lxxxix. 3, 4), and of a priesthood to be connected with it for evermore (Ib. cx. 4) ; but in the mouth of these two prophets those sure mercies of David, which subsequently became the especial subject of Isaiah's prophecy, are first spiritualized and separated from the thought of an earthly kingdom. Hosea's prophecy is one long outpouring of the divine sorrow over the ruin of the ten tribes; and I have already pointed out the remarkable fact that throughout it is God Who in His own person thus shows the tenderness of His love. And this is Hosea's main lesson,—the lesson which John taught so affectionately afterwards,—that God is love. He utters, however, one very remarkable prediction. 'The children of Israel shall abide many days without a king, and without a prince, and without a sacrifice,' and yet free from all stain of idolatry: for there shall be in them 'neither statue of Baal, nor ephod, nor teraphim.' It is an exact prophecy of the state of Israel at the present moment. They have no civil government, and no temple or altar; but neither are they guilty of any form or kind of idolatry. And this is to be their state for many days. How long it shall last is known to Him Who has kept times and seasons in His own hands. But it will not last for ever. 'Afterwards shall the children of Israel return, and shall seek Jehovah their God, and David their king; and shall fear Jehovah and His goodness in the latter days (Hos. iii. 4, 5).'

Now Hosea was an Israelite, and was preaching to the ten tribes. Ephraim, as the head of the great house of Joseph, to whom belonged Reuben's forfeited birthright (1 Chron. v. 1, 2), had never looked upon the lineage of David in any other light than as usurpers who had taken from it its own property. Isaiah thus speaks of the *envy* of Ephraim towards

Judah. Plainly it regarded, as did by far the larger proportion of the tribes, the rising of the Ephraimite Jeroboam as a successful attempt to restore to the house of Joseph that supremacy in Israel which it had ever claimed, and which had generally been readily accorded. Naturally, then, we ask, Had the lineage of David already become among the prophets the symbol of those mercies which in older time had been connected with Abraham, in whose seed all the kingdoms of the earth were to be blessed? Certainly the Israelites would have felt neither pleasure nor pride in the exaltation of David's earthly lineage. It would simply have meant the failure of their own claims to supremacy—claims persistently made during many previous centuries (Jud. viii. 1, xii. 1)—claims subsequently inherited by the Samaritans, and of which we hear the last echo in the discourse of the woman of Samaria with our Lord. The Israelites, then, would only have been irritated by the natural sense of the words. Anyhow the prophecy was painful enough, that, after the loss for long ages of their national independence and national religion, their restoration was to be connected with the object of their envy—Judah. The words, then, must already have become the symbol of spiritual mercies; mercies too large to leave room for envy or national rivalry. And certainly the Jews so understood them. The Targum of Jonathan paraphrases them as follows, 'Afterwards the children of Israel shall repent, and shall enquire for the worship of Jehovah their God, and shall obey Messiah the son of David their king, and shall come in troops to the worship of Jehovah, and great shall be their happiness at the end of days.'

This is plain enough, and it is remarkable that the Targum should describe their worship, even when free from idolatry, as no true worship of Jehovah, till they obey Messiah their king. But Amos is even more explicit. He speaks of a time when 'the house of Israel shall have been tossed about among all nations like as corn is tossed in a sieve,' and yet with so extraordinary a providence watching over it that not the least grain of it, or, more correctly, not even the least stone or bit of gravel that has got into the sieve, in spite of all the tossing, shall fall to the ground. And then there is a time of punishment: 'All the sinners of My people shall die by the sword.' But this is followed by Israel's restoration: 'In that day will I raise up the fallen booth of David, and will wall up their breaches, and restore its ruins; and I will build it as in the days of old: that they may inherit the remnant of Edom, and of all the Gentiles, on whom My name is called, saith Jehovah the doer of this (Amos ix. 9-12).' Now Amos wrote when the house of David had not fallen; the king in his days was Uzziah, who reigned for fifty-two years in great prosperity. Yet Amos calls the royal lineage a booth merely, a contemptuous word, says Gesenius, applicable to a small ruined cottage. Now the mission of Amos, like that of Hosea, was to the ten tribes. Why should he thus describe the royal house of Judah? What comfort would it be to the Israelites to know that the ruling lineage of a neighbouring state, which had not yet fallen, should fall, and be restored again? He represents Israel also as tossed in a sieve, and scattered among the Gentiles. To leave no doubt of his meaning, he says soon afterwards, 'I will bring

again the captivity of My people Israel (Ib. ix. 14).'
Now Amos wrote in the days of Jeroboam II, the
era of Israel's greatest prosperity, when under their
warrior-king they had pushed their conquests north-
ward as far as Hamath, and eastward as far as the
Dead Sea (2 Kings xiv. 25). What scattering, what
captivity would Israel fear then? Fifty years pass
by, and all outward things are changed. The tide
of war has rolled over these lands, and Israel has
fallen. The words of Hosea and Amos have been
in part fulfilled. Israel has no king, but has gone into
captivity. And what of Judah? The army of Assyria
is advancing upon Jerusalem as an easy prey, but it
is to have an extraordinary deliverance, and Isaiah is
commissioned to announce that the pride of Sennacherib shall fall by a sudden and heaven-sent overthrow. In terse and vigorous language he sets before
us that warrior's onward march; describes the rapidity
with which town after town is captured; shows the
terror of the inhabitants, and their flight in hopeless
confusion. And now the conqueror has reached the
capital; Jerusalem is in sight, and, secure of victory,
he shakes his hand in his pride against the mount of
the daughter of Zion, the hill of Jerusalem. Suddenly
he falls by the hand of God, and not of man. 'Behold,
the Lord Jehovah of hosts lops the boughs with terror:
the tall trees are cut down, the lofty trees are felled.
He cuts down the thickets with the axe, and Lebanon
falls by the hand of the Mighty One.' And what
follows without pause or break upon this description
of Jehovah hewing down the army of Sennacherib?
'There shall come forth a sprout from the cut-down

trunk of Jesse, and a sucker shall bud forth from among his roots (Is. x. 33, xi. 1).'

Now it was not very complimentary to Hezekiah, just after Isaiah had been describing Sennacherib's army as a glorious Lebanon felled by God's own hand, for him to speak of David's royal lineage as a dead stump, out of which there springs one poor sucker. Nay, he passes by David. It is no longer a royal lineage, but the lineage of the farmer of Bethlehem. If the prophecies were mere poetry, or if they grew out of the present circumstances of their times, then Hosea, Amos, and Isaiah, wrote what was perfectly inexplicable. The reasonable thing for Isaiah to have done would have been to wind up his prophecy with a few words of encouragement for Hezekiah, some delicate praise of his well-meant reforms, and a timely hint that the services of the prophets might be well repaid by a little seasonable liberality. Isaiah might then have done as well by his prophecy as Virgil by his lines upon Marcellus, which made him a rich man. But he stoops to nothing of the sort. The prophets never turn aside from the path of truth to flatter any man. Nor is this all. In each of the three cases the prophecy of the restoration of David's ruined house comes in so abruptly, and Hosea places it at so distant a time—after Israel has been many days without a king—that I can see but one explanation which satisfactorily accounts for such teaching. They could not have thus spoken had it not been clearly revealed to the prophets, and become a settled truth among them, and one regularly taught in the prophetic schools, that the Messiah was not to come

till after the house of David had fallen into obscurity.
A long period was to separate the earthly splendours
of David's temporal sovereignty from the spiritual
glories of Christ's rule over the hearts of believers [b].
I am not prepared to grant that these three prophets
spake nonsense, or, what is much the same thing, what
was unintelligible to their contemporaries. There
is abundant proof that the prophetic schools had a
settled body of teaching, and that the people generally
were sufficiently trained in it to know what the prophets meant. And thus the ten tribes would perfectly
understand Hosea's meaning, namely, that their captivity would be a very long one,—not limited to
seventy years as in the case of Judah,—and that their
restoration would only be after the Messiah's advent,
'by their obeying Christ, the Son of David, their king,'
as the Targum explains it. They would gather the
same conclusions from the words of Amos. And
Hezekiah would feel no bitterness at Isaiah, though his
words could not but suggest many sad and troubled
thoughts; still there would be no anger, because he
knew that with one accord the prophets all taught
the same truth as Isaiah—that the Messiah, though

[b] Nothing, too, could more plainly show that the true interpretation of those prophecies which promise an era of glory and splendour to the Israelites was to be a spiritual one. The perpetuity of David's throne, for instance, was repeatedly affirmed in the plainest terms by the prophets (2 Sam. vii. 13, 1 Kings viii. 25); in terms equally plain they stripped it of all temporal rule and grandeur (Is. xi. 1, &c.); and then, as if to show that they themselves felt no difficulty in this seeming contradiction, they refer to it long after the last king of David's line had reigned, as an encouragement for rebuilding the second temple (Ps. cxxxii. 11, 12). Surely they must have been fully aware that 'the sure mercies of David' were something higher and better than earthly greatness.

of David's line, would be born in a low place; that He would be a root springing out of dry ground, at Whom kings would purse up their mouths, and Who would have no earthly splendour to make men desire him.

And thus, after the seventy years' exile, David's line was not restored. There was great respect felt for and shown to Zorobabel, but no power was given him. Many psalms 'to David' were written, extolling the promises made to his house. In the Psalms of Degrees, psalms sung by the returning exiles, psalms of joyous praise, pre-eminent even in the Book of Psalms for their beauty and the loving gratitude which they express; in them you have the record of the promise, 'Jehovah hath sworn in truth unto David, He will not turn from it; Of the fruit of thy body will I set upon thy throne (Ps. cxxxii. 11).' But there was no legitimist party among the exiles who proposed to fulfil that promise in a literal sense. In short, neither were the prophets so unintelligible, nor the people so stupid, as the negative critics imagine. They lived in a great circle of thoughts: and these thoughts they were ever urging upon the people: everywhere throughout the land the same truths were taught by thousands whose names are written in no earthly record, but in the Book of Life: in their colleges they had head-quarters for training those whom God called to the ministry, and in which the writings of their great chiefs and leaders were stored up. The recipe for making the prophets unintelligible and the people stupid, is to stand apart from this circle of truth. If the prophecies were mere human presentiments and forebodings, they are absolutely inexplicable. For there could not have been one fixed, settled, and consentient teaching in that which took its colouring from the varying course of events. Isaiah would never have described Hezekiah's lineage as a decaying stump in the same breath as that in which he foretold the overthrow of Sennacherib ; nor Amos have spoken of Uzziah's palace as a ruin, with gaping breaches in its walls, and with a mere booth or hut as all that remained of its former splendour.

The ancient Jews did not misunderstand these prophecies. They mused upon them in sorrow : for they saw in them the overthrow of their nation. Still there was comfort. As Jeremiah so repeatedly affirmed, God would never make 'a full end' of them : or, to use Isaiah's words, 'a remnant would remain.' The ground would be dry, yet out of it a root would spring forth : the stem of Jesse would be prostrate, yet from its stump would come forth a sucker ; the royal palace would be in ruins, yet among them would be a booth or hut for David's son. And thus, after their expressive way, one of their names for the Messiah was 'The Son of the fallen.' Now how came these prophets to know that two such contrary things would be combined in Christ as the fall of David's throne and its establishment for ever? That, like Solomon the Magnificent, He would be the Prince of peace, with the key of government upon His shoulder, and yet one despised and rejected of men ? The Jews could not understand this contradiction, and they divided the prophecies between two Messiahs. To one, the son of Joseph, they gave all those passages which spake of Christ's humiliation and rejection and death. To the other, the Son of David, they applied all those which spake of His kingdom and triumph and glory. In Jesus of Nazareth all these passages are combined in one harmonious yet unexpected solution. All equally find in Him their place and meaning, though in a very different way from what any uninspired expositor had ever imagined. If the negative critics are to effect anything, they must, on their own principles, show that Hosea and Amos and Isaiah lived in the second or third century of the Christian era. They say that prophecy is nothing more than the record of past history, and that the prophets wrote subsequently to the events which they profess to predict. It is one of their established canons of criticism, if that can be called established which rests upon nothing but unsupported assertion. Well, then, let them prove the soundness of their principles by showing us in what century of the Christian era these prophets lived. If I may refer to the Church in the same breath as to the negative critics, I would remind you that St. James had no doubt of the meaning of Amos' prophecy. In the first council of Jerusalem, of whose decrees the apostles ventured to say, 'It seemed good to the Holy Ghost and to us (Acts xv. 28),' St. James quotes these words of Amos as a sufficient justification for his sentence, that the Gentiles should be admitted into the Church without requiring of them obedience to the law of Moses.

With Hosea and Amos closed the long struggle of grace with Israel. It had begun with the man of God sent to rebuke Jeroboam at the very altar of his calves. It had been sustained by the heroic energy of Elijah and Elisha. It ended with Hosea's—or rather

Jehovah's—lamentation over Israel's fall. Their words primarily referred to this struggle, but combined with their message to their own times, they had also grand truths for God's universal Church. The rest of the prophets belong to Judah, except Daniel. He is the link between the prophets and the Church. But already we have seen that the prophets of Judah teach just the same truths as those of Israel. It is quite evident, as regards their doctrine, that the prophetic schools at Gilgal and Jericho taught just the same as was taught at Jerusalem.

Now we have already shown that the two earliest prophets of Judah, Micah, and Isaiah, start with a contradiction in terms. The mountain of the Lord's house is to be desolate and solitary at the very time when it is to be established upon the top of the mountains, and when all peoples—Gentile nations in the plural number—are to be flocking into it. And what have we just been considering? Under a perfectly distinct metaphor, and one that refers primarily not to the Church but to Christ, Hosea and Amos teach you just the same truth. Daniel, as we have seen, dispensed with metaphor altogether. He taught (xii. 11) that the daily sacrifice would be taken away, and that for a vast period after the abomination of desolation had been set up by Titus within the sacred area—a period which he describes as a thousand two hundred and ninety days—the Jews would continue in that very condition described by Hosea. Elsewhere he foretells the destruction of the city and sanctuary, and that the sacrifice and oblation are to cease (ix. 26, 27). But is this the teaching of all prophecy? Plainly it is. The temporary nature of the Jewish

Church and of the Mosaic institutions is as clearly taught as the eternal nature of Christianity, and the certainty of the perpetual existence of the Christian Church. And if we have seen the one set of predictions come true, we may rest perfectly confident that the other will prove equally true, whoever they may be 'who rage and take counsel together against the Lord and against His Christ.'

For, first, it is a mere trifle, but it is something, that the Mosaic religion had for its symbol an ark of gopher-wood, a very lasting material, which with proper care might have existed just about down to the days of our Lord. It was past repair in Josiah's time; it perished when Nebuchadnezzar burnt the temple. The Jews understood its significance, and stoutly denied that it had perished (2 Macc. ii. 5). Jeremiah, they said, had stowed it away safely, and in due time would come again to restore it to them. You have here the contrast between prophecy that grew out of the circumstances of the times—the prophecy of patriotism—and true prophecy. The restoration of the ark was necessary as a proof of the perpetuity of their covenant rights, and hence the predictions of Jeremiah's reappearance to give it them back: but he has never come. Of more importance was the tabernacle: for it involved the fact that Judaism had a local seat, and a definite centre. Such an institution never could be universal. And what were the fortunes of this central seat of Judaism? Once in about every four hundred years it was destroyed. The Philistines destroyed it at Shiloh, and the ark went into captivity. Nebuchadnezzar destroyed it at Jerusalem, and burned the ark. The third temple lasted somewhat longer, but was at last levelled to the ground with a destruction as complete and enduring as that which had befallen Shiloh. Jeremiah, one of the truest patriots that ever lived, foretold this in the most marked and public way (vii. 12-16). And with the temple fell the whole Levitical law. There is no high-priest to enter the Holy of Holies now, and no Holy of Holies for him to enter upon the great day of atonement, and thereby give validity to the sacrifices of the Mosaic ritual. And thus two things combine. The very nature of the Levitical law and the course of Jewish history alike show that Judaism was a temporary religion. And Micah and Isaiah not merely teach this clearly and plainly as I showed in a previous Lecture. That would be a very small truth in itself. What they teach is, that it was to be removed out of the way solely to give room for something better. The imperfect was to be followed by the perfect: the preparatory by the final: the torch of truth by the risen sun. 'God's mountain is to be established, not on the mount Moriah, but upon the mountains everywhere: and exalted above the hills.' 'Out of Zion goes forth the law, and the Word of Jehovah from Jerusalem.' The law was to become the rule of life of all nations, but only as spiritually explained in the Sermon on the Mount. God's mountain was to be established, but it was to be a stone cut out without hands that was to fill all the earth.

I do not suppose that the prophets understood this great truth as fully and exactly as we understand it now: but they understood the main outlines of it. Naturally they used metaphors drawn from the state of Jerusalem in their days. Their city, their temple, their covenant relations with Jehovah, naturally suggested the terms in which they were to speak to the people of their times. And rightly so. Jerusalem was the seat of God's true Church. The Jews were the cluster which contained the new wine of the Gospel (Is. lxv. 8, 9). Christianity is Judaism separated from all that was temporary, and raised to the highest possible perfection. And this is what the prophets say, 'Jacob is to be brought back : Israel is to be gathered [c].' But this redemption of Israel is but a small thing in the prophet's eyes. 'It is a light thing that thou shouldest be My Servant to raise up the tribes of Jacob, and to restore the preserved of Israel: I will also give thee for a light to the Gentiles, that thou mayest be My salvation unto the end of the earth (Ib. xlix. 6).' Messiah's kingdom is to be a religion co-extensive with creation (Mark xvi. 15): yet not won by war and conquest, for its symbol is a mountain, strong, calm, perpetual, and in which none hurt or destroy. And how does Isaiah in this very place—the place where he describes the peace and love which is to prevail in God's holy mountain,—how does he himself explain it? 'The earth,' he says, 'shall be full of the knowledge of Jehovah, as the waters cover the sea (xi. 9).' It is the general prevalence of Christ's religion in which consists this vast and universal monarchy which was to take the place of David's temporal kingdom. Of David's kingdom the symbol in prophecy is the hill

---

[c] There is little doubt that this is the right reading and meaning of Isaiah xlix. 5.

of Zion : the mountain of Jehovah is the Christian Church.

This temporal kingdom was expressly to pass away. 'The Sceptre was to depart from Judah when Shiloh came (Gen. xlix. 10).' 'Ships,' sang Balaam, 'shall come from the coast of Chittim, and shall afflict Asshur, and shall afflict Eber; and he also shall perish for ever (Num. xxiv. 24).' 'They shall come,' says Jerome, 'in triremes from Italy, and shall conquer Assyria, and devastate the Hebrews, and they too shall finally perish.' His translation is the right one, and the temporal dominion and polity of the Hebrews was to fall as certainly as that of the Seleucidæ, the rulers of Asshur at the time referred to in this prophecy[d]. There is nothing, then, so extraordinary in the fact, that Moses in Deut. xxviii. foretold the fall of Jerusalem, and the dispersion of the Jews. What is very remarkable is, that the details are so exactly described, that if the book be a forgery, it must have been forged by some one with Josephus' history of the Jewish war by his side. The general fact that the Jews were to be scattered among the heathen was, so to say, a common place of prophecy. It was declared in the book of Leviticus (xxvi. 33) as clearly as in Deuteronomy; it is referred to by Nehemiah (i. 8) as a prediction of Moses that had become a tradition of the race: but what was only obscurely foreshown by Moses in the way of

---

[d] However absurd may be the attempt of the Romish Church to thrust this version upon nations who do not speak Latin, yet, in itself, Jerome's translation, known as the Roman Vulgate or common edition, will always rank among scholars as a work of primary authority.

warning, and as something conditional upon their conduct, was constantly referred to by the prophets as something that daily was becoming inevitable. There is really but one teaching upon the subject from Moses to Malachi. And this I cannot but think is one of the most extraordinary phenomena ever witnessed in the annals of thought. You have an order of men of the most exalted patriotism; men who are perpetually looking forward to 'latter days,' in which Israel and Judah are to enjoy every temporal and spiritual blessing; and yet these very men with one consent foretell an evil end for everything in their religion and their country. The nation is to be scattered and become a curse, the city is to be destroyed, the temple to be laid in ruins, the sacrifice and oblation to cease, the royal lineage to sink into obscurity. Yet nothing is to perish. The throne of David is to be eternal, his dominion universal; all nations are to enter their Church; in this Church the Jew is to have no exclusive privileges, the Gentile to be subject to no disabilities. It is to be the Church of all nations. I have read many attempts to weaken the force of detached portions of this scheme. I have never read nor expect to read any attempt to explain on naturalistic principles the combined force of this grand teaching of prophecy as a whole.

But when the prophets had thus sketched out the great future of religion,—for, as I have said, the one purpose for which the people of Israel was called by God, and made subject to so extraordinary a providence, was that God by it might give mankind the one true religion,—when, then, the prophets had taught plainly the main outlines of this great purpose, they began to add specific and particular details. And these specific prophecies are so numerous, and have been so wonderfully fulfilled, that naturally they have excited the chief attention on the part of expositors, and have been most frequently appealed to as the sure foundation on which our faith may calmly rest. Now the first of these predictions is found in Micah. From Bethlehem-ephratah, the old home of David's family, but which nevertheless must so dwindle as to become 'too small to be reckoned among the thousands—the princely divisions—of the tribe of Judah, out of it there shall go forth to Me one that shall be ruler in Israel; whose goings forth have been of old, from the days of eternity (v. 2).' Israel, then, is to go back to Bethlehem for a new beginning of the kingly power, and this new king is described by the prophet as one Who had gone forth from all eternity. But I am not going to press this: it belongs to the inner essence of Christianity, to that which is the rightful portion of believers—its doctrines—and not to its outer proof. I take, then, only the fact that Micah affirms that a second kingdom would spring forth from Bethlehem, and I ask you to read the Book of Micah, and follow the order of his thoughts. You will then see the force of his words, not in that haphazard way in which they come before you separately from what leads up to them, and which makes people sometimes speak as if prophecy were a sort of legerdemain, but as the calm, thoughtful, and orderly unfolding of the chart of truth.

Micah, then, begins his prophecy by reproving the Jews for their sins. Zion, he says, is built up by blood, and Jerusalem by improbity. The chiefs judge for bribes, the priests teach for hire, the prophets divine—and I have shown before how strictly all divination was forbidden—for silver. All classes thus are corrupt, and therefore justice requires their removal. It is because of this deep-set and general moral corruption that Zion is to become ploughed as a field, and Jerusalem a heap of rubbish, and the temple-area a desolate place, where the sound of God's true service is never heard. Observe then: moral reasons caused the removal of Israel out of its place. Clearly as that removal was foretold, it was never foretold as a fated necessity. The Jews to the last might have averted it. 'How often would I have gathered thee, even as a hen her chickens!' It is unrepentant man who turns the warnings of prophecy into certainties. And so, then, there was no inevitable reason why the Jews should have been taken captive, and Jerusalem destroyed, except their own immorality. Read the pages of Josephus' Jewish War, and you will find that if ever there was a city ripe for judgment it was Jerusalem. No wonder that our merciful Saviour denounced manifold woes upon its inhabitants, when they were capable of so acting, as their own historian describes. Moral reasons, then, caused them to reject Christianity nationally; had they received Christianity, they might have become the first and foremost of all Christian nations, and their temple have been the St. Peter's of the world. But even in Micah's days the immorality of the nation was too entire for any mild remedies to suffice. It was this immorality which frustrated the earnest attempts of Hezekiah and Josiah to bring about a national reformation. It was the wickedness of the people which made the teaching of our Lord practically so powerless, that at His resurrection the number of the disciples was but one hundred and twenty.

From the hopeless present, therefore, Micah hurries on to the distant future. 'In the last days the mountain of the Lord's house shall be established.' The Jewish Church was to have a great development. Its teaching was not altogether to fail because of the immorality of the nation. Accordingly the justice of God separated first of all at the exile between the good and the bad. It was shown to Jeremiah before the event, that those who would perish at Jerusalem with Zedekiah were the refuse whom God had rejected, while those who had gone captive to Babylon with Jeconiah were men picked out by God's providence, that in them the Jewish Church might survive (ch. xxiv). So too the teaching of our Lord and His apostles gathered out of the festering mass of the Jews all those fit for admission to the Christian Church, and God's Providence notably saved every one of them from perishing with the refuse of the nation at Jerusalem. In both cases the nation by its immorality had separated itself from the Church. But in what way God would still carry on His work Micah could not yet see, though he did see that the Jews were to go to Babylon, and be delivered there (iv. 10). Generally what he saw was that the thorough immorality of all classes of the Jews, while it would put an end to their national existence, would nevertheless remove them only that something better might take their place. As, then, Æneas saw the gods leaving vanquished Troy, so Micah sees the law going out from Jerusalem, but only that it may gather the

Gentiles into a nobler and truer Zion. And, thus, after describing that peace and love which are the necessary effect of Christian principles, and which do not prevail as they ought among Christian nations, because their Christianity is nominal only, or nominal too much — after this he goes on to speak of the Church's triumphs. She was lame, driven out, and afflicted, yet she shall become a great nation. God makes the horn of the daughter of Zion iron, and her hoofs brass, that she may beat in pieces many peoples, and consecrate them and their substance to the use of Jehovah, who is now described as the 'Lord of the whole earth (Micah iv. 13).'

And thus, then, having seen the Church's glory, having seen, in metaphor though it be, a time of vast activity, when nations far and wide are to be won, not for any national god, but for Him Who is Lord of all, he finally couples all this with one of David's race. From the town of Jesse shall go forth the Church's everlasting ruler. And his words about this ruler surpass all reasonable bounds. Yet it could not be flattery; for the prophecy nearly cost the prophet his life. It roused up general and intense indignation against him. But Hezekiah was of a tender conscience, and he urged the people not to destroy the prophet, but to repent. Yet the prophecy does not soften its painful details by connecting this restoration of the Church with Hezekiah's race. As a matter of fact the Messiah did not spring from Hezekiah, nor from any Jewish king but David. He came from an uncrowned branch of his descendants. And it is notable that the prophets never do connect the Messiah with any king but David. This is very unlike flattery: flattery would have coupled the promise with something distinctive of Hezekiah. Micah couples it with a decaying town, where the dynasty lived ere it had achieved greatness.

Time forbids me to speak of the rest of the prophecy—how Micah tells of a waiting-time until she that travaileth hath brought forth, and that then the remnant of his brethren shall return to the sons of Israel, and Israel shall feed in the divine strength, and be magnified even to the ends of the earth: and how the remnant of Jacob shall be scattered among many peoples, no longer as a curse, but as the dew, and as showers, bringing a blessing unasked, and yet strong as a lion amid meaner herds, whom none may resist. Already the Gentiles have been thus blest by the missionary labours of the apostles and early Christians, most of whom were of Jewish parentage: and never have missionary labours been more beautifully described than as the coming of the soft, gentle, refreshing dew, heaven's own gift, but a gift unasked; and of the showers which descend unbidden upon the arid waste, and bid it revive: labours which nevertheless have a lion's strength to break through the bonds and obstacles which sin and error place in the way of God's truth. And a still greater fulfilment will assuredly come: 'for if the casting away of Israel was the reconciling of the world, what shall the receiving of them be but as life from the dead? (Rom. xi. 15).' Upon these and similar points I have not spoken, nor do I intend to speak, because they belong to those who accept the Christian interpretation of the prophecies as given by our Lord and His apostles, and held by the Church. It is the believer's privilege to study such prophecies as are still but partially fulfilled, and search out their deeper lessons. But with those who deny the inspiration of the prophets we can bring forward only the larger and salient points, and say, Here are certain plain facts. Christianity gives of them a straightforward, simple, and natural explanation,—an explanation nevertheless quite different from anything imagined by the Jews, or by any one before the fulfilment came. Of the prophetic teaching, involving apparently a contradiction, we assert that both sides have in Christianity an exact and complete, but unexpected fulfilment, a fulfilment not brought about by human means, but by God. If the critics refuse to accept this fulfilment, then let them offer some tenable theory of the phenomena. What at present they do is to nibble at trifles, pare away a little here and a little there, and insinuate that the rest is unintelligible.

I will only add, as regards Micah, that there is the most striking similarity between his thoughts and those of Isaiah, while, as writers, nothing can be more dissimilar than their style. They both lived at the same time, and though born at Moresheth, a village on the Philistine frontier, yet Jerusalem was evidently the place where Micah laboured. Both he and Isaiah were probably members of that college[e] at

[e] Our version in 2 Kings xx. 4 suggests an entirely wrong notion as to Isaiah's dwelling. It says, 'Afore Isaiah was gone out into the middle court,' whereas the Hebrew is, 'before he had reached the middle of the city.' The substitution of the word *court* for *city* was an absolutely unauthorized change made by the Massorites, to suit a Jewish notion that Isaiah dwelt in the temple. At the time when our version was made, the corrections of the Massorites were supposed to be authoritative; now they are as generally acknowledged to be changes for the worse. Isaiah, then, dwelt in the city, and moved in a circle

Jerusalem, of which we read subsequently as the residence of the prophetess Huldah. Of this college Isaiah was probably the head during the latter part of his life, and Micah no unworthy colleague. But while Isaiah is the most polished of Hebrew writers, Micah's prophecy reads like a series of rough notes. It does, in fact, belong to a period when the prophets were still orators rather than writers: and we may justly consider it as representing only the more important points in a long course of public teaching. The prophecy of Judah in ruins, and of a new kingdom starting afresh at Bethlehem, was no chance expression thrown off by the pen in a moment of enthusiasm. It was the settled conviction of Micah's whole teaching.

Never were there writers whose style is more exactly marked than the prophets, and the idea that large interpolations are possible, and that you may pull a prophecy to pieces and divide its dismembered limbs among a heap of other writers, simply means

separate alike from the king and the priests. But his rank was so high that Hezekiah sent as a deputation to him the highest nobles of his court, Eliakim and Shebna (of whom see Is. xxii. 15-25), together with the elders of the priests (2 Kings xix. 2). Isaiah plainly must have held some position of great power and influence; for we do not find that his prophetic office saved Jeremiah from contumely and personal indignities of the gravest kind (Jer. xx. 2, 8). But if Isaiah was the regularly appointed head of the prophetic order, we can understand his position. It is quite plain that the prophets were a numerous and powerful body: it is but reasonable, therefore, to suppose that they had their own chiefs, and a regular organization and head quarters. Manasseh no doubt broke these institutions down; and though possibly restored afterwards, they never seem to have regained their original strength; for the prophets themselves had lost their old vigour, and in the days of Jeremiah and Ezekiel had become, as far as the mass was concerned, utterly corrupt.

that people know so little of the subject that they suppose that Hebrew literature is unlike every other literature. If I were to affirm that Horace wrote considerable portions of Virgil's Georgics, the assertion would be treated as ridiculous, not because it is more ridiculous than what has been said about Isaiah, but simply because men generally know enough of Latin to be able to form a judgment upon the subject. If a man makes a similar assertion as regards the writers of the Old Testament, he can always count upon the ignorance of his readers. They do not know that the prophets have each one his own marked and peculiar style. Micah's is abrupt and broken. Evidently he was a man of deep feeling, who beheld with intense pain the growing corruption of the people. And thus though he wrote those remarkable Messianic predictions, yet his primary subject was morality. What stirred his whole nature was the violation, by God's own people, of the moral law. And never has any man gone more directly to the root of the whole question of human conduct than Micah in that short code which forms perhaps the best known portion of his whole prophecy :—

> Wherewith shall I come before the Lord,
> And bow myself before the High God?
> Shall I come before Him with burnt offerings?
> With calves of a year old?
> Will the Lord be pleased with thousands of rams?
> With ten thousands of rivers of oil?
> Shall I give my first-born for my transgression;—
> The fruit of my body for the sin of my soul?
> He hath shewed thee, O man, what is good:
> And what doth the Lord require of thee
> But to do justly, and love mercy,
> And to walk humbly with thy God!

In short passages such as this we often see Micah master of a powerful and impressive style. The earnestness of the thoughts is equalled by the beauty of the language, and both the memory readily seizes upon the words, and the heart is moved by their import. His rhythm, too, is good and effective, though far from being so smooth and exact as that of Joel and Amos: and his Hebrew is that pure dialect spoken in Jerusalem by the educated class, and by that class only. Still there is no prophet who requires more minute and patient study. You must think over Micah before you can see how his thoughts grow out of one another, and what is the inner chain which binds his terse, brief, disjointed sentences into a connected whole.

Such, then, is Micah, the contemporary of Isaiah, and no unworthy associate of that great prophet. Not that he ever rises to that height of sublimity and beauty, whither indeed Isaiah mounted alone. Nor is his teaching so complete as that of Isaiah. It is very full as regards the Church, but as regards the person of the Messiah he tells us but little. His great lesson is holiness, that one sole foundation upon which alone Christ can be built. But he never separates this lesson from Him Who made holiness possible for us. Whatever may be their special lesson, the prophets are men whose hearts are ever full of one great subject, the advent namely of the promised Deliverer. And natural as it may seem to us in our cold pedantic way to look for some lower application of each prophecy, something in the prophet's own times to which it may refer; to them and to the people generally it was as natural to look onward to the distant future, and to the coming of that Messiah, in Whom their nation, shorn of its glory and fast sinking under the power of Assyria, was to revive to a grander, a more enduring, a more world-wide, and a more spiritual empire.

LECTURE VIII.

THE PROPHECIES OF ISAIAH.

I pray thee, of whom speaketh the prophet this? of himself, or of some other man? Then Philip opened his mouth, and began at the same scripture, and preached unto him Jesus.—ACTS viii. 34, 35.

WE can well understand the confusion which disturbed the eunuch's mind when reading the fifty-third chapter of Isaiah. The words of that chapter were to be the key wherewith in due time the Church would unlock the mystery of the atonement; they were to explain to us why Christ suffered, why His death was necessary for our acquittal, why His merits avail for our pardon and acceptance. But until 'He was brought as a lamb to the slaughter,' the mystery of a suffering Christ, though clearly taught in prophecy, was something so alien from the usual current of men's thoughts, that they read the words of the prophets without understanding their meaning. Men never do understand anything unless already they have in their minds some kindred ideas, something that leads up to the new thought which they are required to master. Our knowledge grows, but it is by the gradual accumulation of thought upon thought, and by following out ideas already gained to their legitimate conclusions. God followed this rule even in the supernatural knowledge bestowed upon the prophets. It was a growing light, a gradual dawning preparatory to the sunrise, and not a flash of lightning, illuminating everything for one moment with ghastly splendour, to be succeeded immediately by a deeper and more oppressive gloom. It has been our endeavour to trace this growing light. We have seen how the foundation for the revelation of Christ was laid in broad and general doctrines concerning the universality of the Church, the power of prayer and repentance, the necessity of sanctification, the certainty of judgment. Upon these followed exacter teaching as regards the plan of salvation, and the person and offices of Him Whose name is Jesus, a Saviour; and we have seen that this knowledge came in no haphazard way. Carefully, and with prayer, the prophets studied the words of their predecessors, and by the use of the light already given were made fit for more light, and to be the spokesmen of Jehovah in teaching with growing clearness to the Church those truths which have regenerated mankind. For the truths of religion alone give us the power of mastering the baser portion of our nature, and of rising to a nobler and more spiritual, aye! and a more manly, existence!

And this exacter teaching attains to its greatest clearness and highest elevation in Isaiah. There are other inspired writers, whose lessons instruct, as their varied excellencies adorn, that 'goodly fellowship of the prophets,' by whom God gave us the Scriptures. Had time permitted, there are many of whom one would fain have spoken. There is much I would gladly have said of Jeremiah, a man it may be of small natural gifts, but worthy, nevertheless, to stand at the very head of the prophetic choir, and to be in his sorrows the type of Christ; for never was there a character more distinguished for moral excellencies, or one more determined, in spite of the shrinking melancholy of his disposition, at all hazards to do his duty. There is the sublime, but often obscure, prophet of the exile, Ezekiel, whose mysterious teachings appear again in their Christian form in the Revelation of St. John; but it would need a volume in itself to show what are the relations in which these two books stand to one another. There are the prophets of the return, especially Zechariah, whose mind dwelt so exactly among the same thoughts as filled the heart of Isaiah and the old prophets, that Archbishop Newcome[a] argued that he must have been their

---

[a] The portion of Zechariah, so entirely in the style of the old prophets as to have suggested (first of all to Dr. Mede) the idea that it was written before the exile, consists of the last six chapters. Of these, Dr. Newcome assigned chapters ix., x., xi., to a date antecedent even to the carrying away of the ten tribes by Shalmaneser, while chapters xii., xiii., xiv. he thought were by a different author, who flourished between the death of Josiah and the destruction of Jerusalem. Undoubtedly these six chapters are most remarkable. They contain the account of Christ's entry into Jerusalem, riding upon an ass' colt; of His betrayal, and of the thirty pieces of silver being cast to the potter. They contain the weighty prophecies of the two staves, Grace and Union; of the cutting off of the three evil shepherds; of the destruction of Jerusalem, and of its better restoration, when God shall pour out upon the house of David, and upon the inhabitants of Jerusalem, the spirit of grace and of supplication, and they shall look upon Him whom they have pierced. They contain, too, the great prophecy of Christ's divinity, joined with that of His death, 'Awake, O sword, against My shepherd, and against the man that is My fellow, saith Jehovah of hosts:' and, to add but one prophecy more, when Jerusalem has been captured, Jehovah goes forth to fight with the nations: 'And His feet in that day

contemporary. More reasonably we may attribute this fact to his careful examination of their writings, and see in those very many remarkable predictions spoken by him of Christ, God's especial blessing upon his thoughtful study of what had been already revealed. Finally, there is Malachi, whose office it was solemnly for the last time to declare God's purpose of calling the Gentiles, and His rejection of the Jews. 'I have no pleasure in you, Israel, saith Jehovah of hosts, nor will I accept even the unbloody sacrifice at your hand,' to say nothing of the sacrifices of animals, which at Israel's rejection would of course become impossible, and which already among the Jews of the dispersion had ceased to be offered. 'For from the rising of the sun even unto the going down of the same My name shall be great among the Gentiles; and in every place incense shall be offered unto My name, and a pure unbloody offering: for My

shall stand upon the Mount of Olives, and the mount shall cleave beneath them, and living waters shall go forth from Jerusalem, and Jehovah shall be king over all the earth: in that day shall there be one Jehovah, and His name one.'

Now the sole reason for conjuring up several Zechariahs, was the fact of these predictions agreeing so exactly with what the old prophets had taught about the Messiah. It seemed impossible that one who lived in the time of Darius Hystaspes, and whose office it was to encourage the exiles in rebuilding the temple, would foretell a fresh destruction of Jerusalem in as clear a manner as Isaiah and Jeremiah had foretold its capture by the Chaldees. But the minute criticism of the Germans has scattered this theory to the winds. Especially De Wette and Stähelin made a most exact and thorough examination of everything connected both with the language of the book and with its historical allusions, and came to the conclusion, not only that the last six chapters were written by the same author, but that, whoever he was, he also wrote the first eight. Ewald, however, still divides the book into several fragments, which he assigns to different periods, but without giving any adequate reasons for his decisions.

name shall be great among the Gentiles, saith Jehovah of hosts (Mal. i. 10, 11).' The Israelites must have read such a prophecy with sinking hearts, and its ominous meaning was made the more threatening by Malachi being the prophet who was commissioned to foretell in such clear terms the speedy advent of the forerunner, and the sudden appearance immediately afterwards in His temple of the Lord, as the messenger of the new covenant. Clearly too he sets forth that separation between the believing and the unbelieving Israelites, which was to be effected by the preaching of the apostles, as the heralds of this new covenant, even within the lifetime of the very generation who had seen our Lord manifest in the flesh. Nationally it was the last day of acceptance for the Jews, and Christ sat, during the last few years of the Mosaic dispensation, as a refiner and purifier of silver, putting aside for the Christian Church all the faithful and true: leaving for Titus and the armies of Rome all 'impostors, and adulterers, and false-swearers, and those that oppress the hireling in his wages, the widow, and the fatherless, and who turn the stranger from his right, and fear not Me, saith Jehovah of hosts (Mal. iii. 1-5).'

Upon this, and much more, there is no time to speak. For the Bible is like an ever-flowing fountain. Take what we will, and as much as we will, we ever leave more than we take to satisfy the wants of others [b]. Neither the writers nor the thinkers of any

---

[b] Compare the passages culled from St. Augustine in Archbishop Trench's 'Exposition of the Sermon on the Mount,' pp. 5 sqq., expressive of that great father's 'entire confidence that in the Scriptures were laid up all treasures of wisdom and knowledge.'

one age can exhaust its fulness. For nearly eighteen centuries men have thought and written upon that one book, and if for eighteen more centuries men so write, yet will there still remain much to call for fresh examination and fuller enquiry: new knowledge to be won, old truths to be better and more fully understood. I do but submit to the general law in acknowledging that my subject is ten times larger than I can adequately treat. I have but stirred the surface, whereas if I had dug deeper, I should have won a richer harvest. Yet even the slightest stirring of God's Word yields abundant fruit. The books of men have their day, and then grow obsolete. God's Word is ever fresh and new—like Himself, 'the same yesterday, to-day, and for ever.' Time passes over it, but it ages not. As long as the Church shall last, so long will it be the voice of God speaking in it and to it; and that not as a thing of the past, but as a thing of the present. 'The Word of the Lord is quick,—alive,' says the apostle to the Hebrews (iv. 12). Its power is as fresh as if God spake it but yesterday.

All these later prophets, then, add each his own portion to the exact delineation of Christ and the doctrines of the Gospel. But, passing them by, I shall content myself with a few words upon Isaiah, as being the prophet who gives us the clearest possible description of Christ's person and office. In Isaiah all the peculiarities of Hebrew prophecy reach their highest elevation, and especially in the last twenty-seven chapters, concerning which no critic of note abroad any longer holds that they can be distinguished from the first thirty-nine chapters, by any test either of language or matter. If any critic at home still holds that some Babylonian Isaiah wrote the last twenty-seven chapters, it is because criticism with us is, as a rule, at second-hand, and it is only gradually that we learn what is the conclusion arrived at by those abroad, who devote their whole lives to study. What that conclusion is the reader will find in my Preface [c]. It is not what we hold. A routed army will still try to save what it can of its baggage : and with Isaiah the negative critics can have no peace. For the mention of Cyrus by name, and the circumstantial account of the manner in which Babylon was captured, cannot be explained away as mere outlooks and presentiments. Either they were written after the event, or prophecy is supernatural and divine, and 'God the Holy Ghost spake by the prophets.'

Theirs is a hard fate. They have to turn God out of His own word, and out of His own world ; and it is not easy to do either one or the other. When they began what they are pleased to call (modestly ?) the higher criticism, they supposed that if they could suggest doubts about the dates of some few very remarkable prophecies—that if, by the power of reiterated assertion, they could make people suppose that this passage was an interpolation, and that a forgery—then all their work would be done. Knowing the credulity of unbelief, they did reasonably count upon rationalists being childish enough to take upon trust two Isaiahs, two Daniels, and three Zechariahs. But these make-

---

[c] Ewald's view will be seen below, note [e], page 295. Virtually, he acknowledges that more or less of eleven chapters out of the twenty-seven are irreconcilable with Döderlein's theory. A very full discussion of the authorship of these chapters will be found in Mr. Stanley Leathes' 'Witness of the Old Testament to Christ,' pp. 254-300.

shifts are by no means easy to manage; and, behind, there are a multitude of prophecies as exact, as precise, as completely fulfilled, as those more commonly put forward in argument. The prophecy of Cyrus by name, and of the capture of Babylon, does not stand alone: from beginning to end the Bible is a book of special predictions exactly fulfilled. Take it as God's word, and its various parts all unite well together, and are all capable of satisfactory exposition; and the difficulties in it are such only as were reasonably to be expected in a book which gives us all necessary knowledge of another world, but in human language, through the medium of human thoughts and human ideas. There must be mysteries in such a book: places where the human words can give us but a faint and shadowy representation of the Divine reality. But treat the Bible as an ordinary book, as the mere remains of a curious national literature, and you are involved at once in hopeless entanglements. The Divine element in it is too strong, too clearly evident, to yield to this treatment. You must upset all Jewish history, all Jewish chronology; you must cut out large portions of every prophetic writing, and bring them down to a time removed by centuries from that in which the prophet lived: you must say that the rest is obscure, unintelligible, meaningless. Anyhow the Bible cannot be an ordinary book. For if the miracles and prophecies recorded in it are real and true, then must God have been with the writers and workers of those miracles in an extraordinary manner. If they are not true, then the book is an imposture, and every portion of it which contains a prediction must have been written after the event predicted had happened. It is this necessity which requires the invention of those numerous shadowy personages, referred to above, summoned up to write a bit of a book now, and a bit then, as occasion serves. Fortunately, the fertility of the imagination of the negative critics has bounds set to it. They cannot say of any prophecy fulfilled in Christ, or in His Church, that it was written after the event. For, three centuries before Christ came, God was pleased in His providence to cause the Septuagint version of the Old Testament to be made at Alexandria by a colony of Jews placed there by Alexander, and who gradually became greatly estranged from their brethren at Jerusalem. But for this independent testimony, we should have been told that the chief prophecies were fabricated by Christian writers; and that predictions of Christ, so plain and clear, were interpolations put into the Bible after the event [d].

[d] It should also be remembered that the Jews, immediately after the return from the exile, set themselves most earnestly to the study of their sacred books. Their great scribe Ezra is believed on reasonable evidence to have begun the work of settling the canon of Scripture, and tradition ascribes to Nehemiah the gathering of a library, containing the acts of the kings and prophets (2 Macc. ii. 13). The previous age of Hezekiah, as I have shown, was one of very high culture; this culture revived immediately after the return from Babylon, and the style of the three last prophets and of the post-exilian Psalms is far more pure than that of Jeremiah and Ezekiel. Plainly it was an age when the old models were carefully studied. The numerous books quoted or referred to in Chronicles prove how large were the literary resources of Ezra and his contemporaries; and the men of the Great Synagogue continued his work. In Ecclesiasticus we see with what reverence the prophets were regarded, and Isaiah is referred to as the author of these last twenty-seven chapters: 'Esay comforted them that mourn in Sion (Ecclus. xlviii. 24, Is. xl. 1, lii. 9).' The external evidence, in short, gives a strong presumption for the general authenticity of the prophetic writings: and no negative critic, to the best of my knowledge, has

And nowhere are these predictions more clear and plain than in these last twenty-seven chapters of Isaiah. They are, as I believe, the final memorial of the prophet's teaching, a monograph written in the calm seclusion of his later life, when retired from the turmoil of public business, saddened, too, it may be, by the failure of Hezekiah's reforms, viewing with heartfelt sorrow that relapse of the nation into sin, which, upon the succession of the child Manasseh to the throne, amounted almost to national apostasy; in grief at the present, he turned away from the sickening sight of God's own people offering human sacrifices to devils, to concentrate all his powers upon the contemplation of the future and happier times of Messiah. It was a monograph written chiefly for the use and study of that portion of Israel which was true to its calling—the prophetic order. Isaiah had not to combat and struggle, like Jeremiah, with corruption at home. There were many lukewarm prophets it may be (Is. xxx. 10), some utterly corrupt (Micah iii. 5, 11), but the mass was still true. It is, however, abundantly plain to any attentive reader of the Bible that Hezekiah's later days were days of disappointment, when, in spite of all that king and prophet could do, idolatry was generally prevalent. And thus Isaiah represents the people as 'enflaming themselves with idols under every green tree, and slaying the children in the torrent-beds under the clifts of the

---

grappled with it. No one has shown when, or under what circumstances, or by whose hands, this falsification of the Hebrew Scriptures took place. It is a thing unparalleled in any other literature. We ought to have something more than mere subjective criticism. Subjective criticism can do much: but it must be sober and careful. That of the negative critics is usually wilful, capricious, and fanciful.

rocks (Is. lvii. 5).' Now I need scarcely say, that as there are no torrents, but only canals in the flat alluvial soil of Babylonia, so there are no torrent-beds there, but that these form a common feature of the landscape in Palestine as of all other mountainous countries. Such places were the favourite haunts of superstition, and there, in the deep channels worn by the rushing streams of winter, they reared, it seems, altars of the loose stones, and celebrated on them their horrid Moloch-rites. 'Among the smooth stones of the torrent-bed is the place chosen for the sacrifice: they, even they, are Israel's lot.' Its lot, its inheritance, used to be Jehovah: but now their God, their country, their love as parents, all that ennobles man, is rejected and trampled under foot, and nothing valued but what ministers to sin! And so, on these stones placed altar-wise, 'they pour their drink offering, and there they offer their meat offering.' Now this portion of the last twenty-seven chapters Ewald and other great critics have at length been forced to own must have been written in Palestine, and most of them further grant that it describes the state of things before the exile, and that there is no evidence, but rather the contrary, of human sacrifices having been offered at Babylon. They invent, however, for it a shadowy author, who lived, they say, during Manasseh's reign [e].

---

[e] According to Ewald, Proph. d. A. B. iii. 27, several portions of this last prophecy of Isaiah, namely, chaps. xl. 1, 2, lii., liii., liv. 1-12, lvi. 9-12, lvii. 1-11, were written by an unknown prophet, who lived in the time of Manasseh. He invents this mythical personage in a few off-hand lines at the end of vol. i. p. 537, but in this latter place he speaks of him more respectfully, and laments that we possess 'only

Now it is the state of things here described which is the key to the whole monograph. There are periods in every nation's history when it seems to struggle violently against God, and endeavour to free itself from the restraints of religion. In modern days the struggle takes the form of infidelity: with the Jews it took the form of idolatry. There was much idolatry in Jeremiah's time. He, too, speaks of human sacrifices outside the walls of Jerusalem (Jer. vii. 31) in the valley of Hinnom. But in his days it was more the wantonness of idolatry that captivated the people than its darker rites; and so he tells how even in the streets of Jerusalem in

these noble fragments, as evidences of a time so remarkable as the reign of Manasseh—a time of the deepest trial, distraction, and humiliation, but also of endless elevation and high enlightenment on the part of the most pious and the most true in Israel.' See also Ib. iii. p. 102. It is strange that reasonable men do not see the absurdity of these shadowy personages, and how destructive they are to real criticism. Whenever German critics get into a difficulty, and do not know what to do with any portion of the prophetical books, they invent an ancient prophet, or a modern prophet, or a great unknown, or a little unknown, till one is weary of such commonplace makeshifts. Thus the last twenty-seven chapters are written by a 'great unknown' who lived at Babylon at the end of the exile: but first, he did not write the opening words, he borrowed them from an earlier prophet. He wrote, however, the controversy with idols, and the account of the capture of Babylon: but when you reach the very kernel of the book, ch. liii., Ewald owns that it could not have been written at Babylon. He even thinks that it may describe Isaiah's own martyrdom, or if not, then the martyrdom of some one else, but at all events the sorrows there described were suffered under Manasseh (p. 90). Why? Simply because the prophecy would have been almost more remarkable in the mouth of an exile at Babylon than in that of Isaiah. To get rid of its Messianic character you must affirm that it is historical, an account of some past tragedy. Tradition says that Isaiah was sawn asunder; it is certain that Manasseh was a tyrant; *ergo*, by the higher-criticism, it was Isaiah who 'bore our griefs and carried our sorrows.' Well! then come chaps. lvi. 9-lvii. It is a the days of Josiah, and again in Egypt after the destruction of the temple, 'the children gathered the wood, and the fathers kindled the fire, and the women kneaded dough to make cakes to Melcath,' the love-goddess of those days (Ib. vii. 18, xliv. 17, 19). But in Isaiah's later days it was the darker side of idolatry which oppressed the minds of the Jewish people: the idea that sin could be atoned for only by the blood of the young, the beautiful, the innocent. God was no longer, as taught by Moses, a being good, merciful, gracious, long-suffering: he was a dark, malignant, cruel demon, who rejoiced in human woe, and whose envy and

---

passage which in Germany has brought great ridicule upon the negative critics. No one on full consideration could believe that it was written at Babylon, as was at first innocently affirmed. But Ewald is equal to the emergency. It was copied from 'an ancient prophet,' and must be printed in italics. But chaps. lviii. and lix. are almost as unmanageable, so they, too, must be printed in italics, and assigned to a 'modern prophet,' an imitator of Ezekiel (p. 107). And now there are no great difficulties till we come to ch. lxiii. Judah had nothing to fear from Edom and Bosra at Babylon. And so the first six verses are printed in italics again, and the passage is said to be borrowed from the prophet who wrote ch. lviii. (p 119). And as for all the rest Ewald fairly gives it up. The great unknown may have written it, but at a later time, and under different historical circumstances (p. 125). Ch. lxvi. 6, which shows that the city and temple were still standing when the prophecy was composed, must refer, he says, to a time subsequent to the decree of Cyrus and the 'weak commencement of the rebuilding of the holy city.' Observe then; omitting the opening words, *eleven chapters* out of the twenty-seven, i. e. all the crucial passages, are confessedly irreconcileable with the theory of a great unknown having written this magnificent composition at Babylon. Either, then, this book was written by Isaiah, as the Jews constantly affirmed from the most ancient times, or it is a piece of patchwork. Ewald has proved convincingly that it is not the work of a Babylonian Isaiah. Is his own theory more than an unwilling confession that the victory remains with the orthodox critics of Germany?

hatred of man could be appeased only by the violation of the holiest instincts of our nature. If Melcath, the queen, was pleasure-giving, the stern king Moloch [f] could be served only in anguish and despair.

Now it is only too probable that the distress occasioned by the Assyrian invasions had caused this deep gloom of anguish to settle upon the national mind. Isaiah describes Judæa as desolate, its cities burnt with fire, the land devoured by marauding strangers in the very presence of the hopeless inhabitants, watching perhaps from the hill-tops the destruction of their property. Zion alone is left, and it is but as a booth put up for the temporary use of the watchers in a vineyard (Is. i. 7, 8). It was the first time, too, that the land had been thus afflicted, and used as the people were to regard temporal prosperity or adversity as the direct results of religion, their faith seems to have given way. In their anguish Isaiah describes them as multiplying their sacrifices, and busying themselves with all the externals of religion (i. 11–15), but Micah, his contemporary, discloses to us a darker back-ground. He, too, speaks of the thousands of rams they were willing to offer, and of meat-offerings so numerous that the temple ran with rivers of oil. But still unrepentant, and oppressed therefore with a sense of unforgiven sin, they looked round for something wherewith to crush the conscience, and were ready to 'give their first-born

[f] I have little doubt that the right vocalization in Isaiah xxx. 33, lvii. 9, is מֹלֶךְ *Moloch*, not מֶלֶךְ *king*, but it makes no difference whatsoever in the sense.

for their transgression; the fruit of the body for the sin of the soul (Micah vi. 7). It was this despairing unbelief which Hezekiah tried to stem by a national reformation. This, too, was present to Isaiah's mind when he wrote the last twenty-seven chapters of his prophecy. He wished to meet this despair: wished to give them consolation, and to raise their hopes. He shows them, therefore, the powerlessness of idols: tells them that though they must go into captivity, yet that they shall be delivered. And then he sets before them their Messiah—describes Him as the true expiation of sin, the true giver of peace to the conscience: while finally, in terms of mixed upbraiding and comfort, he exhorts them to repentance, and declares to them the future glories of the Church, Christ's love for it, and the high office to which nationally and individually they were called.

For the time both failed. Hezekiah's reforms led to no national repentance, and Isaiah's exhortations reached only that 'remnant,' in whom the Jewish Church was to live on, till the time came for it to do God's work. But, for the present, the nation's faith totally gave way. The long reign of Manasseh was a period of utter irreligion, when everything good and right was persecuted to the death. For unbelief is never a philosophy: a philosophy may be—generally is—tolerant. Unbelief is a propaganda, fierce usually, and intolerant, and eager to crush out belief. And so Jeremiah, speaking of Jerusalem in Manasseh's days, says, 'In thy skirts is found the blood of the souls of the poor innocents: I have not found it by secret search, but upon all these (Jer. ii. 34).' Like Jehoiakim's murder of Urijah, Manasseh's bloodshed was done openly, to strike terror, and put to silence that hateful word of Jehovah, that would still speak of sin and judgment.

This utter failure, then, of Judah's faith was probably the result of that first great wave of trouble (Is. viii. 7, 8) which broke over the land in Hezekiah's days. Their faith had been hollow before, but now it quite gave way. Isaiah describes their unbelief in that stage in which it degrades the outward forms of true religion to superstitious uses. Micah describes it in that further stage when it looks to a false creed for peace, and would appease God, not by serving Him in holiness and truth, but by offerings of pain and anguish and cruelty. And gradually this darker side of unbelief prevailed. The feeling which Micah describes grew more intense in Hezekiah's later years: during Manasseh's reign it became universal. He made his own offspring to pass through the fire (2 Chron. xxxiii. 6), but—poor child—when he came to the throne at twelve years old[g], he could have had little to do with the nation's apostasy. There must

---

[g] It may be answered that children in the East are more precocious than with us, and that Josiah was equally young when he began his reforms. But Josiah is just a case in point. He was surrounded by good men, Hilkiah, Shaphan, and others. For four years he did nothing, though he gave every indication of piety: at twelve years old he began his reforms, but it was not till his eighteenth year that the vigorous proceedings recorded in 2 Kings xxiii. took place. These things depend not upon the precocity of the understanding, but upon the strength of the will, and it may be doubted whether this ripens faster in the East than with us: witness our own Edward VI.

have been strong bad men behind, such as had rejected God in Hezekiah's days. Men like Shebna (Is. xxii. 15–19) had come to the front again, and so those last fifteen years of Hezekiah's life (Ib. xxxviii. 5) were years probably of much sorrow, when the king saw all his efforts for the spiritual good of his people frustrated, and idolatry every day more powerful and rampant throughout the land. To his own soul this sorrow may have been blessed (2 Kings xx. 19), but they were not years in which he could have rejoiced. For evil seemed in them more powerful than good.

During the latter part of Hezekiah's reign Isaiah seems to have withdrawn from public business. The first thirty-nine chapters record his labours during the time when he was strong and active. They are the record of a long life of duty: for when for the last time he left the prophetic college to reprove Hezekiah for his vanity, and forewarn him of the Babylonian captivity, forty-six years had passed since, in the last year of Uzziah, he was called to be a prophet[h]. The time for personal labour was now past, but he was no unobservant spectator of the signs of the times; and thus, in retirement, occupied probably with teaching the sons of the prophets, he gathered into one memorial the great truths which he had

[h] Isaiah was certainly very young at his call. During the reign of Jotham he does not seem to have done much more than prepare for his high office, and write the life of Uzziah. It is in the reign of Ahaz that he first steps forth with great boldness and authority in Jehovah's name, while the period of his greatest activity is the first half of the reign of Jotham's grandson, Hezekiah. If he was about Jeremiah's age when called to be a prophet he would be now (in the fifteenth year of Hezekiah's reign) sixty-two years of age.

taught all life through, and which the present circumstances of his times made more than ever necessary.

The one great subject, then, of this his last writing is God's controversy with idols. With this Isaiah begins: to this he returns. It was the great struggle during Hezekiah's reign. Ahaz, his father, Manasseh, his son, were both open idolaters. Between these two there was an interval of thirty years, during which Hezekiah struggled against the national will; but it prevailed, and Manasseh represented the winning side. Still the triumph of evil is never more than temporary, and Isaiah, mindful of the promises made to the nation, looked forward to a better age, when Judah would again worship the one God in truth. And with this he connected the bestowal of Christ. Necessarily so. Christ cannot come to idolaters, or to atheists. The heart which is occupied by many gods: the heart which believes in no God: in neither of them can Christ dwell. The great preparation for Christ, throughout the Bible, is the teaching that there is but one God, and the teaching what that God is. It is only when men know and feel, more or less thoroughly, that God is a Spirit, that God is good, and that God is love, that it becomes possible to worship Him in spirit and in truth. And thus Isaiah begins by the utter overthrow of all the principles of idolatry. And he does it with a master's hand. Jeremiah—the authors of several psalms—later prophets—apocryphal writers—can but reproduce Isaiah's arguments. They exult in them, repeat them as an unanswerable demonstration of the follies of the heathen creed. They were unanswerable. In due time they did banish idolatry entirely from the minds of the Jews. Naturally a very sensuous people, 'projectissima ad libidinem gens (Tac. Hist. v. 5),' idolatry had a strong hold upon them. They loved it because it was vile. But the combined teaching of the two prophets, Isaiah and Jeremiah, prevailed against their besetting sins. From the close of the Babylonian exile the Jews hated idolatry as decidedly as before they had loved and delighted in it.

This, then, was a very great step onwards in God's purposes. The controversy with idols had begun when Abraham left Ur of the Chaldees. God had set him apart that his seed might grow into a nation, whose office it should be to contend for a spiritual faith. When we roll backward the pages of history, we can generally discern, of all the chief races of mankind, what is the purpose they have served in God's counsels. So plain everywhere is His handwriting. But here we have a nation whose office is marked out for it at the commencement of its history, and which has fulfilled that office exactly. Abraham, indeed, was rather removed from evil influences than commanded to testify publicly to God's unity[i]. It was at the Exodus that the struggle began in earnest; and the result of that struggle was to stamp deeply into the minds of Israel those great spiritual truths which in the Bible alone are expounded clearly and purely. Take all your philosophies, and you will find them only groping darkly and hesitatingly after those

---

[i] See page 55, note c.

grand truths taught in the two first verses of Genesis, that God created everything that is not God, and that there is no progress from darkness to light, from confusion to order, except by the presence of God's Spirit. And for eight centuries after the time of Moses these and the like truths were entrusted to Israel's keeping. Taught in Israel by the law, by the temple ritual, by the psalms, and by the prophets, not merely were they maintained, but were growing in depth and clearness, and both the men were being prepared to teach them, and the truths were being put in such a form as made them ripe and fit for the acceptance of the whole world.

In Isaiah we reach the last stage of this preparation. For mark, as regards these last twenty-seven chapters, what immediately precedes them. It is Isaiah's visit to Hezekiah with the painful message, 'Behold, the days come, that all that is in thine house, and that which thy fathers have laid up in store until this day, shall be carried to Babylon: nothing shall be left, saith Jehovah. And of thy sons that shall issue from thee, which thou shalt beget, shall they take away; and they shall be eunuchs in the palace of the king of Babylon (Is. xxxix. 6, 7).' Now I have not time to stop and ask whether Isaiah was likely to end his prophecies with this announcement? whether any prophet concludes with a prediction of unmitigated evil? But it is necessary to point out that henceforward the idea of Israel's exile is uppermost in Isaiah's mind. Involuntarily the fact clearly breaks through that the writer was living at Jerusalem. Even such small matters as his calling the land Hephzibah, the name of Hezekiah's wife, all agree with this supposition, and with no other. But Judah in exile is the thought uppermost in Isaiah's mind throughout. He seems to have gone home, and to have made this sad prediction to Hezekiah the one subject of his prayers and meditations. There was nothing new in it. Jerusalem a heap of ruins, Zion ploughed as a field, the area of the temple desolate and bare; these, as we have seen, were the opening declarations of Isaiah's prophecy. Yet truths come home to men at various times with fuller force; and the picture of Hezekiah's descendants ministering as eunuchs to the pride of a savage conqueror may well have set Isaiah pondering upon the mysterious ways of God.

Israel in exile, then, is the starting-point of these last twenty-seven chapters, and thus they are a natural sequel to the melancholy announcement made to Hezekiah. As I have repeatedly said, the prophets never predict anything simply that men may know the future: their words have ever a moral purpose. Hezekiah was the first to be benefited by Isaiah's message; but its chief fruits were those which the prophet himself won by prayer and study for the whole Church.

Of these, the first was for the Jews themselves. As I have said, that despairing form of idolatry which then prevailed was partly due to the misery, so utterly beyond anything in previous times, which the Assyrian invasions had brought upon the land. Isaiah heals this by hope. Just as Jeremiah's prediction of the seventy years of captivity became, as time rolled on, the comfort and strength of the exiles at Babylon, so Isaiah's plain and definite predictions of the return, and of the rebuilding of the city and temple, and of the grand and unique though spiritual destiny of the nation, were intended to rouse it from its despair, and quicken it with new hope.

But there was more than this. That exile was itself the first beginning of the fulfilment by Israel of its appointed duties. And this, again, is another key to unlock the meaning of these twenty-seven chapters. Why did Isaiah at this very time come forward with arguments which utterly overthrew the principles of idolatry? If there be a God, and Isaiah was His prophet, it was because it was just the right time for them. If there be not, I have nothing more to say, except that it actually was just the right time, and so you endow chance with a will and a purpose. The captivity of Israel had become a settled decree of prophecy. It was to take place in about a century. As soon as it had happened, the people would find themselves face to face with idolatry. Of this intervening century, half was occupied by the open heathenism of Manasseh's reign, when Jehovah's worship was violently suppressed. Where was the mighty though silent influence which maintained the pure doctrines of the Mosaic teaching during this period, and gave them at the close of it such entire ascendancy, that at Babylon no single doubt about the folly of idol-worship ever entered the people's minds?

At Babylon, then, in the ninth century after Moses, Israel's specific work began. Their training was now all but completed, and the time had arrived when they must begin to make the Gentile world ready for Christ. For this purpose they were scattered far and wide. Other nations when scattered in this way are absorbed. Their influence is often great for a time, as was that of the Greeks who followed in the wake of Alexander's conquests, but at length the race itself disappears. Not so the Jews. To do God's work they must be dispersed, but He endued them with such vitality and tenaciousness, that to this day they remain a distinct and separate people. Now this dispersion began just six centuries before Christ, when Jeconiah was carried into captivity. Up to that time the oracles of truth had been intrusted to Israel's keeping, and confined to their sole use. Yet from the first, account for it how you will, they had been taught by their own chiefs and sages, that they had not received their many privileges for their own good simply, but for the good of others; and that in them all the nations of the earth were to be blessed. Never was there a people who set themselves more obstinately against what their own sacred books told them was the one purpose of their existence. But that purpose was fulfilled in spite of them. Upon the fertile plains of the Euphrates arose vast earthly empires, cruel, merciless, the robbers and oppressors of mankind; not worse, perhaps, than other great military powers, but as bad. And these crushed the independence of Judæa, but the Jews were thereby dispersed throughout the world. Everything proves that the time of Hezekiah was a period of great culture. It was a time when literature had advanced far enough to be interested in and proud of its own past career; and thus we read of the men of Hezekiah making search for and copying out the proverbs of Solomon, and the three first books of the Psalms apparently were collected and arranged by the same hands. So, too, in Isaiah, the prophet of Hezekiah's days, the Hebrew language reached its highest perfection. No such Hebrew was written before or after; and though there were among the prophets who succeeded him his equals perhaps in native power, yet there is none whose style is so pure and perfect. Whence, then, came it that just when there was this palmy state of things at Jerusalem, when the long peace of the reigns of Uzziah and Jotham had led to these happy results, that God's providence should permit those merciless Assyrians to crush and destroy a civilization so infinitely superior to anything that existed at Nineveh or Babylon?

This is the question which the prophet Habakkuk asks in Josiah's days. How could God permit a hasty and bitter nation like the Chaldæans, men that were idolaters, who sacrificed to their net, and burned incense to their drag, to slay the nations continually, and devour those that were more righteous than themselves? Equally were the cruelties of the Assyrians a terrible stumbling-block in Hezekiah's days, and made men turn to Moloch, a demon to be served only by human tears, and by the offerings of despair. Habakkuk gives the answer which suited those times, and quieted, no doubt, many troubled consciences. But he could not give the whole answer. It is ever the weakness of man's judgment when he tries to justify the dealings of God, that he can know only in part. Our judgments are the judgments of ignorance. By Habakkuk, however, God revealed just such a portion of the truth as satisfied men's requirements then. He showed that the Chaldæans were commissioned only to chastise Israel; and that God's justice would visit their sins with a severe and merited retribution. Babylon, the city built with blood, was, as Habakkuk foretold, the scene of murder and usurpation oft repeated till Cyrus captured it, and from that day it has been an independent state no more. But our interest lies not with Babylon, but with Judæa; and now that the whole course of God's Providence is open to us, and not a part only, we can see more clearly why, just when Judæa had reached its highest point of civilization, God allowed those fierce empires to arise and trample it under foot.

For, to use Isaiah's metaphor, it was the crushing of the cluster in order to obtain from it the new wine (lxv. 8, 9). The grapes must be ripe before they are crushed. Had Israel been dispersed earlier, they would not have been fit for their mission. Had the Philistines crushed Israel in Samuel's days, the one true religion would have been trampled out. Had the dispersion taken place soon after the disruption of Solomon's empire, you would have had a set of men of great military capacity, as good soldiers as the Chaldæans, who, until they established their short-lived empire at Babylon, were the great mercenaries of the East: but that would have been all. As you read the books of Judges and Kings, you see the discipline by which God formed the most firm, tenacious, inflexible, and enduring race that ever existed, or that now exists, on the face of the earth. Without the military glory of David's empire, without the fame for wealth and wisdom of Solomon's court, the Jews could not have been that lasting monument of God's dealings with mankind which they are now. No nation can look forward to an abiding position on earth for the future, which cannot look back with pride upon the past. But so false a position as that of earthly empire for God's chosen people lasted but for a short time. Restored to the happier position of a petty monarchy, they slowly ripened under a long succession of good kings till they became fit for God's purposes. And then there came bad kings; for the higher good is never reached without a struggle, and men like Manasseh and Jehoiakim served as a fan to separate the base and mean and unworthy from Jehovah's true followers (Mat. iii. 12). Finally there arose that succession of monstrous earthly empires, which occupy the pages of profane history: empires at first of brute force, but which in time gave way to the learning and commerce of Greece, and to Rome's empire of law. No sooner did these earthly empires arise, than the dispersion of Israel began. 'I will bring forth a seed out of Jacob, and out of Judah an inheritor of my mountains.' They are Isaiah's words just where he had been speaking of the crushing of the grape as a necessary step towards the obtaining of the new wine. The whole passage is one full of all the marked peculiarities of prophecy. It begins with the call of the Gentiles, while it reproaches the Jews as a rebellious people, stained with the worst forms of idolatry and sin. Punished they must be if God be just. This crushing, then, by Assyria, is no harsh decree, serving merely for a future purpose. The dealings of God with Israel—with man always—combine what is most just and merciful and good for the present, with what is also best for the future. Had Israel not sinned, and so deserved the chastening armies of Assyria,

God would have brought about the necessary dispersion of the Jews in other ways, as He did increase it subsequently by the favour of Alexander, and by the aptness of the Jews for trade. The carrying away, then, to Babylon, was primarily the chastisement due to their iniquities. Yet it was also, by a deeper and more mysterious counsel, for the redemption of the whole human race. Crush the cluster: yes! for so will the new wine be found in it, the new spiritual Israel, Abraham's seed by faith in Christ. But 'destroy it not; for a blessing is in it:' the old blessing, 'In thy seed shall all the nations of the earth be blessed.' And therefore he proceeds, 'I will bring forth a seed out of Jacob, and out of Judah an inheritor of my mountains.' Chastised though it be, yet that seed of believers which is to inherit, not mount Zion only, but all God's holy mountains, His Churches everywhere, can be brought forth only by Israel's aid. Scattered far and wide, they carry with them the promise of universal blessing, and immediately begin the work of the renovation of the world.

And just when the time of Israel's dispersion was at hand, Isaiah wrote his prophecy. The elect part of the nation was ripe for it; the teaching of all the prophets had gradually led up to, and prepared for it: and if the Jews were to do their work, it was essential that they should carry with them some such document as this. They were going forth as the advanced guard, comparatively few in number, at a time when idolatry was firmly established everywhere, and none doubted but that the heathen gods were real beings, delighting some in lust and impurity, some in cruelty and bloodshed. They were to shake this belief, and destroy its influence, and lead the thoughtful everywhere to the conviction that there is but one God, and that He is good. And henceforward all Israel's history tends to this one object. They are restored, and Jerusalem rebuilt, not merely because the Messiah must be born of them, and must have Judæa as the scene of His labours, and Jews for His apostles and the propagators of His teaching, but also because it gave stability to the Jews abroad. They went up there at the great feasts, and so their faith was quickened, and their views and doctrines brought back to the standard of the Scriptures. When we read Philo, and the works of other Jews of the Alexandrian school, we see how great a purpose Jerusalem served in the economy of preparation for the giving of the Gospel. The Jews living among the heathen were the connecting link between truth as revealed in the Scriptures, and the truths of natural religion. Open themselves to the influence of Greek philosophy, it was their office to bring the influence of Divine knowledge in return to bear upon the Greek mind. But their teaching, in spite of the extraordinary tenacity of the race, would not have been so powerful or so pure had not the Jews of the dispersion from time to time revisited Jerusalem, and gone forth thence renewed and refreshed for their noble warfare. In no other way could the balance have been maintained. We now see what was the object of the Divine providence in those constant journeyings thrice every year to the holy seat of their religion, so stringently required of every Israelite in the Mosaic law. Thrice in the year there were those great gatherings, and though distance prevented the Jews abroad from being present at every festival, yet there were few who did not often in their lives revisit Zion, to worship there in all the beauty of holiness. This also was the great means by which Christianity was so rapidly propagated. Not at the first Pentecost merely, but constantly, at every feast, 'devout men out of every nation under heaven' were brought into contact with the apostles and the Christian Church at Jerusalem, and returned home to prepare men's minds in every city for the visits of Christian missionaries. But if we suppose that this was the sole use of those great gatherings, we shall lose half the truth. The place held by Jerusalem in the affections of the Jews, and their constant pilgrimages to it, had kept them true to their faith and earnest in their calling during those six centuries before Christ, in which God's providence was yearly dispersing them more and more widely throughout the whole civilized world. So complete, so perfect in every point, externally as well as internally, was the preparation in Judaism for the Christian Church.

The return, then, of Ezra and the exiles from Babylon, the rebuilding of Jerusalem, the restoration of the temple and its glorious ritual, were things absolutely necessary for the establishment and propagation of the Gospel. Without the dispersion of the Jews there would have been nothing to prepare the Gentile mind for Christ: without Jerusalem, and all those influences which knit the hearts of the dispersed Jews in unwavering love and duty to their hallowed home, they could not have maintained that firm adherence to their law, that inflexible determination to be Jews and nothing else, which marks them everywhere, which rouses against them the anger of the philosophic historian, and the satire of the Roman moralist: but without which the influences which the Greek and Roman world brought to bear upon them would have been irresistible. With open indignation Tacitus reviles the Jews for that *superstitionis pervicacia,* that *fides obstinata,* which made them, even at banquets, sit at a separate table, and prevented all intermarriage with the Gentiles. To him it is simply *adversus omnes alios hostile odium* (Tac. Hist. ii. 4, v. 5): a bitter enmity against the whole human race. And this isolation, he says, was simply for a reason so absurd to his philosophic mind as a difference of creed. The Jews, he says, worship God *mente sola,*— worship with them was spiritual, a service of the heart and affections. And then he says, 'they worship but one God, and believe that God to be supreme and eternal, incapable of change and of death: and they reject the worship of images, shaped after the likeness of men, and liable to decay.' To us these truths are worth any price: and we note with wonder the long course of discipline, by which the providence of God formed in the Jews that tenacity of character, and that strength of will, which enabled them to stand up firmly, and resolutely, though alone, amid the thousand reasons that tempted them to conform to the world around them. But no! they were God's witnesses, and while there were many that hated and reviled them for their inflexible steadfastness, the more thoughtful and unworldly listened to their noble teaching about the oneness and goodness of God, and believed that God was one, and was good.

Had not Jerusalem, then, been rebuilt, and the law

of Moses obtained there a local establishment, the Jews could not so easily have maintained themselves in their dispersion as a separate people. But, next, had Judæa been rich, prosperous, successful in war, and thriving in commerce, the Jews would have returned thither, and so again they would not have effected the purpose for which God had formed them. It is a glorious history, that history of the poor exiles restored to their dear country. The martyr-spirit in which they resisted the abominable persecutions of the Syrian kings, the valour and heroism of the Maccabees, this and more sheds a halo of light around God's chosen people during the centuries which preceded the coming of the Messiah. But like most heroic histories, it is a history of the few and the weak striving against the strong, a history, therefore, of endurance, of indomitable resolution, of determined resistance to wrong. But such a state of things does not allure men from more peaceful homes to take part in it. It made the Jews of the dispersion proud of their country; it made them, it may be, hate uncharitably those Gentile kingdoms which so cruelly illtreated the home of their race. But every act of oppression drove many Jews away from their land: and at other times their aptitude for trade, and their many useful, yes, and high qualities, made rulers of large mind invite them as valued settlers to new and rising towns. It was thus that Alexandria became a second metropolis of the Jews, and we may well contrast its fortunes—the fortunes of a city founded for peaceful purposes—with those of Babylon, 'the city built with blood.' Sometimes, then, by violence, occasionally by gentler means, the dispersion of the Jews from the time of Nebuchadnezzar's conquest was continual. On the one hand, there was everything to make them proud of Jerusalem, and love it, and go there from time to time, and have their faith quickened and refreshed by the sight of the temple-services, and by the glorious memories of martyrdoms, and of stern resistance to wrong, and noble deeds of heroism which hallowed every spot there; as well as by intercourse with the great teachers who had made Jerusalem a town wholly devoted to religion: on the other hand, there was no motive to return and settle there. The old did, that they might die and be buried in holy ground: the young and active sought their fortunes in more prosperous lands. I may even add, that physical causes conspired with political in producing this effect. The soil of Palestine, owing perhaps to the destruction of the trees, owing certainly to the continual ravages of war, has undergone an extraordinary deterioration since the days of the monarchy. Districts where at every turn you meet the ruins of wine-presses, and every mark of a large and thriving population, will now scarcely maintain a few half-starved sheep. It was possibly with the Assyrian invasions that this deterioration began.

I ask you, then, to notice that Isaiah wrote rather more than a century before this dispersion of the Jews began. The interval just about served for the book of his prophecies to become widely and generally known: and silently, I doubt not, it was working during Manasseh's evil reign, and was the secret root of Josiah's piety, and the teacher of those holy men who stood in such goodly numbers round him.

Notice, too, that this dispersion is the third great stage of God's dealings with His people. The first was the Exodus, the second was the monarchy, the third the dispersion. Moses was God's representative, His great chief and spokesman, for the first period; Samuel for the second; Isaiah for the third. Is it, then, so incredible that Isaiah, after having predicted the Babylonian captivity to Hezekiah, should have been inspired by God to give that instruction which so great a crisis required? and that God should have set His seal to Isaiah's words by the express prediction that Cyrus would let the Jews go free, and restore them to their land? Grant that it is, in some respects, a more express prediction than you usually find in Holy Scripture: yet is there not a sufficient cause? Our Lord's miracles were greater and more wonderful than those of any preceding period. They offer no difficulty to the believer, for he knows that it was the last and final stage of God's revelation. His purposes were then full, and so He sent no longer a servant, but the Son — Himself God blessed for evermore. If miracles and prophecy, when Christ came, necessarily reached their highest elevation, is it not reasonable that at the third stage Isaiah should also be in some way or other more plainly accredited by God as a messenger from Him? Was there not the same necessity for a special proof of Isaiah's mission as there had been at the first stage when God sent Moses as His prophet?

And still I must notice one thing more. Prophecy ceased at the dispersion. It belongs distinctly to the second stage of God's dealings with Israel. It began with Samuel, and ended with Isaiah, Jeremiah, and

Daniel. Moses, as I have shown, occupied different ground from those who were 'the prophets.' He stands in direct relation to our Lord. In our Lord, with John the Baptist as His forerunner, and the apostles as His messengers to all the world, there was a fulness of every grace, by which all the blessings and gifts of every previous period were poured out afresh in riper and larger measure upon the Church. But prophecy distinctively belongs to the age from Samuel to the dispersion. It was not withdrawn abruptly. It still lingered in those beautiful Psalms of Degrees sung by the returning exiles, and in those prophets who helped in rearing the second house. But at the dispersion it had done its work. The Jews wondered that no prophet more arose. We can see why the gift was withdrawn. The time of teaching had ceased. The Jews were children no longer, but grown men; and like grown men they must leave home, and go out into all lands to carry to others the truths which the prophets had taught them. They must study their Scriptures: must translate them: must gather their teaching into one focus, and bring their concentrated light to shine upon the dark regions of heathenism. You never find the Jews of the dispersion falling away into idolatry. They had their faults, I do not deny it. But their faults did not lie in their creed or their teaching: and the reason why the heathen world so hated them was their evident superiority to the heathens both in doctrine and in morals. At Jerusalem, when the Christian Church had gathered into it the elect, I read with sorrow the painful picture drawn of the rest in the pages of Josephus. But it is the description of the threshing-

floor after the wheat has been separated from the
chaff. His pages also tell us how rapid had been the
progress of corruption at Jerusalem during the last
few festering years. We must not judge by his
narrative of the moral state of the Jews at an earlier
time, nor of that of the Jews of the dispersion. There
were bad among them as well as good : but the good
and true were numerous. There were those everywhere who were themselves ripening for Christ's
kingdom, and preparing others for it. Of the Jews
at home and abroad, of those called to be God's
people everywhere and in all times, mournfully we
own the painful fact that Christ's is ever a 'little flock.'
' Semen Abrahae,' says St. Augustine, speaking of
those who shared Abraham's faith, ' Semen Abrahae,
in comparatione multitudinis impiorum, profecto in
paucis est (De Civ. xvi. 21).' This mysterious law
of God's providence held good, I doubt not, of the
Jews of the dispersion : but few, comparatively, as
may have been God's saints among them, yet all
nationally held firmly to the great doctrines of the
prophets : and upon the foundation laid by the Jews
of the dispersion rose the Christian Church. To this
day, in our forms of worship, in our rites of burial,
in our graces before and after meals, and much more
besides, we still follow the modes and habits of those
scattered and exiled Jews.

And now to conclude. Were those Jews of the
dispersion to carry with them, as their manual, only
an unanswerable demonstration of the absurdity of
idolatry ? Read for yourselves those last twenty-
seven chapters. You will find Israel described in
them as Jehovah's servant—the epithet applied in

so remarkable a way to Moses, the legislator, who first established God's Church upon earth, and gave to the one true religion the necessary support of external forms and ordinances. But now all Israel is Jehovah's servant, and I have endeavoured to show that this was an absolute fact. I have shown you what their work and mission was, and that the time had come for them to enter upon it. Could it be that Israel's mission as Jehovah's servant was only to throw down evil? Lucretius did that. He overthrew the superstitions of heathen Rome, and left it, as regards faith, a blank. And when the house is empty, swept, and garnished, there can be but one result. There will come seven devils worse than that ejected, and the last state of that man, or empire, or people, will be worse than the first. Those who pull down without having anything to put into its place are simply doing Satan's work. God's servants pull down the false, the wicked, the corrupt, but only that they may build in its place the true, the good, the sound, the eternal and abiding verities of God.

And thus, then, Isaiah's teaching is not destructive but constructive. He pulls down the motley superstitions of a debasing heathenism, to build up in its place the ennobling service of the one true God. And oh! how great is the mystery of that teaching! He sets forth Him Who in very deed is Jehovah's servant, the prophet like unto Moses, bearing in Isaiah's pages the same distinctive name, but ruling by no delegated power, but as a Son in His own house. Yes, He was a servant—for though 'in the form of God and very God, He took upon Him the form of a servant and became very man.' But inasmuch as when He was man He ceased not to be very God, therefore He could by one sacrifice of Himself offered once for all make that atonement for sin, whereby God's justice was appeased and man's salvation won.

I need not dwell upon Isaiah's teaching of Christ: so full, so mysterious, so admirably adapted to keep the Jews everywhere in an attitude of expectation, to make them ask with the eunuch, 'Of whom speaketh the prophet this?' and wait with minds open and ready for the answer when the fulness of time should come. Without Isaiah, I doubt whether the Jews could have preserved their faith and maintained their isolation during those long centuries of dispersion: without Isaiah I doubt whether the Christian Church could have been so quickly, so surely founded. Christ, His apostles, the early Christians, always appeal to the Old Testament as the great proof of Christianity being the one true religion: that proof is plain everywhere, but nowhere so plain and concentrated as in Isaiah. Nowhere else do we find Christ suffering, and Christ triumphant, and the character and duties and destinies of Christ's Church, so clearly taught.

And with Isaiah I conclude. Jeremiah must yet strive to the very last with the disobedient Jews, till Zedekiah flees by night from the beleaguered city. His was a strife for God, hopeless as long as he lived, successful, triumphant, as he himself foresaw, among the exiles at Babylon. He could not save Jerusalem, he did save the Church in banishment. In that strife Ezekiel was his true yokefellow. They were really the men who won for Israel its restoration. And amid the mingled tears and rejoicings of that restoration prophecy uttered its last grand words : after Malachi it ceased till He came Who as the Divine Word is the Author of all revelation. I have endeavoured, feebly I know, and unworthily, to trace the development of this wonderful gift of God ; to show in what institutions it took its rise, how it grew, what was its outer form, what its purpose, what its lower and political aspect, what its higher and diviner life, and how the prophets as an order became corrupt at the very time when prophecy itself attained its highest elevation in Isaiah and Jeremiah. What may have been the effect of these Lectures upon the minds of others I know not. But when, for my own part, I think upon what Christianity is, what it has done for mankind, what it is still capable of doing if men would but give it fuller obedience, and then look at this marvellous preparation for it, so complete and perfect, carried on through so vast a length of time, and answering so perfectly to Christianity, combining so exactly with it, and forming in fulfilled prophecy so trustworthy a proof of its divine origin, I cannot believe that in all this there is nothing more than empty mockery, and the foolish play of blind chance. I believe that I can see His hand Who, with perfect wisdom and almighty power, doeth all things well, and Who instructs me by this proof to worship that Messiah Whom these prophets foretold as my Lord and my God.

THE following Lecture forms no part of the Bampton Course, but is added as constituting a necessary part of the argument (see Lect. I. p. 25). My object in the foregoing Lectures has been to show that there was in the Old Testament a real, large, and thorough preparation for Christianity; and that this preparation was no chance work, but the definite and systematic carrying out of a settled purpose, not kept secret, but publicly proclaimed from the very first, and constantly referred to in every stage of the fulfilment. But it is necessary also to meet a counter theory, which does not deny the close connection between the Old and New Testaments, but affirms that it was the fanatic belief of the Jews in the assertions of the prophets which brought about their seeming accomplishment. Wrought up to the very fever-point of excitement by the long series of cruelties suffered by them at the hands of the Seleucidæ and the Romans, they surrounded with a halo of romance a simple Galilæan peasant, and invested him with powers and qualities which were the mere result of their own over-heated imaginations. In opposition to this theory I have shown that the fulfilment of prophecy in Jesus of Nazareth contradicted all the preconceived ideas of the Jews both in Palestine and abroad. Clear as it is to us, it was utterly at variance with the deductions of their teachers. This Lecture was preached before the University as the sermon upon 'the Jewish Interpretation of Prophecy,' in Lent, 1867.

LECTURE IX.

THE JEWISH INTERPRETATION OF PROPHECY AT VARIANCE WITH THAT TAUGHT BY CHRIST AND HIS APOSTLES.

What think ye of Christ?—MATT. xxii. 42.

WHEN our Lord put this question to the Pharisees, their hesitation showed how great was the confusion and uncertainty of their views respecting both the person and the attributes of the Messiah. They knew that He was to be David's son; the voice of prophecy was too plain and consentient for there to be any doubt so far: but whether He was to be David's son lineally, or only politically, as the restorer of David's throne, upon this they had no settled convictions. They were even uncertain whether all the prophecies respecting the Messiah would be fulfilled in David's son. Many seemed to them so unworthy of Him, and spake so confidently of His humiliation and dishonour and death, that they shrank from connecting them with One in Whom all the glories of David's empire were to revive. Nor had they any certain opinions as to His attributes, and therefore when our Lord asked them for a solution of but one of the many apparent contradictions contained in prophecy concerning the Christ, they had none to offer. Prophecy had described Him as at once David's superior and inferior, his Lord and yet his son, and they could not tell how this could be. They had not reflected upon Micah's words, that though born in time at Bethlehem, yet 'His goings forth had been from of old, from everlasting (Micah v. 2).'

Nor is this the only place which bears witness to the unformed character of the opinions of the Jews respecting Christ. When, for instance, the wise men from the East came at the appearance of the star to worship Him, the scribes at Jerusalem, being asked by Herod where the Messiah should be born, answered, 'in Bethlehem of Judæa,' and adduced in proof the words of the prophet Micah. But in St. John's Gospel we find that Micah's words were by no means universally regarded as conclusive. Some held—and many famous expositors among the Jews have since maintained the same opinion —that the Messiah would come suddenly, like a bright and unexpected meteor. 'We know this man whence He is: but when Messiah cometh, no man knoweth whence He is (John vii. 27).' The popular opinion, however, agreed with the answer of the scribes to Herod: for many asked, 'Hath not the Scripture said that Christ cometh of the seed of David, and out of the town of Bethlehem, where David was? (Ib. 42).'

Now it would be erroneous to suppose that the opinion of those who held that at Christ's coming no man would know His origin, was groundless, or fanciful. It rested upon all those passages of the Old Testament which refer to our Lord's divine sonship. To us the doctrine of the divine and human natures indissolubly united in Christ is a cardinal article of the faith: and trained in this belief we reconcile by its aid, almost without conscious effort, those many statements of the prophets which externally are at variance with one another. But this twofold aspect of our Lord must have been a serious difficulty to those who had only the teaching of the prophets without the exposition of that teaching given in the New Testament: nor can I see anything absurd in the expectation that, like a second Melchizedek, He would appear suddenly, with no human lineage, no natural parentage, and no place of earthly birth and education. More correctly we may regard this idea as only a confused anticipation of the truth that the Messiah was not only David's son but also 'the Son of God.'

Now this very title is more than once given to our Lord. Thus Nathanael says, 'Rabbi, Thou art the Son of God! (John i. 49).' So, too, Peter confessed, 'Thou art the Christ, the Son of the living God (Matt. xvi. 16).' Even more remarkable is it that the high priest adjured our Lord to tell him, whether He were the Christ, the Son of God (Ib. xxvi. 63). For his words bear witness to the recognized existence among the Jews of this most pure and spiritual conception of the Messiah's nature. Caiaphas himself probably put the question contemptuously, as representing what he deemed to be the most extreme form of Messianic doctrine: but there were other and better men who held it devoutly as a truth. But could those noble souls, who did hold this doctrine, make it harmonize with the equally plain prophetic teaching that the Messiah was to be a man, a descendant of David, and born at Bethlehem? Many attempts no doubt were made to harmonize this and other apparent discrepancies of the Old Testament. One such we read in Justin Martyr's Dialogue with the Jew Trypho (c. 8). Trypho there affirms 'that the Messiah at His birth would remain unknown, and unacquainted with His powers until Elias appeared, who would anoint Him, and proclaim Him as the Christ.' Attempts such as this only show that the difficulty was a real one, and was felt to be such.

In the Talmud the most conflicting opinions are found respecting the Messiah's advent. In one place it is said that the Messiah will first manifest Himself at Rome: in another that the place will be Babylon: in a third that He will not appear at all unless the Jews reform their manners. More frequently, however, it asserts that Jerusalem would really be the place of His birth. Did not the Psalmist say, 'Of Zion it shall be reported that He was born in her?' (Ps. lxxxvii. 5).' Was not Zion the one source of all that was good? 'Out of Zion shall go forth the Law, and the Word of Jehovah from Jerusalem (Is. ii. 3):' 'Out of Zion, the perfection of beauty, God hath shined (Ps. l. 2).' Who could read such passages, and not draw from them the conclusion that the Messiah would be born on Zion's holy hill? By a similar argument the Jewish zealot who wrote the Second Book of Esdras was led to place at Jerusalem the scene also of the last judgment. The Messiah when He comes again as judge is to rebuild the hill of Zion, and stand upon it to pass sentence upon the nations gathered at its foot (2 Esdras xiii. 6, 35, etc.).

Now, however confused and mistaken may have been the expectations of the Jews concerning Christ, still the knowledge of their opinions seems to me in two respects to be of value. For, first, it helps us in understanding what the prophets wrote: and, secondly, it is not without use in the interpretation of the New Testament. We have in their opinions an exposition of the Old Testament entirely independent of that given by our Lord and His apostles. Too often it seems to be the result rather of national prejudice than of sober reflection: it expresses rather what they hoped than what they read. Still it often gives us one side of the meaning, and usually that side which we are in danger of not seeing. It contributes, then, something to our knowledge of the Old Testament, but for the interpretation of the New it is of direct importance. How, for instance, could we possibly understand that extraordinary ferment of the popular mind at Jerusalem, occasioned by our Lord's teaching and miracles, and so forcibly set before us by St. John in the seventh and three following chapters of his Gospel, unless we knew something of the various and conflicting views respecting the Messiah, which were struggling in the hearts of the Jews? Those chapters seem to me to have been written for the express purpose of explaining to us what were the feelings at work in the minds severally of the Pharisees and Sadducees, which made them combine in putting to death One Whose teaching contradicted and irritated the prejudices of them both. No doubt the Gospels themselves throw great light upon the theories then current among the Jews, but to understand these marvellous chapters fully, and much besides in the New Testament, we need a more complete and exact knowledge of the doctrines which the scribes had gathered from the words of the prophets, and which they taught as their authorized interpretation.

In recent times an additional interest, perhaps, has been given to the enquiry by the theory of Strauss, who argued that the Gospels were not the record of a real life, but the result of fancies and notions generally prevalent among the Jews in the era immediately preceding the destruction of their city; and that their present external form had been given to them under the influence of an overwrought and unnatural excitement. This excitement undoubtedly existed, but it is not the fact that the Gospels embody any explanation of the prophetic writings current or generally received by the Jews of that time either in Palestine or in Egypt. On the contrary, our Lord's death, humanly speaking, was caused by the intense disappointment of all parties at finding one endowed with such remarkable powers steadily opposing and refuting all their received opinions. Strauss' theory itself had never much intrinsic value, but owed its importance chiefly to the skilful manner in which the author had combined with it every objection in detail which had usually been brought against the credibility of the Gospels. In the last edition of his work he has virtually abandoned his theory, and the current of thought now sets in the exactly opposite direction. Thus Rénan ascribes

Christianity to the extraordinary personal qualities of our Lord, and to the enthusiasm excited by Him in the minds of His disciples: while in the pages of Ecce Homo we begin with a man, but a man endowed with the power of working miracles, and as we proceed, and learn more of His doings, no other conclusion seems possible than that to which, perhaps, the writer meant to lead us, namely, Ecce Deus. But independently of this, the enquiry has a legitimate source of interest in the fact that our materials for learning what the Jews thought of Christ have been very greatly increased during the course of the present century.

I propose, therefore, to consider what were the conclusions arrived at by the Jews during those four hundred years in which the voice of prophecy was silent, and also during the first century of the Christian era. The materials are so large that I can only offer a very cursory review of them, and that rather in the hope of awakening interest in a very important field of study, than of giving full information concerning it [a].

The question, then, has often been asked, What was the purpose and intention of that long interval between the last utterance of prophecy in the Old Testament and the Advent of our Lord? When Malachi closed the roll of the Hebrew Scriptures it

[a] For a fuller account of these materials, consisting chiefly of works belonging to what is called 'apocryphal' literature, I must refer the reader to the valuable treatise of Dr. Joseph Langen, Professor of Catholic Theology in the University of Bonn, entitled 'Das Judenthum in Palästina zur Zeit Christi,' Freiburg im Breisgau, 1866, to which I am perpetually indebted throughout this lecture.

was with so spirit-stirring an announcement of the speedy coming of Elijah, that the minds of the Jews could not but have been roused to the earnest study of those priceless records, which told them of the future glories of their race. And this study was the appointed work of those four centuries. The Jews were already widely dispersed throughout the Greek empire; they were everywhere being brought into contact with the heathen world: and that world they were gradually to leaven with principles far higher and holier than any to which its philosophers had been able to attain by the light of nature. Up to this time they had been at school, shut up in a narrow region, and subject to a sharp and incisive discipline. That was now over: for prophecy had spoken for the last time. Daniel had told them that there were but a few more weeks unto Messiah the prince: Malachi had bid them listen to the approaching footsteps of the Forerunner. Everything, therefore, both in their outward circumstances and in their relations with God was altered. His word was no longer growing: it was perfect and complete as far as their Church could receive it. They must now study it, and find out its meaning, and learn what it taught them of their duties now that their scattering had begun, and what would be the next stage of God's dispensation. And they did study it: for everything combined to make them love and value it more and more. The very fact that prophecy was silent made them feel more deeply how priceless were those oracles which God had entrusted to their keeping (Rom. iii. 1, 2).

And their study was not fruitless. Two invaluable results of their labours remain to this day in the Septuagint and the Chaldee Targums, the one the work of the Jews in Egypt, the other that of the Jews in Palestine. Of these the former is the more valuable. For, first, it is the more ancient. Though the Targums had an earlier beginning, and embody many a traditional rendering of great antiquity, and much knowledge gathered by a long course of teachers in the schools of Jerusalem, yet the very earliest—that of Onkelos—probably was not committed to writing till about the first, or even the second, century of our era. Much indeed of its matter was far more ancient, and no less an authority than M. Neubauer [b] considers that it very possibly embodies much of the very Targum made immediately after the return from exile (Neh. viii. 7, 8). The other great Targum, that of Jonathan, was the work of the Jews in Babylonia, and though probably not written down till the fourth century, it, too, is a trustworthy record of traditions far more ancient than that date. But the Septuagint is beyond all price. For it was made far away from Jerusalem by the Jews in Egypt, who were a numerous and learned body. At Alexandria, at Leontopolis, and at other places there existed a large literary class, of whom some studied philosophy, like Philo, and the author of the Book of Wisdom. Others studied history, and we have a specimen of their labours in the Second Book of Maccabees. But their great strength lay in apocryphal writings. Two goodly volumes still exist of Sibylline oracles forged by them, but re-

---

[b] Géographie du Talmud, Préface, p. xi.

garded as genuine by many of the fathers. Excepting the Second Book of Esdras they wrote all the more worthless portion of our Apocrypha, and much besides of a similar kind not contained in our collection. But they also wrote the Septuagint. It is the work of many hands, was probably a long time in making, and is of very unequal merit, some books being very well and closely rendered, and others very loosely and badly, but its very mistakes show that the translators had substantially the same text before them as we possess now [c]. It is not too much to say, that without the Septuagint, and the Targums of Onkelos and Jonathan, instead of that comparative certainty which we now enjoy, very great uncertainty would rest upon the genuineness of the Hebrew Text. Owing to the prejudices of the Christian Church against the Jews, Hebrew manuscripts were destroyed as things unholy. None exist of great antiquity, but the ancient versions happily take their place, and give us full assurance that the Hebrew Scriptures were neither, on the one hand, corrupted or interpolated by Christians, nor on the other hand, have the Jews been able to weaken their testimony to Christ and the doctrines of the Gospel.

But for my present purpose it is necessary to notice that these works also teach us what the Jews thought. The Targums are professedly paraphrases: the Septuagint, though nominally a translation, is throughout largely influenced by the opinions of the translators. In both alike the hopes and fears,

[c] They had, however, a somewhat different text of the Book of Jeremiah, and this again furnishes most valuable aid for the criticism of the Old Testament.

the prejudices, the current philosophy and theories of the times respecting the nature of God and man and of the earth, are freely substituted for the inspired words of the Hebrew Text. The Septuagint, for instance, in its opening words substitutes the Greek notion of a chaos in the place of the very different ideas contained in the Hebrew. The earth, it says, was ἀόρατος καὶ ἀκατασκεύαστος, a mass of matter, but of matter not discernable by the sight, because its separate atoms were still uncombined. Even more remarkable is the care with which both the Targums and the Septuagint soften down, and alter, or entirely omit all those expressions in which human actions or attributes are ascribed to the Deity.

We must confine ourselves, however, to one point, namely, the conclusions at which the Jews arrived respecting Christ. And here first, generally, we find an entire disagreement between the opinions of the Jews of Palestine and those of Egypt. To the former the Messiah was a man, a hero, a soldier: to the latter he was an allegory, an idea only, and not a reality.

Now, vast as is the difference between the two theories, they both grew out of Holy Scripture. Errors generally are but one-sided and partial statements, and have their origin in half-truths, which gradually are pushed onward and developed till the grain of truth in them is lost in the mass of falsehood. And thus the Jews of Palestine and of Egypt divided between them those statements of the prophets, which, when combined, present to us the perfect delineation of our Lord. We find in

Scripture a twofold sonship of the Christ: on the one hand, Jehovah says unto Him, 'Thou art My Son (Ps. ii. 7);' on the other, He is but a root growing in a dry soil, an off-shoot merely of a lineage fallen to decay (see page 267). Now He is the Son of David, and now the seed of a woman. So, too, he is described at one time as suffering, at another as triumphant. In some places He is represented as a man of sorrows, universally despised and rejected; elsewhere He is God, and His throne is established for ever. So again, He is sometimes the judge, and sometimes is Himself led to judgment and cut off by an unrighteous sentence. Finally, the very times of the Messiah are sometimes described as a period of earthly glory and universal empire, and again as a disastrous period, in which the city and sanctuary are destroyed, the sacrifice and oblation cease, and pagan symbols profane the temple area. What wonder if uninspired men could not reconcile these conflicting statements!

Were the Jews of Palestine unreasonable when they put a literal interpretation upon words such as these: 'God will extend peace to Jerusalem like a river, and the glory of the Gentiles like an overflowing torrent? (Is. lxvi. 12).' Or these, 'The righteous bud of David shall reign as a king and prosper, and shall execute judgment and justice in the earth? (Jer. xxiii. 5).' Even words incapable of being literally understood, yet seemed to portend an era of surpassing earthly magnificence: 'Thy sun shall no more go down, neither shall thy moon withdraw itself: for the Lord shall be thine everlasting light, and the days of thy mourning shall be ended

(Is. lx. 20):' for they followed upon a promise of changing the brass of Jerusalem into gold, and its iron into silver; of making its officers peace, and its exactors righteousness, and of stilling all violence, wasting, and destruction within its borders. There were prophecies of successful war. 'Ephraim and Judah shall fly upon the shoulders of the Philistines towards the west; they shall spoil them of the east together (Ib. xi. 14).' 'The house of Jacob shall be a fire, and the house of Joseph a flame, and the house of Esau for stubble (Obad. 18).' 'Proclaim ye this among the Gentiles; Prepare war, wake up the mighty men. Beat your ploughshares into swords, and your pruninghooks into spears (Joel iii. 9, 10).' There were also prophecies of peace. 'They shall beat their swords into ploughshares, and their spears into pruninghooks: nation shall not lift up a sword against nation, neither shall they learn war any more (Micah iv. 3).' 'They shall not hurt nor destroy in all God's holy mountain (Is. xi. 9).' In short, while some of the prophets describe the Messiah's advent as a time of blessedness at home, and dominion abroad; a time when Israel shall possess the heathen, and David's son 'break them with a mace of iron (Ps. ii. 9):' other prophets as clearly declare that the heathen shall then conquer Jerusalem, defile the sanctuary, and cause the sacrifice and oblation to cease. It 'shall be a time of trouble,' says Daniel, 'such as never was since there was a nation even to that same time (Dan. ix. 26, 27.' xii. 1, 11).'

In the interpretation of the prophecies given in the New Testament, all these conflicting statements fall naturally and easily into their place. To the Jews before Christ's advent they could not but be a difficulty, and we have no right to be surprised if we find that in Palestine a literal interpretation prevailed, while in Egypt all was turned into allegory. The Jews of Palestine, however, attempted to combine the two sides of prophecy into a whole, and held either that there would be two Messiahs, or that the one Messiah after being slain (Zech. xii. 10, 11) would be raised again to life. They held, too, that His coming was to be accompanied by a fierce struggle, during which they would as a nation suffer terrible calamities, but finally would gain the victory, and attain to universal empire. But here they had a difficulty. The Messiah would be the first king of the whole earth, but they could not make up their minds whether He would found a dynasty, and sons born of Him succeed to His crown, or whether He would restore the theocratic government, and, after His death, Jehovah rule again by the Urim and Thummim. A small school seems even to have held that the Messiah would not die at all. But among the Jews in Egypt a belief in a personal Messiah soon entirely ceased. Already in the Septuagint we find them obliterating from the text all reference to Christ's birth in the flesh. Thus, whereas in Ps. cx. 3 the words of the Hebrew are, 'Of the womb of the morning is the dew of thy birth,' the Septuagint paraphrases it thus, 'Of the womb have I begotten thee before the morning dawn.' They acknowledge the pre-existence of the Messiah, but are offended at the doctrine of His birth in time. We must not, however, conclude that therefore they confessed His

Divinity. For in Isaiah ix. 6, where the prophet speaks of the birth of the child, Whose name shall be called 'The Mighty God,' they reject a statement so contrary to all philosophy as that God could be born, and, omitting this title altogether, they paraphrase the passage thus: 'His name shall be called the angel of the great counsel.' Now, according to the Alexandrian philosophy, the angels were born of God before the world was, and the idea which the translators of the Septuagint seem to have formed of the Messiah was, that He might possibly be a being similar to and sharing the nature of the angels.

It is, however, in the Book of Wisdom that we find the open expression of those philosophical opinions which finally ruined the Alexandrian school. Beautiful as is this book, and ready as we are to acknowledge that its influence upon the Christian Fathers has been less unwholesome than might have been expected, yet nothing can be more unsound than its philosophy; and the respect felt for it in old times did introduce principles into the Church contrary to the teaching of the New Testament. Apparently it was the work of a man of singular richness of imagination, and great command of language, and his description of the shortness of life, and the greatness of immortality, is the noblest and most powerful passage in the whole of the apocryphal scriptures. In his attempt, however, to combine the philosophy of the Greeks with the teaching of the Old Testament, he adopts principles entirely at variance with the revealed word. Thus he teaches that matter is eternal (xi. 17), and that creation consisted in fashioning what already existed, though only as ἄμορφόν τινα ὕλην, a mass of chaotic shapelessness. Like Plato, he also teaches the pre-existence of the human soul (viii. 19, 20), a passage, however, which the fathers interpreted of the pre-existence of Christ. But the most dangerous of the principles which he adopted from Plato, was that of the essential opposition between matter and spirit, and the inherent badness of matter. The body is no temple of the Holy Ghost, as with St. Paul, but a heavy clog and dull prison-house of the soul; and the Christian hope of a resurrection, in which body and soul will once again be joined together, and mutually perfect one another's happiness, was a thought which he would have rejected with horror. Worse in itself than even this dualism, was his conception of the Divine Logos, or Wisdom of God. It becomes with him mere pantheism, a sort of cosmical life pervading the universe, with not a trace of a personal existence. The Book of Ecclesiasticus may be, as Dean Milman argues, the programme of Sadducæanism. It gives, as he shows, no word of comfort to the dying, no hope of any life after death. In the universe it acknowledges neither angel nor spirit, but two beings only, God and man[d]. But in the main it is a noble book, and as regards the doctrine of the Divine Wisdom, its teaching is sober, thoughtful, judicious, and scriptural. As a rule, it adheres closely to the inspired words of the Book of Proverbs; but the Book of Wisdom sets before us a refined but thorough pantheism.

In fact, these two books illustrate in a remarkable

---

[d] Milman, History of the Jews, ii. 32, note.

manner what I have said before of the tendencies of the two great divisions of the Jews. The Palestinian book is religious, but in a hard, worldly, matter of fact way; the Alexandrian book is religious, but in a mystic way. In neither of them is the Messiah a living reality, and in this respect the Palestinian book is not a fair representative of the views of the great mass of the Jews in Judæa. It belonged to a sect who believed in no future world, nor had any hope beyond the grave.

Time will not permit me to trace the gradual disappearance in Egypt of the doctrine of a personal Messiah, as shown in other apocryphal works, like the Fourth Book of Maccabees[e], the Sibylline Oracles, and other products of the Jews of Alexandria and Leontopolis. Living under a foreign rule, losing gradually their hold of the Hebrew language, occupied with trade, and thereby brought into daily contact with the Greeks, powerfully influenced by their ideas and literature, and daily growing cosmopolitan rather than patriotic, their efforts were directed chiefly to recommending their books to the heathen by explaining away in them everything Jewish, and by detecting the chief tenets of Greek philosophy under the veil of the facts and laws and doctrines and institutions of the Old Testament. Probably, too, they wished to find some authority in their sacred books for ideas which had seized upon their own minds with all the charm of novelty and power. But in embracing the new they parted with

[e] An edition of the Syriac version of this interesting work will shortly be published, with much illustrative matter, by Mr. Bensly, Sub-Librarian of the Cambridge University Library.

the old. Gradually their Messiah ceased to be a person with a real existence. He became a mere abstraction, a phantom. Thus Philo teaches that the Jews are to be delivered solely by their own virtues. Their heathen masters will grow ashamed of keeping in slavery people of such extraordinary merit. And as they return to their land he describes them as 'guided on their way by a kind of human figure divine beyond the limits of nature, invisible to the rest but visible to those who are being saved[f].' The idea is taken from the pillar of fire and cloud which led the Israelites through the wilderness: here the returning host is guided by a phantom visible only to the eyes of believers.

Throughout the Alexandrian theosophy the Messiah never once appears as King, or Ruler, or Conqueror, or Judge: in Palestine, on the contrary, the tendency was to separate from Him every religious element, and see in Him a great national hero. It was the doctrine of the theocracy, but degraded till it was simply human, carnal, earthly. No doubt many noble minds struggled against this debasing tendency: like Nathanael they believed that He would be the Son of God. Others stopping short of this yet held that He would be a prophet, and regarded therefore Christ's miracles as His proper credentials. 'When the Messiah hath come, will He do more miracles than these which this man hath done? (John vii. 31).' But with none, except the Sadducees, was the doctrine allowed to fall into the back-ground. Under some

---

[f] Ξεναγούμενοι πρός τινος θειοτέρας ἢ κατὰ φύσιν ἀνθρωπίνης ὄψεως, ἀδήλου μὲν ἑτέροις, μόνοις δὲ τοῖς ἀνασωζομένοις ἐμφανοῦς, Philo de Execrat. § 8, 9. Cf. Langen, Judenthum, p. 398.

form or other all believed in a Messiah, all daily looked for Him, and were ready to join Him, and even to draw the sword for the restoration of David's throne. Their opinions were confused, incoherent, contradictory; but all held opinions, and those strong ones, upon His coming: and while the mass expected only a hero to fight for them, there were doubtless those who had higher conceptions of His nature, and were thus prepared to understand and embrace the spiritual interpretation put upon the writings of the prophets in the New Testament.

The first work to which I shall refer, for a more exact statement of the views entertained by the better class of Jews respecting the Messiah, is the Book of Enoch. To this University belongs the honour of having first published both an English translation (Archbp. Laurence's, Oxford, 1821), and subsequently the Ethiopic text (in 1838) of this, the most valuable of all the apocryphal writings, though apparently it was not from our present work that St. Jude made the quotation contained in the 14th verse of his Epistle. As regards its date, the best authorities ascribe it to the time of the Maccabees, and consider that its object was to defend and protect the teaching of the Old Testament against the errors and encroachments of Greek philosophy as held by the partizans of the Seleucidæ. Probably, however, very considerable additions have been made to the work at various times, and as all that we possess is a translation made for the use of a Christian Church, there is nothing surprising in the fact that a more directly Christian bearing has been given to certain portions of it. Like the Second Book of Esdras, it bears many marks of having been worked over by Christian hands. As a whole, however, the book represents the spirit of Judaism in its better days. Religion with it is not a matter of Rabbinical scrupulousness about externals, nor of the exact observance of the minuter precepts of the law, but of mercy, judgment, and truth. In its lofty tone, its earnest spirit, its wealth of thought, and its sincere piety, it is no unworthy companion of the canonical writings of the Jews [g].

It is thus the earliest of a large mass of literature which had its origin in the inspired Book of Daniel. With him first Jewish prophecy left the comparatively narrow circle within which it had hitherto worked, and contemplated the progress of the world from a Gentile point of view. With all the other prophets

[g] In 1851 Dillmann edited a text of the Book of Enoch, founded upon the collation of five manuscripts, and two years afterwards published a German translation with a most valuable and elaborate Introduction. Till the publication of these works the materials for criticism were not sufficiently definite to enable scholars to arrive at any certain conclusions as to the date of the book. Dillmann's own view, supported by very satisfactory arguments, is that it was written about 110 years before the birth of Christ (p. xliv): Ewald makes it still older, about 144 B.C. (See his Abhandlung über des Buches Henokh Entstehung, Göttingen, 1854.) Both of them consider that new matter has from time to time been interpolated, but Dillmann maintains that the great mass of the work was written by one and the same author. On the other hand, Philippi asserts that the book was written after the destruction of Jerusalem, at the end of the first century of our era (Das Buch Henoch, Stuttgart, 1868. p. 30, see also p. 142). It is, however, so thoroughly Jewish, in spite of its having been worked over by Christian hands, that I cannot believe that it was from the first a Christian work. Unfortunately there was a period when Christians rivalled the Jews of Egypt in the number of their forgeries, but they are all very clumsy performances, and their authors never attempt to give them any appropriate colouring. Philippi's is, however, a very clever essay, though not to be set against the judgment of Ewald and Dillmann.

the reign of Christ had ever been associated with the thought of a time of glory for their nation. Messiah's throne was the throne of David's son; the Levitical law was the law of His empire; His abode Jerusalem; Mount Zion the seat of His glory; the Jew foremost among His subjects; and the place of their worship a temple the very measurements of which had been given by Ezekiel. Whatever mercy there was for the Gentiles could be won only by their joining themselves to God's chosen people. No doubt this was but the outward aspect of Jewish prophecy. There were not wanting plain and definite indications that Christ's kingdom would be something far nobler and greater than these metaphors seemed at first sight to signify. In Daniel all is altered, as well the outer form as the inner essence. The prime minister of Chaldæan, Median, and Persian monarchs, he traces the course of Gentile history till the God of heaven sets up a kingdom that shall never be destroyed: and contemporaneously with its establishment 'the people of the prince destroy the city and the sanctuary,' and everything distinctly Jewish ceases to exist.

Naturally it was not this part of Daniel's predictions which formed the staple of Jewish apocalyptic literature. Such teaching may well be found in an inspired book, because the facts taught were the predeterminate counsel of God. But no Jew, especially in so spirit-stirring a struggle against heathenism as that of the Maccabæan age, could of himself have conceived or endured the thought that all that he was fighting for was very soon to be destroyed in order that Messiah's Gentile Church might be delivered from an element alien to her free development. The part of

Daniel generally imitated in apocalypses like those of Enoch and Esdras is his description of the Gentile kingdoms under the form of fierce and raging animals. Thus in the Book of Enoch, Judas Maccabæus is described as a lamb with a mighty horn, against which the Syrian kings of the race of Seleucus wage war in the shape of ravens. In a similar way in the Second Book of Esdras the Roman empire appears as an eagle, and the Cæsars are its twelve feathered wings; and in another place it is described as the fourth beast, which by the capture of Jerusalem had 'destroyed the dwellings of them that brought forth fruit (xi. 42).'

Now the doctrine of the Book of Enoch respecting the Messiah is very remarkable. He is usually spoken of as 'the Elect' or chosen one, a title equivalent to that more than once given to our Lord in the Gospels, 'the Holy One of God.' (Mark i. 24, Luke iv. 34, and in John vi. 69 in the Sinaitic and Vatican copies.) But he is also called the Anointed, the Son of Man, as in Daniel, and the Son of God, as by Nathanael. He is even called the Son of Woman, a name more strongly indicative of His human nature than even the title of the Son of Man. As regards His dignity, sometimes He holds a place very near to God; He sits upon the throne of majesty; all address to Him their prayers, and He rules over all: but in other places He is classed with the angels. Like them He has an existence prior to the founding of the world, a view adopted from the speculations of the Jews of Alexandria, and held, as we have seen, by the translators of the Septuagint. He is, moreover, the Teacher and Prophet of His people, and the spirit of the old prophets lives again in Him. It is worth noticing, too, that the Messiah is the Light, not of the Jews only, but also of the Gentiles. He is the teacher of virtue everywhere, the comforter of the distressed, the healer of those wounded in heart. He is also the Judge, before whose tribunal not mankind only, but Azazel and the fallen angels must stand. Finally, after the great judgment, heaven and earth will be changed and renovated, and henceforward no sinner will be found, nor sin exist, in Messiah's realm. No wonder that some of the fathers raised this book almost to the level of the inspired Scriptures [h].

And here I must notice, that while some of the Palestinian Jews recognized the Messiah as the Great Judge of the world, they never formed the idea of His second advent for the purpose of sitting in judgment. So to speak, there was no perspective in their views, but everything that every prophet had foretold as belonging to the Messiah was all compressed into one narrow period. Thus we find the apostles sorely puzzled when our Lord said that He was going away

[h] Tertullian, de Habitu Muliebri, § 3, argues that the book was actually written by Enoch, and was inspired. It is remarkable that he says that it was not received by the Jews, 'in armarium Judaicum non admittitur,' and in fact it does not represent their ordinary views respecting Christ. Clement of Alexandria also supposed it to be authentic, but the more critical Origen rejected its claims for himself, though leaving it as an open question for others. Jerome unhesitatingly calls it an apocryphal book, and destitute therefore of authority (Hieron. ad Ps. cxxxii. 3). Augustine (de Civ. Dei, xv. 23) thinks that Enoch wrote something, but denies that it was the so-called Book of Enoch: and he also mentions (Ib. xviii. 38), that the Jews rejected it. After Augustine's time it disappeared, excepting some long quotations from it in George Syncellus, till the famous traveller Bruce brought from Abyssinia the copy now in the Bodleian Library.

for a little while, and would then come again. Hence, too, the grief of the two disciples going to Emmaus, because He Who, they trusted, would have delivered Israel had died a malefactor's death. And again, in St. John's Gospel, where we find the most numerous allusions to the current opinions of the Jews, when Christ foretells His death the people make this objection, 'We have heard out of the law that the Messiah abideth for ever, and how sayest Thou, The Son of Man—another name for the Messiah—must be lifted up? (John xii. 34).' Now this view, too, is found in the Book of Enoch. The Messiah at His advent first sets His people free, then holds a general judgment, and finally reigns for ever upon a renovated earth over a people incapable of sinning.

Another interesting work is the Psalter of Solomon, consisting of eighteen Psalms, written in the style of the Old Testament, and bewailing the sufferings of the chosen people. From the account given of these sufferings there can be little doubt that the writer's just indignation was stirred at the barbarities inflicted upon Jerusalem by Pompey, after it had of its own accord opened its gates to receive him. The siege and profanation of the temple, the merciless slaughter of its defenders, and of many of the inhabitants of the city, and the leading away into captivity of its sons and daughters, are regarded as so many chastisements brought upon the nation by the godless misrule of the later princes of the Maccabæan line. Naturally the writer turns for comfort to the promises made to the Jews of a Messiah, who will avenge these cruelties, but unfortunately the Hebrew original was translated by some Christian hand, and we can put no confidence in the genuineness of its Messianic teaching[i]. The two most important passages (Ps. xvii. 33-51, xviii. 6-10) are probably even interpolations. All we can safely affirm is, that the public calamities of the nation had filled the writer with an eager longing for the Messiah's advent, and for that display of supernatural power whereby He was to save the nation. The work was much valued at one time by Christians, as is proved by its being the only specimen of Jewish apocryphal literature inserted as an appendix to the New Testament in our own Codex Alexandrinus.

But, after all, the Targums are the most trustworthy evidence of the views and opinions of the Jews at the very time when our Lord was manifest in the flesh. The oldest of these paraphrases — that of Onkelos upon the Pentateuch—keeps very closely, as a general rule, to the Hebrew original. Twice, however, it refers to Christ passages of very great importance. The first of these is the well-known text respecting Shiloh in Jacob's blessing, which Onkelos renders as follows: 'A sultan shall not pass away from the house of Judah, nor a scribe—an interpreter of the law—from his sons' sons for ever, until Messiah shall come, Whose is the kingdom, and Him shall the Gentiles obey (Gen. xlix. 10).' We have a proof here that the Jews were expecting the speedy arrival of the day of their deliverance, and that they believed that the Gentiles would then be subject unto them. The

---

[i] Movers, Dillmann, Ewald, Delitzsch, Langen. all agree that the style is too Hebraizing for the work possibly to have had any other than a Hebrew original. Huet, on a less critical examination of the Psalter, had thought it was written in Greek. Fuller information will be found in the Church Lexicons of Wetzer and Welte (Romanist), and Herzog (Protestant).

other passage is Balaam's prophecy of the star, which Onkelos paraphrases thus: 'A king shall arise out of Jacob, and Messiah shall wax great [k] out of Israel, and shall kill the princes of Moab, and rule over all the sons of men (Num. xxiv. 17).' Again, we find Messiah as a king, invested with universal empire, slaying ruthlessly, and giving the Jews that vengeance which the long and cruel wrongs inflicted upon Jerusalem had made the inhabitants of Palestine so eagerly desire, a feeling, however, of which we find no trace among the more prosperous Jews of Egypt. The Septuagint version of both these places is entirely destitute of interest. The Alexandrians do not seem to have attached any importance to either of these prophecies.

The other Targum, that of Jonathan [1] upon the historical books of the Old Testament and the Prophets, is distinguished first of all by its division of

[k] This is usually translated, 'shall be anointed,' but the passages alleged in proof of this rendering seem to me rather to mean, 'to be made the high priest.' I have given the ordinary and usual signification of the verb.

[1] The Targum of Jonathan, though probably committed to writing at Babylon two or three centuries after Christ, is yet satisfactory evidence of the opinions of the Jews of previous ages, because of the tenacity of the hold which tradition had over their minds. Thus the Massorites, who began their work in the sixth century after Christ, seem to have given us little of their own, but have put into writing, with the most minute accuracy, that system of reading Hebrew which was elaborated in Judæa in the first and second centuries of our era, and which rested even then upon an older basis. So the translation of the Hebrew text into Chaldee had begun with Ezra (Neh. viii. 8), and without doubt its interpretation became a matter of tradition, from which neither Onkelos nor Jonathan departed very widely. The other Targums I pass by as too late in date and too Haggadic in character to be trustworthy. All the Targums are entirely Jewish, and have never been coloured by Christian scribes or translators.

time into that before Messiah's advent, and Messiah's own time. Thus to the account of Solomon's wisdom, his 3000 proverbs, and 1005 songs, Jonathan adds these extraordinary words, 'And he prophesied of the kings of the house of David, that shall reign in this world and in the coming world of the Messiah (1 Kings iv. 32).' He thus seems to have imagined that when the Messiah had restored David's throne, a new line of kings sprung from His body would reign over Israel. Elsewhere, however, he speaks as if Messiah Himself would be their perpetual king. For in Isaiah's prophecy, 'Unto us a Son is born,' he paraphrases the names of the Messiah thus; ' God wonderful in counsel, man enduring to eternity, even Messiah, Whose peace shall be multiplied upon us in His days (Is. ix. 6).' Apparently he expected a restoration of the theocracy in the person of an immortal and divine [m] Christ.

[m] We must not, however, conclude too much from his calling the Messiah ' God wonderful in counsel.' The divinity of Christ was certainly not a Jewish dogma. We find no trace of it elsewhere in Jonathan. Thus if we turn to crucial passages like Micah v. 2 we find him rendering the prophet's words thus, ' Out of thee, Bethlehem, shall Messiah go forth before Me to exercise dominion over Israel, Whose name has been spoken from of old, from the days of eternity.' So in Zech. xiii. 7 his rendering is, ' Unsheath thyself, O sword, against the king, and against the prince, who is his companion and equal.' Even in the Book of Enoch, which gives so high a place to the Messiah, He stands among the angels to worship God (lxi. 10). So, too, the words of ch. xlviii. 6, ' He was chosen and concealed before God before the world was created, and even to eternity will He be before Him,' belong to that connection of the idea of the Messiah with the divine Wisdom, which produced the Alexandrian teaching of the Logos, and which made even the Sadducees acknowledge a sort of eternity in Wisdom, see Ecclus. xxiv. It was not a personal existence, and yet Jonathan avoids even granting this (Micah v. 2), though immediately before he had been speaking (Ib. iv. 8) of the concealment of Israel's Messiah, and the delay of His kingdom

In those magnificent chapters of Isaiah, which treat of the Servant of Jehovah, the Targum refers all to Christ, yet so as to exclude from Him every note of suffering. Every word there of sorrow and affliction Jonathan transfers to the Jewish people: it is they who suffer, while the Messiah is a victorious warrior. Thus the words, ' He hath no form nor comeliness' are paraphrased as follows : 'His aspect shall be no common aspect, nor His fear like the fear of a private person: but His beauty shall be the beauty of holiness ; whosoever seeth Him shall look at Him with admiration. He shall be despised, indeed, but He shall strip all kings of their glory ; they shall be feeble and in pain, like a man of sorrows, and one delivered over to diseases (Is. liii. 3).' In the following verses it is the Jewish people who are smitten of God for their own sins: and the Messiah, so far from being the Lamb, is the Judge, Who 'shall sentence the mighty among the Gentiles like lambs to the slaughter, and like a sheep silent before its shearers, nor shall any one venture to open his mouth and speak in His presence (Ib. 7).' And when thus He has given over the

---

because of their sins. In short, Trypho in Justin Martyr's dialogue gives the ordinary Jewish view, even though there were better schools of thought, which held that in some sense or other the Messiah would be the Son of God. Trypho says, ' We all expect that the Messiah will be a man born of men (c. 49):' and again ; ' It is an incredible and well-nigh impossible thing that thou undertakest to prove, that God submitted to be born and become a man (c. 68).' Naturally, therefore, he denied that the Messiah's birth was miraculous, and said that the virgin of Isaiah vii. 14 meant a young woman (c. 71): and when Justin affirmed that He would not be the seed of man's race, Trypho answered. ' How then does the Scripture say to David that God will take to Himself a son of his loins. and will establish his kingdom, and seat him upon the throne of his glory? (c. 68).'

wicked [n] to the grave, explained as Gehenna, the place of the lost, He purifies His own people, and accompanied solely by the righteous He takes great nations for His prey, and strong states for His spoil. And so, generally, in this Targum the Messiah appears often as King, as Judge, as High Priest, as Prophet: He never appears as a Saviour, as one Who will make atonement for His people's sins and die in their stead. As regards the actual passages, Jonathan refers to Christ, as a rule, the same texts that we do; but there is an impassable gulf between his interpretation of them and that of the Christian Church.

Now the Targum of Jonathan was a book of authority among the Jews, and was regarded as only less venerable than the inspired text itself. We may be sure, therefore, that it embodies no private views, but is the record of the received opinions of the scribes and teachers of the Law. Nevertheless, it is a far worse corruption of the sense of Holy Scripture than anything contained in the Book of Enoch, and may be almost called a systematic perversion of the

---

[n] The exact sense of Jonathan's words in this place may be elucidated by his rendering of Isaiah xi. 4, 'By the speaking of His lips He shall slay the wicked Armillus.' Armillus is the great opponent of the Jewish Messiah, the personal representative and captain of the Gentiles on whom Messiah is to wage war. In subsequent times, Armillus became with the Rabbins the symbol of the Christian Church, and they described him as the offspring of Belial and a beautiful female statue at Rome, made to conceive by magical arts. Beneath his banners all the sons of Esau were to gather to attack Jerusalem, where, according to some, he would slay Messias ben Joseph, but finally would himself be slain by the breath of the true Messiah, according to Isaiah xi. 4. A full account of the various legends concerning him will be found in Buxtorf's Rabbinic Lexicon.

teaching of the prophets. And these were the views which prevailed at the time of our Lord's advent. The mass of the people expected a Messiah armed with supernatural powers, but he was to use these powers for earthly purposes, to drive the Romans from their land, and lead the armies of Israel to the conquest of the world. Hence their eagerness to make our Lord a king after the miracle of feeding the thousands, and the care with which He frustrated their endeavours, and ever taught His disciples that the Messiah was to suffer. Hence the constant disputes of the apostles about place and dignity, and the request of Zebedee's wife that James and John might be the two chief officers of state in Christ's kingdom. Hence, too, the constant uprisings of the populace, their readiness to follow Theudas, and Judas of Galilee, and Bar-Cochba. They were living in a very fever of expectation for the coming of their deliverer; they saw that Judah's sceptre had departed; they knew that Daniel's weeks had expired; but they would not believe that at the end of those weeks their sanctuary would be destroyed, their city captured, their temple-service suppressed, and 'the power of the holy people scattered.' And so their very fanaticism led to the exact fulfilment of the words of the prophets in their true meaning. They joined in cutting off their Messiah because he was no fierce warrior but a preacher of holiness, Whose kingdom was not of this world. And then they brought by their restlessness the avenging armies of Rome upon their city, and from that time the sacrifice of the great day of atonement has been offered no more.

Even before the Jews ceased to be a nation, they

had ceased to be God's Church. But that separation between the believing and the unbelieving Jews which Malachi had described as the Messiah's great work (iii. 1–5) at His first advent, became then complete, and God's covenant from that day forth has been with those who had accepted the Gospel of His Son. God cannot have two Churches; still less can the preparatory Church and that final and perfect Church for which it was to prepare exist at the same time. But Jews founded the Christian Church. Jews were everywhere its first teachers, its missionaries and apostles, its bishops and pastors. Jews everywhere were the first converts, and the nucleus in every town round which the Gentiles gathered. The forms of worship in their synagogues became those of Christian congregations, their scriptures are our inspired law, and to this day our very name testifies that we are those who have accepted a Jewish Messiah. All this had been foreshown before. When the Chaldæans encamped before Jerusalem, Jeremiah (xxiv.) warned the Jews that in destroying city and temple, with the high priests, the king, the princes, and the people, Nebuchadnezzar was not destroying the Jewish Church: for it had departed from Jerusalem with the believing Jews, who went into captivity with Jeconiah to Babylon. So Titus did not destroy God's covenant-people. They had gone to Pella as the believers in His Christ. Those who remained at Jerusalem were the refuse merely whom God had cast out, because in their greed for earthly dominion they had rejected the spiritual blessings offered them by the true Messiah.

Plainly, the Christ of the Gospels was not the creation of uninspired thought. His wondrous character, His spiritual teaching, His kingdom of grace in the hearts of men, His future kingdom of heavenly blessedness, all this the prophets had taught, but the Jews had not found it in their writings. Their imagination had seized only upon metaphors and symbols drawn from earthly things, and these, grossly materialized, had entirely obscured in their minds all the better and deeper teachings of their scriptures. The doctrine of a suffering Saviour was not revealed even to Peter ' by flesh and blood, but by the Father Who is in Heaven (Matt. xvi. 17).' To the mass of the Jews, when our Lord came, the Messiah was scarcely more than a mere political character, a warrior who would bid them rise against Edom—the Roman empire—to battle, and give them Zarephath and Sepharad—the fertile regions of France and Spain—for a possession (Obad. 1, 19, 20). As usual, man's necessity was God's opportunity. When Scribes and Pharisees had done their worst to blot out and darken the teaching of the Scriptures concerning the Messiah, He came Who is our true Light, and the words of the prophets were set forth for the first time in their real meaning, and that a meaning so clear, so simple, so straightforward, so consistent, that we wonder how any other interpretation could ever have been put upon their teaching.

There are numerous other writings of this period, chiefly of an apocalyptic character, which, if time permitted, would serve to show conclusively how entirely the Messiah of the Jews of Palestine had become a mere man, from whom every thought of heavenly dignity, and every diviner attribute, had been completely removed. I must content myself, however, with a very brief reference to two works written at the end of the first century of our era, and both expressive of the honest indignation of the Jews against the Romans for the cruelty with which they had destroyed Jerusalem and treated its inhabitants. These two are the Second Book of Esdras, and the Ascension of Moses[o]. Of the latter, however, I shall make no further use than to say that it proves to us that the creditable view of the Messiah set before us in the Book of Esdras was not the chance product of one religious thinker, but was held at the end of the first century, at all events, by the better class of minds. For substantially the two works agree, and both stand in agreeable contrast with the Targum of Jonathan, and with the unpatriotic Josephus, who was base enough to apply to Vespasian the predictions of the prophets respecting Christ.

No doubt the capture of Jerusalem by Titus was a terrible blow to those who were at that very time eagerly anticipating in their Messiah an able general to lead them on to victory, and may have led many

[o] This work, which is quoted by Clement of Alexandria, Origen, Œcumenius and other fathers, had long been regarded as lost, but in the year 1861 a fragment of a Latin translation of it was found by Ceriani in the Ambrosian Library at Milan, and published in the first volume of his Monumenta Sacra et Profana. It is a slavishly literal translation of a Hebrew original, which was probably written about the same time as the Second Book of Esdras. Both books describe the Roman empire under the similitude of an eagle with many necks and wings; and both have the same object, namely, to comfort the Jews for the destruction of their city and temple by Titus. A time of retribution, they teach, draws near, and then shall Israel mount up to heaven on eagles' wings, and sit among the stars, while their enemies lie humbled upon the earth. 'Of Christian view and interpretation not the least trace can be discovered in this fragment: we have in it a genuine product of the Jews of Palestine.' Langen, Judenthum, p. 106.

others besides Josephus to open infidelity. The disappointment and pain caused by the abandonment of false religious tenets too often produces this effect, but there are others whom it leads to search for a more true interpretation. And thus, in the Second Book of Esdras, we find the Messiah invested with religious attributes. The book itself, which was known in early times to Jerome and Ambrose, has long disappeared, but in the year 1462 a Latin translation of it was appended to the Vulgate. It exists also in various oriental versions, but has not hitherto been discovered in Greek; and it ought to be mentioned that, though appended to the Vulgate, its pages are separately numbered, and it has nothing of that critical apparatus which accompanies those books which the Church of Rome considers in any sense canonical. Readers are in fact warned in the Preface to the Vulgate, that neither the Third nor Fourth Books of Esdras—our first and second—are anything more than *adscititium et extraneum quid*. Our own Church, not using the uncanonical Scriptures for the establishment of doctrine, inserts both the Books of Esdras among its Apocrypha, but it does not thereby give them any more authority than that possessed by the Book of Enoch, the Third and Fourth Books of Maccabees, the Ascensions of Moses and Isaiah, the Book of Jubilees, and the Testament of the twelve Patriarchs. There was a vast apocryphal literature, of which the works appended to our Bible are specimens, but most of those mentioned above have been brought to light again in modern days, since the time when our version was made. The First Book of Esdras is an Alexandrian work of very little value.

The Second Book is really most interesting, but is known to us at present only in a bald Latin translation; and this has been so interpolated by Christian hands, that whole chapters are a mere tissue of phrases taken from the New Testament. Even the name of Jesus occurs in it (vii. 28), where no doubt in the Hebrew original the word was Messiah. Nevertheless, the Jewish part is easily separable from the rest, and is the work of a man of deep religious feeling, but entirely ignorant of Christianity. It burns with intense indignation against the Romans for their cruel treatment of Jerusalem, and finds in the hope of Messiah's advent consolation under the miseries of the times.

The main portion of the book is a vision of the Roman empire under the figure of an eagle. Its twelve wings, as I mentioned before, are the twelve Cæsars: of these the two first, Julius Cæsar and Augustus, are more fully described, as also the last three of the Flavian house, Vespasian, Titus, and Domitian, who naturally are the objects of the writer's ill-concealed aversion. Rapidly they fall, and with them the empire of the twelve Cæsars is brought to a disastrous close. A double pair of wings next arises; they are the Emperor Nerva, and Trajan, his chosen successor. And now the purpose of the vision discloses itself. A roaring lion[p] from the wood, speaking with man's voice to the eagle, condemns it for unjust and tyrannous rule, and proclaims its speedy downfall. That lion is the Messiah, come to deliver the Jew from the intolerable yoke of Rome.

---

[p] Compare Revelation v. 5.

It might have been dangerous to speak openly, but surely it must have been a relief to apostrophize the Romans thus: 'Thy wrongful dealing hath come up to the Highest, and thy pride to the Mighty One. The Highest hath also looked upon the proud times, and behold they are ended, and their abominations fulfilled. And therefore appear no more, thou eagle, nor thy horrible wings, nor thy wicked feathers, nor thy malicious heads, nor thy hurtful claws, nor all thy vain body: that all the earth may be refreshed, being delivered from thy violence (ch. xi. 43–46).' The cruelties practised by Titus upon Jerusalem were still fresh in the writer's mind, but probably it was not merely the feebleness of Nerva's reign, but still more the prophecies of Daniel, which made him hope that a speedy retribution for these cruelties was at hand.

But this retribution is confined within the limits of justice, and we find in the vision of Esdras no trace of that lust of conquest which would have raised the Jews to an equally wicked eminence with the four great military empires of Daniel's dream (vii). Titus had crushed them too utterly for such of them at least as lived in Italy still to dream of battle and war. And thus we find only a tame anticipation of a millennium, if one may so call it, limited to four hundred years, in which the Jews will rejoice in Christ's personal reign. 'My son Jesus[q] shall be revealed with those that be with Him, and they

---

[q] Ambrose, on Luke ii. 21, had already pointed out that the word Jesus has been substituted for something else. It is morally certain that the translator was a Christian, and, finding Messiah in the Hebrew text, instead of rendering it by Christus, or unctus, he put Jesus as the exact equivalent, in his view, of the original word. See above, p. 359.

that remain shall rejoice within four hundred years (2 Esdras vii. 28).' If in these words we are struck by the absence of the fierce fanaticism of the Targum of Jonathan, even more remarkable is the next verse, 'After these years shall My son Christ die, and all men that have life, and the world shall be turned into the old silence seven days, like as in the former judgments.' It seems, then, that in his view there had been a perpetual series of dispensations, between each of which there was upon earth the silence of death for a period as long as the creative week; and the end of the present dispensation he thought was approaching, but before it came the Jews would have at least a moderately long period of consolation. And then they and their Messiah and all living things would die, and after the seven days' silence the dead would rise, and God hold a judgment. If in all this there was a religious conception of the Messiah's character, yet it was a very mean one, nor does the writer attempt any exposition of the actual words of prophecy, but rather substitutes for them his own notions.

There is, then, an impassable gulf between the Christ of the Jewish interpretation of prophecy and the Christ of the Gospels. That interpretation was in no sense a preparation for the teaching of our Lord: His Gospel was no culmination of ideas which had long been at work in the Jewish mind. Christ at Alexandria had become an allegory with the mass, and a metaphysical Logos with the philosophers; in Palestine He was a warrior, with no attributes but those of strength and cruelty; and if in certain apocryphal works we find a religious conception of His character, it was the view probably of minor sects only, and had little influence over the popular mind. Even these works fall utterly short of the teaching of the Gospel, and had little or nothing to do with its success. The reception of that teaching was not effected without a violent wrench alike to the Jew of Jerusalem and the Jew of Egypt. It involved a revolution in all their habits of thought, and this was not accomplished without a fierce and bitter struggle. In the Acts of the Apostles we find abundant evidence of the violence of the conflict, and the battle there gathered chiefly round St. Stephen and St. Paul, the two men who most clearly saw that Christianity implied the abolition of Judaism. In the history of the Christian Church the traces of the struggle are equally plain. We see the marks of it in the deep hatred which grew up between the Christian and the Jew; we see it in the general neglect of Hebrew by the Fathers, in the upgrowth of sects which rejected the Jewish Scriptures, and in the doctrine of books like the Apostolical Constitutions, which taught that the mass of the Old Testament was a Deuteronomy, a second law, bad in itself, and imposed upon the Jews because of the badness of their hearts.

In short, we now in these latter days see only, or chiefly, the profound inner agreement between the Old and the New Testament. Men at first saw chiefly their external antagonism, and to thousands of devout men, brought up to love and venerate and to believe in the eternal obligation of the Mosaic law, it must have been an intense and heartfelt misery which they had to endure, before they could bring themselves to believe that that law was a mere παιδαγωγός, a slave, with no higher function than to lead on the heir, while still under the beggarly elements of the world, to the true teacher Christ (Gal. iii. 24); and that the Christian was that heir, no longer in his nonage, but arrived at man's estate, and in full possession of his heritage.

Nor did the Jew alone thus feel. The key to most of the heresies which troubled the early Church, was the conviction of an antagonism, instead of an agreement, between the two Covenants. If Marcion, in his Book of Oppositions ('Ἀντιθέσεις), wrought the theory out, the strength of his party lay in the fact that the Christian interpretation of the prophets was something new, and entirely contrary to the interpretation current among the Jews.

And thus, then, in the first place, cursory as is this view of what the Jews thought of Christ, it may make it easier to understand the cause of the general indignation aroused in the mind of the populace at Jerusalem by the teaching of Jesus of Nazareth. He had those, indeed, who loved Him: Galilæans, it may be, chiefly, who lived too far away from the centres of thought to hold very settled theories as to what the Messiah ought or ought not to be; but plainly some of the Jews in Jerusalem also believed in Him. The mass saw in Him one Who contradicted and frustrated all their hopes; and if the Galilæans were content to follow a lowly king with their hosannas, their own cry was, Crucify Him! Peter and the few said, 'Lord to whom shall we go? Thou hast the words of eternal life.' What was eternal life to the populace? They wanted the empire of the world, and if the Messiah would not give it them, then they would destroy Him. And, secondly, the Christ of the Gospels is no human invention. Men did not at all learn what He would be from the words of prophecy, plain though they be. Give men what proof you will, but seldom do they find more than what it suits them to find. If what is said agrees with their preconceived notions, well: if not, they reject it. So was it with the oracles of truth. The Jew did not find the interpretation, because he never sought to find it. If we see it, it is because the Holy Ghost has given us the true exposition of those Scriptures which He Himself inspired.

NOTES.

NOTE A, p. 16.

The following Note, conclusively showing that Buddhism is a religion destitute of historical credibility, has been kindly furnished me by one able to speak with authority upon the subject, E. B. Cowell, Esq., M.A., Professor of Sanskrit in the University of Cambridge.

BUDDHISM cannot be called an historical religion, if we mean by that term a religion whose origin is to be traced in contemporary annals.

S'ákya Muni himself (like Socrates) left no writings behind him; his teaching was only oral; and there are two separate streams of tradition for his history and doctrines. These are found in the Sanskrit books of Nepal, i.e. the *Northern* tradition, current in Nepal, Tibet, China, and Mongolia; and in the Pali book of Ceylon, i.e. the *Southern*, current in Ceylon, Burmah, and Siam. These books are said to have been gradually arranged in the celebrated Three Councils, in a threefold form—the discourses of Buddha (*sútra*), the ceremonies and discipline (*vinaya*), and the metaphysics (*abhidharma*). But the dates of these Councils differ in the two traditions. The Southern fixes them as respectively held (1) shortly after the founder's death; (2) 100 years after it, under king Kálás'oka; and (3) 235 years after it, under

Dharmásoka; while the Northern fixes the two latter as held 110 years after his death, under Asoka, and more than 400 years after in Cashmir, under Kanishka. The Ceylonese say nothing of a reduction to writing even at the third Council, and their great chronicle the Maháwanso, expressly states that the canonical traditions, which were introduced into Ceylon by the missionaries from the third Council, were not committed to writing till the reign of Wattagámini, B.C. 100–88. The Northern traditions may have been reduced to writing at their third Council, 400 years after S'ákya Muni's death. We can hardly, in fact, believe that nothing was written even at an earlier date; but we have no reason to suppose that any text which we at present possess goes back even to Kanishka's time.

The Lalita Vistara, our great authority for the early life of Buddha, has been published in Sanskrit. There are said to be four Chinese translations of it: the first was made between A.D. 70 and 76, the second A.D. 308, the third about A.D. 652; of the fourth and latest I do not know the date, but as only the third and fourth have the same division as our present Sanskrit text, into 27 chapters, it would appear that the two earlier may represent another text; but on this point we want fuller information. The Lalita Vistara is legendary in the highest degree—it has miracles in every chapter, and is written in the most hyperbolical style. Every event is related twice, first in a very bald mediæval Sanskrit, and then in a poetical version of very corrupted Sanskrit. The latter appears to be the older version, representing these legends in their popular ballad shape.

No doubt the same legends are to a great extent current in every Buddhist country; but directly we proceed to analyse them, we find the usual divergencies which characterize a legendary, as distinguished from an historical, period. Thus, to take only one instance, the Northern tradition calls the bride whom S'ákya Muni wins by his skill in arts and arms, Gopá, the daughter of Daṇḍapáṇi, but the Southern calls her Yaśodhará, the daughter of S'ákya Suprabuddha. It is well known that there are at least twenty different dates of S'ákya Muni's death, varying between B.C. 2422 and 543; and even the last date (that of the Ceylonese) has been falsified, and has been conjecturally corrected by modern scholars to B.C. 477.

We know with historical accuracy what Buddhism was three or four centuries after its founder's death, and we may conjecture with great probability what his own teaching actually was; but the details of his life are wrapt in the same cloud of fiction which envelopes every event in ancient Indian history. We must never forget Elphinstone's remark at the commencement of his 'Hindu period,' 'no *date* of a public event can be fixed before the invasion of Alexander, and no *connected* relation of the national transactions can be attempted until after the Mohammedan conquest;' or, in other words, we can only get historical light when other nations, possessing an authentic history of their own, come in contact with the Hindus; but they, of course, can be of no use with regard to events which they could only learn from legends current in India.

[The best account of Buddha and his doctrines is to be found in the first volume of Koeppen's 'Die Religion des Buddha und ihre Entstehung,' Berlin, 1857. Its tone is decidedly anti-Christian, but it contains a store of information collected together from different sources.]

NOTE B, p. 42.

NOTHING can be more contrary to the teaching of Holy Scripture than that view of inspiration which confines it to words. In the Bible most of the great acts of the heroes of old time are ascribed to the presence of God's Spirit.

When Othniel stirred up the military ardour of Judah, and led that great tribe to battle against the king of Mesopotamia, it was 'because the Spirit of Jehovah was upon him (Judges iii. 10). Such, too, was the case with Gideon (Ib. vi. 34), with Jephthah (Ib. xi. 29), with Samson, when he rent the lion (Ib. xiv. 6), and when, having burst the new cords with which he was bound, he slew of the Philistines a thousand men (Ib. xv. 14). The Bible speaks in the same way of gifts of artistic skill. Bezaleel's hand was cunning in gold and silver work, and in cutting of stones, and wood-carving, because 'he was filled with the Spirit of God (Ex. xxxi. 3).' Such, too, was the case with Aholiab (Ib. xxxv. 35). Even the ordinary operations of agriculture 'come forth from Jehovah of Hosts: He hath made counsel wonderful, He hath magnified skill (Is. xxviii. 29).' If Isaiah uses words such as these of the labours of the farm, may we not apply them with even fuller meaning to the wonderful enterprizes of the engineer, and to all the works of genius?

But here, as also where St. James tells us that all good and perfect gifts come down to us from God, the difficulty is to draw the right line of distinction between God's gifts where they are the result of His working in nature, and where that working was special and extraordinary. It may be that these two methods of working, apparently so different to us, are not different in themselves. At all events in the workings of Providence we cannot distinguish them. We believe that not a hair of our heads falls to the ground without Divine permission; that our smallest and most ordinary acts are not separable from God's working: while in the great crisis of our spiritual lives we feel that there have been special interventions in our behalf. God has been working by and in natural laws, and yet, apparently, has controlled them for our individual good (1 Cor. x. 13, Phil. ii. 13). Believers have the fullest conviction of this, and yet might hesitate about saying that God had wrought a miracle for them, or that the laws of nature had not held on their undeviating course. They are content with saying that such interpositions are providential. So, if we were to say that these operations of the Spirit of Jehovah, spoken of especially in the Book of Judges, were providential, many might think this a sufficient explanation, because they imagine that some sort of distinction can be drawn between the providential and the miraculous. Really, the terms miracle and miraculous are unknown to the Bible: they are the products of the Latin language, which has done so much by the inaccuracy of its words to vitiate theology. The working of God is so much more perfect than man's working, that that which seems to man miraculous, because unusual, may be perfectly natural to God. If you drive God out of the world, and exalt nature into His place, understanding by nature a working of matter only, neither originating in, nor sustained or controlled by any intelligent mind, then of course you leave for God only such operations as are unnatural, and it does not much matter what you call them, miraculous or not. Not only scientific men, but theologians, I presume, would join in disbelieving in the existence of such actions. But if 'in God we live and move and have our being,' our natural actions cannot be separated from Him, and to Him all actions may be alike natural, though they differ according to the degree in which His presence in them is apparent to our perceptions. In fact, in these things we are reasoning about that of which we know nothing. In all the discussions that have lately taken place about prayer, there has been out of sight the assumption of the postulate that God is a man, acts as a man, and is subject in His working to the same limitations as man. Grant this, and of course prayer cannot produce any effect: providence is impossible: a revelation absurd, and miracle monstrous. Grant it, and *post mortem nihil*. But if God be God and not man, and not subject to human limitations, these results do not follow. If a flock of sheep were to discuss man's nature, they could form no idea of him but that he was a very strong and mischievous kind of sheep. Man's discussions about God's nature are about as wise and convincing. But worthless as they are, after all we cannot form any idea of God except as a very powerful and perfect man, because no being can rise to any idea higher than that of itself freed from all imperfections. But while we may feel sure that God's absolute attributes, such as love, goodness, justice, must be in accordance with our ideas, we ought to recognize that His negative attributes are only veils to our ignorance. We can form no idea of infinity, immutability, eternity. And thus all our discussions must stop at a certain point, and all negative conclusions be worthless. Enough, then, to notice that the Bible does not draw a distinction between the action of God's Spirit upon Samson when rending the lion, and upon Isaiah when prophesying of the Messiah. To us the difference may be vast. In ordinary language we might call the one a natural impulse, or, at most, speak of it as providential : the other we should call supernatural. Really, the difference may be that in one God reveals His presence more than in the other : in natural operations His arm is hidden, in supernatural He makes it bare in the sight of all His people.

INDEX OF SUBJECTS.

Aaron, Moses' prophet, 56.
Abraham, a prophet, 54.
— chief of a clan, 82.
Advent, Christ's second, not a Jewish doctrine, 347.
Ahithophel, counsel of, 135.
Alexandria, Jews of, see 'Israelites.'
Amos, not trained at a prophetic college, 111, 143.
— his mission temporary, 113, 199.
— his literary skill, 147 and *note*.
— prophecy of the booth, 262.
— quoted at Council of Jerusalem, 268.
Angels, ministry of in times of Judges, 65.
— Alexandrian theory of, 339.
Ark, superstitious use of, 100.
— its significance, 270.
— Jewish myths about, 270.
Armillus, Jewish legends of, 353 *n*.

Baal, used as a name in Saul's family, 110 *n*.
Babylon, its prosperity of short duration, 309.
— contrasted with Alexandria, 315.
Babylonia, alluvial nature of its soil, 295.
Bible, its circulation, 4 *n*.
— a collection of numerous books, 200 *n*.
— conditions it has to fulfil, 246.
— its meaning exhaustless, 290.
— not an ordinary book, 292.
See also 'Hezekiah' and 'Testament.'
Bethel, old prophet of, 159, 182.
Buddhism, unhistorical nature of, 365 *n*.
Burden, meaning of, 34 *n*., 47, 223.

Canaanites, their position in Palestine, 91.

Catholicity of Church, taught by prophets, 221, 230.
— resisted by Jews, 226.
Chozeh, name for prophet, 47, 48.
Christ, Son of the Fallen, 267.
— not sprung from any king but David, 278.
— two expected by Jews, 267.
— Jewish views about His advent, 326.
— conflicting views of, in Palestine, 337.
— His twofold sonship, 326, 336.
— cause of His crucifixion, 330.
— His personality not believed in Jews of Egypt, 335, 341.
— regarded in Palestine as a soldier, 335, 342.
— His personal reign, as taught in 2nd Book of Esdras, 360.
— His sufferings not understood by Jews, 226, 267, 285.
Christianity not incompatible with progress, 9.
— influence of, increases with civilization, 14.
— its relation to Judaism, 272, 355.
Church, its type, mountain of Jehovah, 273.
— prophesied of by Micah, 278.
— its forms taken from Jews of the dispersion, 319, 355.
— its relation to Jewish Church, 355.
Clergy, analogy of, to prophets, 106, 113.
— originators of religious movements, 162.
College, see 'Prophets.'
Cosmogony, Indian, 9.
Creation, two accounts of, 36.
— view of, in Septuagint, 335.
Criticism, negative, see 'Rationalism.'

Daniel, differs from all other prophets, 214, 269, 344.
— Book of, why not placed among writings of Prophets, 215.
— not educated in prophetic schools, 215.
— origin of apocalyptic literature in Book of, 346.
— clearly teaches a resurrection, 258.
David, trained by Samuel, 131.
— rebuked by Nathan, 161.
— evil effects of his wars, 198.
— sure mercies of, 259, 261, 265 *n*.
— prophecies relating to fall of his dynasty, 265 *n*.
— his dynasty not restored, 266.
Deioces contrasted with Samuel, 104.
Deuteronomy, meaning of, in Fathers, 194 and *note*.
Didascalia Apostolorum, its teaching as regards the Jews, 194.
Divination absolutely forbidden, 155, 222, 276.

Ecclesiasticus, teaching of Book of, 340.
Egypt, Jews of, see 'Israelites.'
Elijah, why raised up in northern kingdom, 162.
— his work on Mount Carmel, 176.
— why present at Transfiguration, 186, 210.
Elisha, rector of prophetic colleges, 140, 151.
— progress of education under, 138.
— learning of, 147.
Enoch, Book of, its date, 343, 344 *n*.
— its teaching concerning Christ, 346, 351 *n*.
— view of the Fathers concerning, 347.
Ephraim, its claim to supremacy, 260.
Ereb, account of, 88.
Esdras, 1st Book of, worthless, 358.
— 2nd Book of, symbol of Roman empire in, 346, 359.
— not included by Church of Rome among Apocrypha, 358.
— criticism of, 359.
Evidences, internal, value of, 16, 18.

Ezekiel, his imagery reproduced in the Apocalypse, 287.
Ezra, his work on canon of Scripture, 293 *n*.

Family, see 'Mishpachah.'
Farhad, his teaching respecting the Jews, 195 *n*.
Feasts, Jewish, their purpose, 312.
Field, meaning of, 152.
Flood, narrative of, 36.

Gehazi, rank of, 139 *n*.
Genealogies, omission of names in, 119 *n*.
Genesis, Book of, its opening words, 210; grand truths in, 304.
Gourd, Elisha's, what, 152 *n*.
Grove, meaning of, 182 *n*.

Habakkuk, his prophecy written, not spoken, 199.
— difficulty of God's providence only partially answered by, 308.
Hebrew, neglect of study of, 247, 282.
— manuscripts destroyed by Christians, 334.
Heman, a grandson of Samuel, 217.
Hezekiah, malady of, 164.
— reign of, period of high culture, 293, 307.
— last fifteen years of, 301.
History, special study of prophets, 203.
Hosea, Book of, its lesson God's love, 251, 260.
— remarkable prediction in, 260.
Houses, families divided into, 87 *n*., 92.
Hymns, doctrinal, origin of, 212 *n*.

Idolatry, overthrown by Isaiah, 302.
Immortality of soul, why not taught by Moses, 192, 193.
Inspiration of Old and New Testaments equal, 34.
— two errors concerning, 109 *n*.
— wider meaning of, 367 *n*.
Isaiah, medical skill of, 165.
— programme of, 206.
— his dwelling and rank, 280 *n*.
— his teaching of Christ's passion, 196, 321.
— why so attacked by negative critics, 291.

INDEX OF SUBJECTS. 373

Isaiah, summary of German criticism on, 295 n.
— length of his prophetic labours, 301.
— perfection of style of, 308.
— ch. i, purpose of, 205.
— chs. xl-lxvi, a written, not a spoken prophecy, 199.
— leading idea of, 305.
— written for Israel's use in dispersion, 311.
— ch. liii, how paraphrased in Targum, 352.
— pseudo-, theory of, 295 n.
Israel, meaning of, after time of Hosea, 24.
— kings of, nominally worshippers of Jehovah, 182.
— final rejection of, 188, 224; see also 'Judaism.'
— purpose of its existence, 191, 274, 303.
— struggle of, against idolatry, 303.
— began its work at exile, 306.
— why scattered, 307, 309.
— discipline, by which it was fitted for the dispersion, 309.
— merged in Christendom, 355.
Israelites, not all descended from Jacob, 81, 119 n.
— state of, under the Judges, 93.
— length of their sojourn in Egypt, 119 n.
— trained in the wilderness, 120.
— their literary tastes, 126.
— their rejection foretold, 224, 288.
— utter destruction of, impossible, 267.
— the remnant of, not the nation, heirs of the promise, 267, 277, 355.
— probable fate of, if they had accepted Christ, 276.
— views of, respecting Christ's birth, 326.
— how preserved in isolation, 313, 315.
— three stages of God's dealing with, 317.
— views of, at the time of Christ's advent, 354.
— of Alexandria, worthless nature of their apocryphal literature, 334.

Israelites of Palestine, views of, respecting Christ, 335, 356.

Jacob, brethren of, 83.
— number of his lineal descendants at the exodus, 119 n.
Jair, wealth of, 86.
Jehovah, meaning and spelling of, 68 n.
Jeremiah, unwilling to become a prophet, 49.
— mission of, for life, 113.
— sorrows of, 114.
— his knowledge of other prophetic writings, 142.
— Book of, 199.
— his reputation among the Jews, 223 and note.
— his excellences, moral, 287.
Jeroboam, calf-worship of, 182.
Jerusalem, destruction of, caused by moral reasons, 276.
Jews, see 'Israelites.'
Jezebel, fanaticism of, 182, 183.
Joel, teaching of, 199, 241, 257.
— founder of spiritual prophecy, 231.
— prepares the way for Isaiah, 232.
— occasion of his prophecy, 241.
— teaches God's providence, 243.
— teaches coming of Holy Ghost, 244.
— and general judgment, 249.
— often quoted by Apostles, 247.
— only partially understood by St. Peter, 247.
Jonah, Book of, earliest written prophecy, 231.
— teaching of, 232.
— shows nature of prophecy, 233.
— foretells call of Gentiles, 241.
— gives type of Christ's death and resurrection, 241.
Joseph, history of, 36, 84 n.
Josephus, his baseness, 357.
Judah, its strength in David's reign accounted for, 121 n.
Judaism, insufficient to account for Christianity, 228.
— its temporary nature foretold, 270, 273, 274.
Judges, in what way moved by the spirit, 65, 66 n., 106, 368.
— state of Israel under, 93.

Judgment, general, foretold by Joel, 249.
— revelation a necessary consequence of teaching of, 249, 258.
— not fully revealed till Christ came, 250, 258.
Justin Martyr, Jewish view of Christ's advent in, 328.

Kenezites, in what way Israelites, 85 *n.*
Knowledge, human, imperfect, 237.
— grows gradually, 285.

Land, how divided among the Israelites, 89 *n.*
Law of Moses, temporary, 270, 271.
Learning, progress of, in days of Samuel, 126 : of Elisha, 138.
Levites, largely trained in prophetic schools, 132,
— had charge of Temple service, 133 and *note.*
Little ones, meaning of term, 81 *n.*
Locusts, description of in Joel, 241.

Malachi, foretells rejection of Jews, 288, and state of things preparatory to fall of Jerusalem, 289.
Mantle, Elijah's, 168.
Marcion, his Book of Oppositions, 363.
Massorites, labours of, 5 *n.*, 280 *n.*, 350 *n.*
Mediator, necessity of, 58.
Medicine, studied by prophets, 154, 163.
— practised by Christ, 166.
Melcath, her worship in time of Jeremiah, 297.
Melote, see 'Sheepskin.'
Messiah, see 'Christ.'
Micah, prophecy of, 199.
— predicts destruction of Jerusalem, 206, 276.
— is repeated by Isaiah, 207.
— earliest prophet who gives specific predictions, 275.
— how these predictions were prepared for, 276.
— style of, 280.
— morality of, 282.
— prophecies chiefly of Church, 283.
Mishpachah, meaning of, 87 *n.*

Missionary labours, how described by Micah, 279.
Mixed multitude, see 'Ereb.'
Moloch, prevalence of his worship in Isaiah's time, 297.
Morality, laws of, taught by Gospel, 15.
Mosaic period parallel to Christianity, 107 *n.*
Moses, the servant of Jehovah, 72.
— elevation of his views, 93, 97.
— grandson of, 95.
— greatness of, 95, 97, 98.
— gives outline of whole Gospel, 192, 196. See 'Pentateuch.'
— why present at Transfiguration, 210.
— foretold fall of Judaism, 273.
— Ascension of, 357 *n.*
Mountain of Lord's House, 269, 271, 272, 273, 277.
Music, prophets trained in, 128.
— its influence in barbarous times, 129.

Nabhi, name for prophet, 48.
— meaning of, 54.
— head of prophetic schools, 139.
Nahum, prophecy of, 200.
Naioth, meaning of, 105.
Nations, teleology of, 303.
Nature, meaning of its laws, 243.
Neubauer, his view of Targums, 333.
Nineveh, purpose of its empire, 310.

Obadiah, his quotations from Jeremiah, 142.

Palestine, Jews of, see 'Israelites.'
— its physical deterioration, 316.
Patriarchs, why called prophets, 56.
Paul, St., evidential value of epistles of, 17.
— the first active missionary, 220.
Pentateuch, archaic style of, 54 *n.*
— contains the Gospel, 75, 79, 97.
— nature of revelation in, 193.
People, in singular the Jews, in plural the Gentiles, 221.
Philistines, early presence of in Gerar, 82 *n.*
— supremacy of, 99.
Philo, his view of the Messiah, 342.
Preparation for Christ twofold, 22.
— vastness of, 202.

INDEX OF SUBJECTS. 375

Progress, this world one of, 255 *n*.
— law of, requires preparation for Christianity, 255 *n*.
Prophecy, the witness to Christian truth, 26.
— not identical with prediction, 30, 38, 108 *n*., 222, 305.
— meaning of Hebrew verb *to prophecy* in various conjugations, 49, 50.
— idea of, associated with madness, 53.
— four great periods of, 107.
— not confined to any class, 113, 136.
— development of, in northern kingdom, 182, 184.
— development of, in Judah, 188.
— period of unwritten, 203.
— Assyrian period of, 203.
— Chaldaean period of, 204.
— work of prophets of Assyrian period, 205.
— written, object of, 209.
— written, result of prophetic schools, 210.
— secondary sense of, not a Jewish, but a Christian view, 225, 226.
— nature of, taught by Jonah, 233.
— opposed to fatalism, 234.
— conditional, 236, 238, 276.
— general in early prophets, 253, 254.
— specific first in Micah, 275.
— contradictions of, reconciled in Christianity, 280.
— plan of, 253, 254, 286.
— why and when it ceased, 317, 332.
— its external view of Christ, 345.
Prophet, see 'Chozeh,' 'Nabhi,' 'Roëh.'
— speaker for Jehovah, 33 *n*., 65.
— a mediator, 58, 59, 68.
— higher than priest, 63.
— the, like unto Moses, 67, 74.
— how called, 106, 111, 112.
— teacher of spiritual truth, 123.
— and priest, how opposed, 112, 133.
— meaning of name in New Testament, 108 *n*.
Prophets, schools of, 105, 110, 111, 124, 137, 139, 141, 150, 152.
— of Samaria, 111, 138.
— uninspired, 106, 147.

Prophets, urge subjective side of religion, 112.
— why called to life of endurance, 114.
— decline and fall of, 115, 146, 155, 166.
— majority of, priests, 133.
— personal probation of, 140 *n*., 158.
— their knowledge of one another's writings, 141, 256.
— had a college at Jerusalem, 142, 280.
— a powerful class, 145 and *note*.
— wives of, 148, 149.
— houses of, 148, 149.
— collegiate life of, 150.
— offerings made to, 151.
— maintenance of, 153, 166.
— dress of, 167, 172.
— journeys of, 171.
— asceticism of, 174.
— political activity of, 175, 178.
— crown conferred by, 177.
— set free from office of Judge, 197.
— early, work of, 199, 201.
— later, work of, 201.
— Books of, ill-arranged, 231.
— teach imperfection of Judaism, 256.
— unity of teaching of, 266.
— metaphors of, whence drawn, 271.
— style of, marked, 281.
— external evidence of authenticity of writings of, 293 *n*.
Providence, the main lesson of Joel, 243.
— verges on miracle, 368.
Psalmody, beginning of, 129, 203.
Psalms, doctrines of, 213.
— prove nature of teaching of early prophets, 213, 214, 217.
— of degrees, 266.
Psalter of Solomon, 348.

Ramah, 124, 125, and *note*.
Rationalism, credulity of, 291.
— weakness of, 292.
Renan, theory of, 330.
Repentance, nature of, 244.
Revelation, manner of, in Old Testament, 35.
— nature of proof of, 39.
— nature of knowledge given by, 61.
Roëh, meaning of, 41.

INDEX OF SUBJECTS.

Samuel, bringing up of, 100.
— three great acts of, 104.
— reformation wrought by, 121, 127, 196, 197.
— later years of, devoted to schools of the Prophets, 197.
— most of the courses of singers descended from, 217.
Saul, high qualities of, 42.
— among the prophets, 131.
Seer, popular name for prophet, 42; see also ' Chozeh ' and ' Roëh.'
Septuagint, value of, 293, 333.
— work of many hands, 334.
— translates according to preconceived notions, 335, 337.
Servant of Jehovah, title of Moses, 72.
— of Israel, 320.
— of Messiah, 320.
Sheepskin, dress of prophets, 169.
Shiloh, destruction of, 99, 271.
Sibylline oracles, forged by Jews, 333.
Sinai, fertility of wilderness of, 88 *n*.
Slavery, nature of Jewish, 70, 86.
Solomon, evils of his reign, 198.
Son of God, Jewish title of Messiah, 327.
Spirit, gift of, first taught by Joel, 244.
Strauss, theory of, 330.
Synagogue, model of Christian church, 129.

Tabernacle, significance of, 270.
Tacitus, character of Jews by, 314.
Talmud, teaching of, 25, 328.
Taph, see ' Little ones.'

Targum of Jonathan, 261, 350, 353.
— of Onkelos, 349.
Targums, Chaldee, account of, 333.
Tents, the ordinary Jewish dwelling, 127 and *note*.
Testament, Old, the proof of Christ's ministry, 219.
— use of, by St. Paul, 220.
— prophetic of Christ, 227.
— Old and New not opposed, 362. See also ' Bible.'
Theocracy, meaning of, 62.
Towns, low moral state of, 92.
Transfiguration, why Moses and Elias there, 210.
Tribes, different in rank, 80.
— Ten, their revolt, 198.

Unbelief, intolerance of, 299.
University, Ramah the first Jewish, 125 and *note*.
Urijah, fate of, 223.
Urim and Thummim, 62, 63 *n*., 66, 135, 178.

Vision, why prophecy so called, 47.
Vulgate, value of, 273 *n*.

War, condemned by Prophets, 122.
Wisdom, Book of, 339.
Writing, antiquity of, 105 *n*.
— not common till time of Elisha, 139.

Zachariah, genuineness of Book of, 287 *n*.
Zion, hill of, type of what, 272.

INDEX OF TEXTS EXPLAINED.

	PAGE.		PAGE.
Gen. iii. 15	5 n.	Is. x. 28–34	263
— xviii. 32	28	— xi. 1	264
— xxxi. 46, 54	83	— xi. 4	353 n.
Exod. vii. 1	56	— xx. 2	172
Num. xi. 17, 25–27	50	— xlix. 5	272 & n.
— xii. 5–8	69	— lxv. 8, 9	272, 309, 311
— xxiv. 24	273	Jer. xv. 17	114
Deut. xviii. 15	67	— xxiii. 14	167
Judg. v. 14	126	— xxiv. 5, 8	277
— vi. 25	182 n.	Ezek. xxxvii. 4–12	51
1 Sam. iii. 20	64 n.	Hos. iii. 4, 5	260
— ix. 9	42 n.	Joel ii. 28	247
— xviii. 10	52	Amos vii. 14	143
1 Kings iv. 25	90 n.	— ix. 9–12	262
— xvi. 33	182 n.	Micah iv. 10	277
2 Kings i. 8	168	— v. 2	275
— ii. 9	169	Zech. xiii. 4	168
— ii. 15	128	Mat. iii. 4	169
— iv. 39	150 n.	Luke xii. 47, 48	252
— ix. 25	47	John vii. 27	326
— xx. 4	280 n.	— vii. 31	342
1 Chr. xxix. 29	46	— xii. 34	348
2 Chr. xix. 2	43 n.	1 Cor. ix. 5	149 n.
— xx. 37	51	Heb. iv. 12	33 n., 35
Ps. lxxxix. 3, 4	259	— xi. 37	170
— cx. 3	338	1 Pet. i. 10, 11	256
— cx. 4	259	— v. 13	149
— cxxxii. 11, 12	265 n., 266	2 Pet. i. 19	228
Is. ix. 6	339	1 John iii. 2	238